Refactoring

The Addison-Wesley Object Technology Series

Grady Booch, Ivar Jacobson, and James Rumbaugh, Series Editors
For more information, check out the series web site at www.awprofessional.com/otseries.

The Component Software Series

Clemens Szyperski, Series Editor
For more information, check out the series web site at www.awprofessional.com/csseries.

Refactoring

Improving the Design of Existing Code

Martin Fowler

With contributions by Kent Beck, John Brant, William Opdyke, and Don Roberts

▲▲▼

ADDISON–WESLEY

Boston • San Francisco • New York • Toronto • Montreal
London • Munich • Paris • Madrid
Capetown • Sydney • Tokyo • Singapore • Mexico City

For more information about buying this title in bulk quantities, or for special sales opportunities (which may include electronic versions; custom cover designs; and content particular to your business, training goals, marketing focus, or branding interests), please contact our corporate sales department at corpsales@pearsoned.com or (800) 382-3419.

For government sales inquiries, please contact governmentsales@pearsoned.com.

For questions about sales outside the U.S., please contact international@pearsoned.com.

Library of Congress Cataloging-in-Publication Data

Fowler, Martin,
　　　Refactoring : improving the design of existing code / Martin
　Fowler.
　　　　　p.　m. — (The Addison-Wesley object technology series)
　　　Includes bibliographical references and index.
　　　ISBN 0-201-48567-2
　　　1. Software refactoring.　2. Object-oriented programming (Computer
　science)　I. Title.　II. Series.
　　　QA76.76.R42F69　1999
　　　005.1'4—dc21　　　　　　　　　　　　　　　　　　99–20765
　　　　　　　　　　　　　　　　　　　　　　　　　　　　CIP

Executive Editor: J. Carter Shanklin
Project Editor: Krysia Bebick
Editorial Assistant: Kristin Erickson
Production Manager: John Fuller
Production Coordinator: Genevieve C. Rajewski
Copy Editor: Catherine Judge Allen
Composition: Kim Arney
Index: Irv Hershman
Proofreader: Amy Finch

ISBN 0-201-48567-2
Text printed in the United States on recycled paper at LSC Communications in Crawfordsville, IN.
34　17

For Cindy

Contents

Foreword

"Refactoring" was conceived in Smalltalk circles, but it wasn't long before it found its way into other programming language camps. Because refactoring is integral to framework development, the term comes up quickly when "frameworkers" talk about their craft. It comes up when they refine their class hierarchies and when they rave about how many lines of code they were able to delete. Frameworkers know that a framework won't be right the first time around—it must evolve as they gain experience. They also know that the code will be read and modified more frequently than it will be written. The key to keeping code readable and modifiable is refactoring—for frameworks, in particular, but also for software in general.

So, what's the problem? Simply this: Refactoring is risky. It requires changes to working code that can introduce subtle bugs. Refactoring, if not done properly, can set you back days, even weeks. And refactoring becomes riskier when practiced informally or ad hoc. You start digging in the code. Soon you discover new opportunities for change, and you dig deeper. The more you dig, the more stuff you turn up. . .and the more changes you make. Eventually you dig yourself into a hole you can't get out of. To avoid digging your own grave, refactoring must be done systematically. When my coauthors and I wrote *Design Patterns,* we mentioned that design patterns provide targets for refactorings. However, identifying the target is only one part of the problem; transforming your code so that you get there is another challenge.

Martin Fowler and the contributing authors make an invaluable contribution to object-oriented software development by shedding light on the refactoring process. This book explains the principles and best practices of refactoring, and points out when and where you should start digging in your code to improve it. At the book's core is a comprehensive catalog of refactorings. Each refactoring describes the motivation and mechanics of a proven code transformation. Some of the refactorings, such as Extract Method or Move Field, may seem obvious.

But don't be fooled. Understanding the mechanics of such refactorings is the key to refactoring in a disciplined way. The refactorings in this book will help you change your code one small step at a time, thus reducing the risks of evolving your design. You will quickly add these refactorings and their names to your development vocabulary.

My first experience with disciplined, "one step at a time" refactoring was when I was pair-programming at 30,000 feet with Kent Beck. He made sure that we applied refactorings from this book's catalog one step at a time. I was amazed at how well this practice worked. Not only did my confidence in the resulting code increase, I also felt less stressed. I highly recommend you try these refactorings: You and your code will feel much better for it.

—Erich Gamma
Object Technology International, Inc.

Preface

Once upon a time, a consultant made a visit to a development project. The consultant looked at some of the code that had been written; there was a class hierarchy at the center of the system. As he wandered through the hierarchy, the consultant saw that it was rather messy. The higher-level classes made certain assumptions about how the classes would work, assumptions that were embodied in inherited code. That code didn't suit all the subclasses, however, and was overridden quite heavily. If the superclass had been modified a little, then much less overriding would have been necessary. In other places some of the intention of the superclass had not been properly understood, and behavior present in the superclass was duplicated. In yet other places several subclasses did the same thing with code that could clearly be moved up the hierarchy.

The consultant recommended to the project management that the code be looked at and cleaned up, but the project management didn't seem enthusiastic. The code seemed to work and there were considerable schedule pressures. The managers said they would get around to it at some later point.

The consultant had also shown the programmers who had worked on the hierarchy what was going on. The programmers were keen and saw the problem. They knew that it wasn't really their fault; sometimes a new pair of eyes are needed to spot the problem. So the programmers spent a day or two cleaning up the hierarchy. When they were finished, the programmers had removed half the code in the hierarchy without reducing its functionality. They were pleased with the result and found that it became quicker and easier both to add new classes to the hierarchy and to use the classes in the rest of the system.

The project management was not pleased. Schedules were tight and there was a lot of work to do. These two programmers had spent two days doing work that had done nothing to add the many features the system had to deliver in a few months time. The old code had worked just fine. So the design was a bit more "pure" a bit more "clean." The project had to ship code that worked, not code that would please an academic. The consultant suggested that this cleaning up be done on other central parts of the system. Such an activity might halt the project for a week or two. All this activity was devoted to making the code look better, not to making it do anything that it didn't already do.

How do you feel about this story? Do you think the consultant was right to suggest further clean up? Or do you follow that old engineering adage, "if it works, don't fix it"?

I must admit to some bias here. I was that consultant. Six months later the project failed, in large part because the code was too complex to debug or to tune to acceptable performance.

The consultant Kent Beck was brought in to restart the project, an exercise that involved rewriting almost the whole system from scratch. He did several things differently, but one of the most important was to insist on continuous cleaning up of the code using refactoring. The success of this project, and role refactoring played in this success, is what inspired me to write this book, so that I could pass on the knowledge that Kent and others have learned in using refactoring to improve the quality of software.

What Is Refactoring?

Refactoring is the process of changing a software system in such a way that it does not alter the external behavior of the code yet improves its internal structure. It is a disciplined way to clean up code that minimizes the chances of introducing bugs. In essence when you refactor you are improving the design of the code after it has been written.

"Improving the design after it has been written." That's an odd turn of phrase. In our current understanding of software development we believe that we design and then we code. A good design comes first, and the coding comes second. Over time the code will be modified, and the integrity of the system, its structure according to that design, gradually fades. The code slowly sinks from engineering to hacking.

Refactoring is the opposite of this practice. With refactoring you can take a bad design, chaos even, and rework it into well-designed code. Each step is simple, even simplistic. You move a field from one class to another, pull some code out of a method to make into its own method, and push some code up or down a hierarchy. Yet the cumulative effect of these small changes can radically improve the design. It is the exact reverse of the normal notion of software decay.

With refactoring you find the balance of work changes. You find that design, rather than occurring all up front, occurs continuously during development. You learn from building the system how to improve the design. The resulting interaction leads to a program with a design that stays good as development continues.

What's in This Book?

This book is a guide to refactoring; it is written for a professional programmer. My aim is to show you how to do refactoring in a controlled and efficient manner. You will learn to refactor in such a way that you don't introduce bugs into the code but instead methodically improve the structure.

It's traditional to start books with an introduction. Although I agree with that principle, I don't find it easy to introduce refactoring with a generalized discussion or definitions. So I start with an example. Chapter 1 takes a small program with some common design flaws and refactors it into a more acceptable object-oriented program. Along the way we see both the process of refactoring and the application of several useful refactorings. This is the key chapter to read if you want to understand what refactoring really is about.

In Chapter 2 I cover more of the general principles of refactoring, some definitions, and the reasons for doing refactoring. I outline some of the problems with refactoring. In Chapter 3 Kent Beck helps me describe how to find bad smells in code and how to clean them up with refactorings. Testing plays a very important role in refactoring, so Chapter 4 describes how to build tests into code with a simple open-source Java testing framework.

The heart of the book, the catalog of refactorings, stretches from Chapter 5 through Chapter 12. This is by no means a comprehensive catalog. It is the beginning of such a catalog. It includes the refactorings that I have written down so far in my work in this field. When I want to do something, such as *Replace Conditional with Polymorphism (255)*, the catalog reminds me how to do it in a safe, step-by-step manner. I hope this is the section of the book you'll come back to often.

In this book I describe the fruit of a lot of research done by others. The last chapters are guest chapters by some of these people. Chapter 13 is by Bill Opdyke, who describes the issues he has come across in adopting refactoring in commercial development. Chapter 14 is by Don Roberts and John Brant, who describe the true future of refactoring, automated tools. I've left the final word, Chapter 15, to the master of the art, Kent Beck.

Refactoring in Java

For all of this book I use examples in Java. Refactoring can, of course, be done with other languages, and I hope this book will be useful to those working with other languages. However, I felt it would be best to focus this book on Java because it is the language I know best. I have added occasional notes for refactoring in other languages, but I hope other people will build on this foundation with books aimed at specific languages.

To help communicate the ideas best, I have not used particularly complex areas of the Java language. So I've shied away from using inner classes, reflection, threads, and many other of Java's more powerful features. This is because I want to focus on the core refactorings as clearly as I can.

I should emphasize that these refactorings are not done with concurrent or distributed programming in mind. Those topics introduce additional concerns that are beyond the scope of this book.

Who Should Read This Book?

This book is aimed at a professional programmer, someone who writes software for a living. The examples and discussion include a lot of code to read and understand. The examples are all in Java. I chose Java because it is an increasingly well-known language that can be easily understood by anyone with a background in C. It is also an object-oriented language, and object-oriented mechanisms are a great help in refactoring.

Although it is focused on the code, refactoring has a large impact on the design of system. It is vital for senior designers and architects to understand the principles of refactoring and to use them in their projects. Refactoring is best introduced by a respected and experienced developer. Such a developer can best understand the principles behind refactoring and adapt those principles to the specific workplace. This is particularly true when you are using a language other than Java, because you have to adapt the examples I've given to other languages.

Here's how to get the most from this book without reading all of it.

- **If you want to understand what refactoring is,** read Chapter 1; the example should make the process clear.

- **If you want to understand why you should refactor,** read the first two chapters. They will tell you what refactoring is and why you should do it.

- **If you want to find where you should refactor,** read Chapter 3. It tells you the signs that suggest the need for refactoring.

- **If you want to actually do refactoring,** read the first four chapters completely. Then skip-read the catalog. Read enough of the catalog to know roughly what is in there. You don't have to understand all the details. When you actually need to carry out a refactoring, read the refactoring in detail and use it to help you. The catalog is a reference section, so you probably won't want to read it in one go. You should also read the guest chapters, especially Chapter 15.

Building on the Foundations Laid by Others

I need to say right now, at the beginning, that I owe a big debt with this book, a debt to those whose work over the last decade has developed the field of refactoring. Ideally one of them should have written this book, but I ended up being the one with the time and energy.

Two of the leading proponents of refactoring are **Ward Cunningham** and **Kent Beck**. They used it as a central part of their development process in the early days and have adapted their development processes to take advantage of it. In particular it was my collaboration with Kent that really showed me the importance of refactoring, an inspiration that led directly to this book.

Ralph Johnson leads a group at the University of Illinois at Urbana-Champaign that is notable for its practical contributions to object technology. Ralph has long been a champion of refactoring, and several of his students have worked on the topic. **Bill Opdyke** developed the first detailed written work on refactoring in his doctoral thesis. **John Brant** and **Don Roberts** have gone beyond writing words into writing a tool, the Refactoring Browser, for refactoring Smalltalk programs.

Acknowledgments

Even with all that research to draw on, I still needed a lot of help to write this book. First and foremost, Kent Beck was a huge help. The first seeds were planted in a bar in Detroit when Kent told me about a paper he was writing for the *Smalltalk Report* [Beck, hanoi]. It not only provided many ideas for me to steal for Chapter 1 but also started me off in taking notes of refactorings. Kent helped in other places too. He came up with the idea of code smells, encouraged me at various sticky points, and generally worked with me to make this book work. I can't help thinking he could have written this book much better himself, but I had the time and can only hope I did the subject justice.

As I've written this, I wanted to share much of this expertise directly with you, so I'm very grateful that many of these people have spent some time adding some material to this book. Kent Beck, John Brant, William Opdyke, and Don Roberts have all written or co-written chapters. In addition, Rich Garzaniti and Ron Jeffries have added useful sidebars.

Any author will tell you that technical reviewers do a great deal to help in a book like this. As usual, Carter Shanklin and his team at Addison-Wesley put together a great panel of hard-nosed reviewers. These were

- Ken Auer, Rolemodel Software, Inc.

- Joshua Bloch, Sun Microsystems, Java Software

- John Brant, University of Illinois at Urbana-Champaign

- Scott Corley, High Voltage Software, Inc.

- Ward Cunningham, Cunningham & Cunningham, Inc.

- Stéphane Ducasse

- Erich Gamma, Object Technology International, Inc.

- Ron Jeffries

- Ralph Johnson, University of Illinois

- Joshua Kerievsky, Industrial Logic, Inc.

- Doug Lea, SUNY Oswego

- Sander Tichelaar

They all added a great deal to the readability and accuracy of this book, and removed at least some of the errors that can lurk in any manuscript. I'd like to highlight a couple of very visible suggestions that made a difference to the look of the book. Ward and Ron got me to do Chapter 1 in the side-by-side style. Joshua Kerievksy suggested the idea of the code sketches in the catalog.

In addition to the official review panel there were many unofficial reviewers. These people looked at the manuscript or the work in progress on my Web pages and made helpful comments. They include Leif Bennett, Michael Feathers, Michael Finney, Neil Galarneau, Hisham Ghazouli, Tony Gould, John Isner, Brian Marick, Ralf Reissing, John Salt, Mark Swanson, Dave Thomas, and Don Wells. I'm sure there are others who I've forgotten; I apologize and offer my thanks.

A particularly entertaining review group is the infamous reading group at the University of Illinois at Urbana-Champaign. Because this book reflects so much of their work, I'm particularly grateful for their efforts captured in real audio. This group includes Fredrico "Fred" Balaguer, John Brant, Ian Chai, Brian Foote, Alejandra Garrido, Zhijiang "John" Han, Peter Hatch, Ralph Johnson, Songyu "Raymond" Lu, Dragos-Anton Manolescu, Hiroaki Nakamura, James Overturf, Don Roberts, Chieko Shirai, Les Tyrell, and Joe Yoder.

Any good idea needs to be tested in a serious production system. I saw refactoring have a huge effect on the Chrysler Comprehensive Compensation system (C3). I want to thank all the members of that team: Ann Anderson, Ed Anderi, Ralph Beattie, Kent Beck, David Bryant, Bob Coe, Marie DeArment, Margaret Fronczak, Rich Garzaniti, Dennis Gore, Brian Hacker, Chet Hendrickson, Ron Jeffries, Doug Joppie, David Kim, Paul Kowalsky, Debbie Mueller, Tom Murasky, Richard Nutter, Adrian Pantea, Matt Saigeon, Don Thomas, and Don Wells. Working with them cemented the principles and benefits of refactoring into me on a firsthand basis. Watching their progress as they use refactoring heavily helps me see what refactoring can do when applied to a large project over many years.

Again I had the help of J. Carter Shanklin at Addison-Wesley and his team: Krysia Bebick, Susan Cestone, Chuck Dutton, Kristin Erickson, John Fuller, Christopher Guzikowski, Simone Payment, and Genevieve Rajewski. Working with a good publisher is a pleasure; they provided a lot of support and help.

Talking of support, the biggest sufferer from a book is always the closest to the author, in this case my (now) wife Cindy. Thanks for loving me even when I was hidden in the study. As much time as I put into this book, I never stopped being distracted by thinking of you.

Martin Fowler
Melrose, Massachusetts
fowler@acm.org
http://www.martinfowler.com
http://www.refactoring.com

Chapter 1

Refactoring, a First Example

How do I begin to write about refactoring? The traditional way to begin talking about something is to outline the history, broad principles, and the like. When someone does that at a conference, I get slightly sleepy. My mind starts wandering with a low-priority background process that polls the speaker until he or she gives an example. The examples wake me up because it is with examples that I can see what is going on. With principles it is too easy to make generalizations, too hard to figure out how to apply things. An example helps make things clear.

So I'm going to start this book with an example of refactoring. During the process I'll tell you a lot about how refactoring works and give you a sense of the process of refactoring. I can then provide the usual principles-style introduction.

With an introductory example, however, I run into a big problem. If I pick a large program, describing it and how it is refactored is too complicated for any reader to work through. (I tried and even a slightly complicated example runs to more than a hundred pages.) However, if I pick a program that is small enough to be comprehensible, refactoring does not look like it is worthwhile.

Thus I'm in the classic bind of anyone who wants to describe techniques that are useful for real-world programs. Frankly it is not worth the effort to do the refactoring that I'm going to show you on a small program like the one I'm going to use. But if the code I'm showing you is part of a larger system, then the refactoring soon becomes important. So I have to ask you to look at this and imagine it in the context of a much larger system.

The Starting Point

The sample program is very simple. It is a program to calculate and print a statement of a customer's charges at a video store. The program is told which

1

movies a customer rented and for how long. It then calculates the charges, which depend on how long the movie is rented, and identifies the type of movie. There are three kinds of movies: regular, children's, and new releases. In addition to calculating charges, the statement also computes frequent renter points, which vary depending on whether the film is a new release.

Several classes represent various video elements. Here's a class diagram to show them (Figure 1.1).

I'll show the code for each of these classes in turn.

Movie

Movie is just a simple data class.

```java
public class Movie {

    public static final int  CHILDRENS = 2;
    public static final int  REGULAR = 0;
    public static final int  NEW_RELEASE = 1;

    private String _title;
    private int _priceCode;

    public Movie(String title, int priceCode) {
        _title = title;
        _priceCode = priceCode;
    }
```

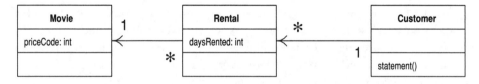

Figure 1.1 *Class diagram of the starting-point classes. Only the most important features are shown. The notation is Unified Modeling Language UML [Fowler, UML].*

```
    public int getPriceCode() {
        return _priceCode;
    }

    public void setPriceCode(int arg) {
      _priceCode = arg;
    }

    public String getTitle (){
        return _title;
    };
 }
```

Rental

The rental class represents a customer renting a movie.

```
class Rental {
    private Movie _movie;
    private int _daysRented;

    public Rental(Movie movie, int daysRented) {
      _movie = movie;
      _daysRented = daysRented;
    }
    public int getDaysRented() {
      return _daysRented;
    }
    public Movie getMovie() {
      return _movie;
    }
 }
```

Customer

The customer class represents the customer of the store. Like the other classes it has data and accessors:

```
class Customer {
  private String _name;
  private Vector _rentals = new Vector();

  public Customer (String name){
      _name = name;
  };

  public void addRental(Rental arg) {
    _rentals.addElement(arg);
  }
  public String getName (){
      return _name;
  };
```

Customer also has the method that produces a statement. Figure 1.2 shows the interactions for this method. The body for this method is on the facing page.

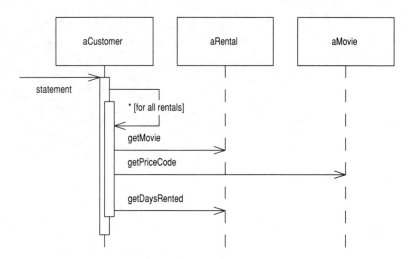

Figure 1.2 *Interactions for the statement method*

```
public String statement() {
      double totalAmount = 0;
      int frequentRenterPoints = 0;
      Enumeration rentals = _rentals.elements();
      String result = "Rental Record for " + getName() + "\n";
      while (rentals.hasMoreElements()) {
          double thisAmount = 0;
          Rental each = (Rental) rentals.nextElement();

          //determine amounts for each line
          switch (each.getMovie().getPriceCode()) {
              case Movie.REGULAR:
                  thisAmount += 2;
                  if (each.getDaysRented() > 2)
                      thisAmount += (each.getDaysRented() - 2) * 1.5;
                  break;
              case Movie.NEW_RELEASE:
                  thisAmount += each.getDaysRented() * 3;
                  break;
              case Movie.CHILDRENS:
                  thisAmount += 1.5;
                  if (each.getDaysRented() > 3)
                      thisAmount += (each.getDaysRented() - 3) * 1.5;
                  break;

          }

          // add frequent renter points
          frequentRenterPoints ++;
          // add bonus for a two day new release rental
          if ((each.getMovie().getPriceCode() == Movie.NEW_RELEASE) &&
              each.getDaysRented() > 1) frequentRenterPoints ++;

          //show figures for this rental
          result += "\t" + each.getMovie().getTitle()+ "\t" +
              String.valueOf(thisAmount) + "\n";
          totalAmount += thisAmount;

      }
      //add footer lines
      result +=  "Amount owed is " + String.valueOf(totalAmount) + "\n";
      result += "You earned " + String.valueOf(frequentRenterPoints) +
            " frequent renter points";
      return result;

  }
```

Comments on the Starting Program

What are your impressions about the design of this program? I would describe it as not well designed and certainly not object oriented. For a simple program like this, that does not really matter. There's nothing wrong with a quick and dirty *simple* program. But if this is a representative fragment of a more complex system, then I have some real problems with this program. That long statement routine in the Customer class does far too much. Many of the things that it does should really be done by the other classes.

Even so the program works. Is this not just an aesthetic judgment, a dislike of ugly code? It is until we want to change the system. The compiler doesn't care whether the code is ugly or clean. But when we change the system, there is a human involved, and humans do care. A poorly designed system is hard to change. Hard because it is hard to figure out where the changes are needed. If it is hard to figure out what to change, there is a strong chance that the programmer will make a mistake and introduce bugs.

In this case we have a change that the users would like to make. First they want a statement printed in HTML so that the statement can be Web enabled and fully buzzword compliant. Consider the impact this change would have. As you look at the code you can see that it is impossible to reuse any of the behavior of the current statement method for an HTML statement. Your only recourse is to write a whole new method that duplicates much of the behavior of statement. Now, of course, this is not too onerous. You can just copy the statement method and make whatever changes you need.

But what happens when the charging rules change? You have to fix both statement and htmlStatement and ensure the fixes are consistent. The problem with copying and pasting code comes when you have to change it later. If you are writing a program that you don't expect to change, then cut and paste is fine. If the program is long lived and likely to change, then cut and paste is a menace.

This brings me to a second change. The users want to make changes to the way they classify movies, but they haven't yet decided on the change they are going to make. They have a number of changes in mind. These changes will affect both the way renters are charged for movies and the way that frequent renter points are calculated. As an experienced developer you are sure that whatever scheme users come up with, the only guarantee you're going to have is that they will change it again within six months.

The statement method is where the changes have to be made to deal with changes in classification and charging rules. If, however, we copy the statement to an HTML statement, we need to ensure that any changes are completely consistent. Furthermore, as the rules grow in complexity it's going to be harder to figure out where to make the changes and harder to make them without making a mistake.

You may be tempted to make the fewest possible changes to the program; after all, it works fine. Remember the old engineering adage: "if it ain't broke, don't fix it." The program may not be broken, but it does hurt. It is making your life more difficult because you find it hard to make the changes your users want. This is where refactoring comes in.

> *When you find you have to add a feature to a program, and the program's code is not structured in a convenient way to add the feature, first refactor the program to make it easy to add the feature, then add the feature.*

The First Step in Refactoring

Whenever I do refactoring, the first step is always the same. I need to build a solid set of tests for that section of code. The tests are essential because even though I follow refactorings structured to avoid most of the opportunities for introducing bugs, I'm still human and still make mistakes. Thus I need solid tests.

Because the statement result produces a string, I create a few customers, give each customer a few rentals of various kinds of films, and generate the statement strings. I then do a string comparison between the new string and some reference strings that I have hand checked. I set up all of these tests so I can run them from one Java command on the command line. The tests take only a few seconds to run, and as you will see, I run them often.

An important part of the tests is the way they report their results. They either say "OK," meaning that all the strings are identical to the reference strings, or they print a list of failures: lines that turned out differently. The tests are thus self-checking. It is vital to make tests self-checking. If you don't, you end up spending time hand checking some numbers from the test against some numbers of a desk pad, and that slows you down.

As we do the refactoring, we will lean on the tests. I'm going to be relying on the tests to tell me whether I introduce a bug. It is essential for refactoring that you have good tests. It's worth spending the time to build the tests, because the tests give you the security you need to change the program later. This is such an important part of refactoring that I go into more detail on testing in Chapter 4.

Before you start refactoring, check that you have a solid suite of tests. These tests must be self-checking.

Decomposing and Redistributing the Statement Method

The obvious first target of my attention is the overly long statement method. When I look at a long method like that, I am looking to decompose the method into smaller pieces. Smaller pieces of code tend to make things more manageable. They are easier to work with and move around.

The first phase of the refactorings in this chapter show how I split up the long method and move the pieces to better classes. My aim is to make it easier to write an HTML statement method with much less duplication of code.

My first step is to find a logical clump of code and use *Extract Method (110)*. An obvious piece here is the switch statement. This looks like it would make a good chunk to extract into its own method.

When I extract a method, as in any refactoring, I need to know what can go wrong. If I do the extraction badly, I could introduce a bug into the program. So before I do the refactoring I need to figure out how to do it safely. I've done this refactoring a few times before, so I've written down the safe steps in the catalog.

First I need to look in the fragment for any variables that are local in scope to the method we are looking at, the local variables and parameters. This segment of code uses two: each and thisAmount. Of these each is not modified by the code but thisAmount is modified. Any non-modified variable I can pass in as a parameter. Modified variables need more care. If there is only one, I can return it. The temp is initialized to 0 each time around the loop and is not altered until the switch gets to it. So I can just assign the result.

The next two pages show the code before and after refactoring. The before code is on the left, the resulting code on the right. The code I'm extracting from the original and any changes in the new code that I don't think are immediately obvious are in boldface type. As I continue with this chapter, I'll continue with this left-right convention.

```java
public String statement() {
    double totalAmount = 0;
    int frequentRenterPoints = 0;
    Enumeration rentals = _rentals.elements();
    String result = "Rental Record for " + getName() + "\n";
    while (rentals.hasMoreElements()) {
        double thisAmount = 0;
        Rental each = (Rental) rentals.nextElement();

        //determine amounts for each line
        switch (each.getMovie().getPriceCode()) {
            case Movie.REGULAR:
                thisAmount += 2;
                if (each.getDaysRented() > 2)
                    thisAmount += (each.getDaysRented() - 2) * 1.5;
                break;
            case Movie.NEW_RELEASE:
                thisAmount += each.getDaysRented() * 3;
                break;
            case Movie.CHILDRENS:
                thisAmount += 1.5;
                if (each.getDaysRented() > 3)
                    thisAmount += (each.getDaysRented() - 3) * 1.5;
                break;

        }

        // add frequent renter points
        frequentRenterPoints ++;
        // add bonus for a two day new release rental
        if ((each.getMovie().getPriceCode() == Movie.NEW_RELEASE) && each.getDaysRented() >
1) frequentRenterPoints ++;

        //show figures for this rental
        result += "\t" + each.getMovie().getTitle()+ "\t" + String.valueOf(thisAmount) +
"\n";

        totalAmount += thisAmount;

    }
    //add footer lines
    result +=  "Amount owed is " + String.valueOf(totalAmount) + "\n";
    result += "You earned " + String.valueOf(frequentRenterPoints) + " frequent renter
points";
    return result;

}
```

```java
public String statement() {
    double totalAmount = 0;
    int frequentRenterPoints = 0;
    Enumeration rentals = _rentals.elements();
    String result = "Rental Record for " + getName() + "\n";
    while (rentals.hasMoreElements()) {
        double thisAmount = 0;
        Rental each = (Rental) rentals.nextElement();

        thisAmount = amountFor(each);

        // add frequent renter points
        frequentRenterPoints ++;
        // add bonus for a two day new release rental
        if ((each.getMovie().getPriceCode() == Movie.NEW_RELEASE) &&
            each.getDaysRented() > 1) frequentRenterPoints ++;

        //show figures for this rental
        result += "\t" + each.getMovie().getTitle()+ "\t" +
            String.valueOf(thisAmount) + "\n";
        totalAmount += thisAmount;

    }
    //add footer lines
    result +=  "Amount owed is " + String.valueOf(totalAmount) + "\n";
    result += "You earned " + String.valueOf(frequentRenterPoints) +
        " frequent renter points";
    return result;

  }
}
private int amountFor(Rental each) {
    int thisAmount = 0;
    switch (each.getMovie().getPriceCode()) {
        case Movie.REGULAR:
            thisAmount += 2;
            if (each.getDaysRented() > 2)
                thisAmount += (each.getDaysRented() - 2) * 1.5;
            break;
        case Movie.NEW_RELEASE:
            thisAmount += each.getDaysRented() * 3;
            break;
        case Movie.CHILDRENS:
            thisAmount += 1.5;
            if (each.getDaysRented() > 3)
                thisAmount += (each.getDaysRented() - 3) * 1.5;
            break;
    }
    return thisAmount;
}
```

Whenever I make a change like this, I compile and test. I didn't get off to a very good start—the tests blew up. A couple of the test figures gave me the wrong answer. I was puzzled for a few seconds then realized what I had done. Foolishly I'd made the return type amountFor int instead of double:

```
private double amountFor(Rental each) {
    double thisAmount = 0;
    switch (each.getMovie().getPriceCode()) {
        case Movie.REGULAR:
            thisAmount += 2;
            if (each.getDaysRented() > 2)
                thisAmount += (each.getDaysRented() - 2) * 1.5;
            break;
        case Movie.NEW_RELEASE:
            thisAmount += each.getDaysRented() * 3;
            break;
        case Movie.CHILDRENS:
            thisAmount += 1.5;
            if (each.getDaysRented() > 3)
                thisAmount += (each.getDaysRented() - 3) * 1.5;
            break;
    }
    return thisAmount;
}
```

It's the kind of silly mistake that I often make, and it can be a pain to track down. In this case Java converts doubles to ints without complaining but merrily rounding [Java Spec]. Fortunately it was easy to find in this case, because the change was so small and I had a good set of tests. Here is the essence of the refactoring process illustrated by accident. Because each change is so small, any errors are very easy to find. You don't spend a long time debugging, even if you are as careless as I am.

Refactoring changes the programs in small steps. If you make a mistake, it is easy to find the bug.

Because I'm working in Java, I need to analyze the code to figure out what to do with the local variables. With a tool, however, this can be made really simple. Such a tool does exist in Smalltalk, the Refactoring Browser. With this tool refactoring is very simple. I just highlight the code, pick "Extract Method" from the menus, type in a method name, and it's done. Furthermore, the tool doesn't make silly mistakes like mine. I'm looking forward to a Java version!

Now that I've broken the original method down into chunks, I can work on them separately. I don't like some of the variable names in amountFor, and this is a good place to change them.

Here's the original code:

```
private double amountFor(Rental each) {
    double thisAmount = 0;
    switch (each.getMovie().getPriceCode()) {
        case Movie.REGULAR:
            thisAmount += 2;
            if (each.getDaysRented() > 2)
                thisAmount += (each.getDaysRented() - 2) * 1.5;
            break;
        case Movie.NEW_RELEASE:
            thisAmount += each.getDaysRented() * 3;
            break;
        case Movie.CHILDRENS:
            thisAmount += 1.5;
            if (each.getDaysRented() > 3)
                thisAmount += (each.getDaysRented() - 3) * 1.5;
            break;
    }
    return thisAmount;
}
```

Here is the renamed code:

```
private double amountFor(Rental aRental) {
    double result = 0;
    switch (aRental.getMovie().getPriceCode()) {
        case Movie.REGULAR:
            result += 2;
            if (aRental.getDaysRented() > 2)
                result += (aRental.getDaysRented() - 2) * 1.5;
            break;
        case Movie.NEW_RELEASE:
            result += aRental.getDaysRented() * 3;
            break;
        case Movie.CHILDRENS:
            result += 1.5;
            if (aRental.getDaysRented() > 3)
                result += (aRental.getDaysRented() - 3) * 1.5;
            break;
    }
    return result;
}
```

Once I've done the renaming, I compile and test to ensure I haven't broken anything.

Is renaming worth the effort? Absolutely. Good code should communicate what it is doing clearly, and variable names are a key to clear code. Never be afraid to change the names of things to improve clarity. With good find and replace tools, it is usually not difficult. Strong typing and testing will highlight anything you miss. Remember

---

Any fool can write code that a computer can understand. Good programmers write code that humans can understand.

Code that communicates its purpose is very important. I often refactor just when I'm reading some code. That way as I gain understanding about the program, I embed that understanding into the code for later so I don't forget what I learned.

Moving the Amount Calculation

As I look at amountFor, I can see that it uses information from the rental, but does not use information from the customer.

```
class Customer...
  private double amountFor(Rental aRental) {
      double result = 0;
      switch (aRental.getMovie().getPriceCode()) {
          case Movie.REGULAR:
              result += 2;
              if (aRental.getDaysRented() > 2)
                  result += (aRental.getDaysRented() - 2) * 1.5;
              break;
          case Movie.NEW_RELEASE:
              result += aRental.getDaysRented() * 3;
              break;
          case Movie.CHILDRENS:
              result += 1.5;
              if (aRental.getDaysRented() > 3)
                  result += (aRental.getDaysRented() - 3) * 1.5;
              break;
      }
      return result;
  }
```

This immediately raises my suspicions that the method is on the wrong object. In most cases a method should be on the object whose data it uses, thus the method should be moved to the rental. To do this I use *Move Method (142)*. With this you first copy the code over to rental, adjust it to fit in its new home, and compile, as follows:

```
class Rental...
   double getCharge() {
       double result = 0;
       switch (getMovie().getPriceCode()) {
           case Movie.REGULAR:
               result += 2;
               if (getDaysRented() > 2)
                   result += (getDaysRented() - 2) * 1.5;
               break;
           case Movie.NEW_RELEASE:
               result += getDaysRented() * 3;
               break;
           case Movie.CHILDRENS:
               result += 1.5;
               if (getDaysRented() > 3)
                   result += (getDaysRented() - 3) * 1.5;
               break;
       }
       return result;
   }
```

   In this case fitting into its new home means removing the parameter. I also renamed the method as I did the move.

   I can now test to see whether this method works. To do this I replace the body of Customer.amountFor to delegate to the new method.

```
class Customer...
   private double amountFor(Rental aRental) {
       return aRental.getCharge();
   }
```

   I can now compile and test to see whether I've broken anything.

The next step is to find every reference to the old method and adjust the reference to use the new method, as follows:

```
class Customer...
    public String statement() {
        double totalAmount = 0;
        int frequentRenterPoints = 0;
        Enumeration rentals = _rentals.elements();
        String result = "Rental Record for " + getName() + "\n";
        while (rentals.hasMoreElements()) {
            double thisAmount = 0;
            Rental each = (Rental) rentals.nextElement();

            thisAmount = amountFor(each);

            // add frequent renter points
            frequentRenterPoints ++;
            // add bonus for a two day new release rental
            if ((each.getMovie().getPriceCode() == Movie.NEW_RELEASE) &&
                each.getDaysRented() > 1) frequentRenterPoints ++;

            //show figures for this rental
            result += "\t" + each.getMovie().getTitle()+ "\t" +
                String.valueOf(thisAmount) + "\n";
            totalAmount += thisAmount;

        }
        //add footer lines
        result +=  "Amount owed is " + String.valueOf(totalAmount) + "\n";
        result += "You earned " + String.valueOf(frequentRenterPoints) +
            " frequent renter points";
        return result;

    }
```

In this case this step is easy because we just created the method and it is in only one place. In general, however, you need to do a "find" across all the classes that might be using that method:

```
class Customer
    public String statement() {
        double totalAmount = 0;
        int frequentRenterPoints = 0;
        Enumeration rentals = _rentals.elements();
        String result = "Rental Record for " + getName() + "\n";
        while (rentals.hasMoreElements()) {
            double thisAmount = 0;
            Rental each = (Rental) rentals.nextElement();

            thisAmount = each.getCharge();

            // add frequent renter points
            frequentRenterPoints ++;
            // add bonus for a two day new release rental
            if ((each.getMovie().getPriceCode() == Movie.NEW_RELEASE) &&
                each.getDaysRented() > 1) frequentRenterPoints ++;

            //show figures for this rental
            result += "\t" + each.getMovie().getTitle()+ "\t" +
                String.valueOf(thisAmount) + "\n";
            totalAmount += thisAmount;

        }
        //add footer lines
        result += "Amount owed is " + String.valueOf(totalAmount) + "\n";
        result += "You earned " + String.valueOf(frequentRenterPoints) +
            " frequent renter points";
        return result;

    }
```

Figure 1.3 *State of classes after moving the charge method*

When I've made the change (Figure 1.3) the next thing is to remove the old method. The compiler should tell me whether I missed anything. I then test to see if I've broken anything.

Sometimes I leave the old method to delegate to the new method. This is useful if it is a public method and I don't want to change the interface of the other class.

There is certainly some more I would like to do to Rental.getCharge but I will leave it for the moment and return to Customer.statement.

```
public String statement() {
    double totalAmount = 0;
    int frequentRenterPoints = 0;
    Enumeration rentals = _rentals.elements();
    String result = "Rental Record for " + getName() + "\n";
    while (rentals.hasMoreElements()) {
        double thisAmount = 0;
        Rental each = (Rental) rentals.nextElement();

        thisAmount = each.getCharge();

        // add frequent renter points
        frequentRenterPoints ++;
        // add bonus for a two day new release rental
        if ((each.getMovie().getPriceCode() == Movie.NEW_RELEASE) &&
            each.getDaysRented() > 1) frequentRenterPoints ++;

        //show figures for this rental
        result += "\t" + each.getMovie().getTitle()+ "\t" +
            String.valueOf(thisAmount) + "\n";
        totalAmount += thisAmount;

    }
    //add footer lines
    result +=  "Amount owed is " + String.valueOf(totalAmount) + "\n";
    result += "You earned " + String.valueOf(frequentRenterPoints) +
        " frequent renter points";
    return result;

}
```

The next thing that strikes me is that thisAmount is now redundant. It is set to the result of each.charge and not changed afterward. Thus I can eliminate thisAmount by using *Replace Temp with Query (120):*

```
public String statement() {
    double totalAmount = 0;
    int frequentRenterPoints = 0;
    Enumeration rentals = _rentals.elements();
    String result = "Rental Record for " + getName() + "\n";
    while (rentals.hasMoreElements()) {
        Rental each = (Rental) rentals.nextElement();

        // add frequent renter points
        frequentRenterPoints ++;
        // add bonus for a two day new release rental
        if ((each.getMovie().getPriceCode() == Movie.NEW_RELEASE) &&
            each.getDaysRented() > 1) frequentRenterPoints ++;

        //show figures for this rental
        result += "\t" + each.getMovie().getTitle()+ "\t" + String.valueOf
            (each.getCharge()) + "\n";
        totalAmount += each.getCharge();

    }
    //add footer lines
    result +=  "Amount owed is " + String.valueOf(totalAmount) + "\n";
    result += "You earned " + String.valueOf(frequentRenterPoints)
          + " frequent renter points";
    return result;

    }
}
```

Once I've made that change I compile and test to make sure I haven't broken anything.

I like to get rid of temporary variables such as this as much as possible. Temps are often a problem in that they cause a lot of parameters to be passed around when they don't have to be. You can easily lose track of what they are there for. They are particularly insidious in long methods. Of course there is a performance price to pay; here the charge is now calculated twice. But it is easy to optimize that in the rental class, and you can optimize much more effectively when the code is properly factored. I'll talk more about that issue later in Refactoring and Performance on page 69.

Extracting Frequent Renter Points

The next step is to do a similar thing for the frequent renter points. The rules vary with the tape, although there is less variation than with charging. It seems reasonable to put the responsibility on the rental. First we need to use *Extract Method (110)* on the frequent renter points part of the code (in boldface type):

```
public String statement() {
    double totalAmount = 0;
    int frequentRenterPoints = 0;
    Enumeration rentals = _rentals.elements();
    String result = "Rental Record for " + getName() + "\n";
    while (rentals.hasMoreElements()) {
        Rental each = (Rental) rentals.nextElement();

        // add frequent renter points
        frequentRenterPoints ++;
        // add bonus for a two day new release rental
        if ((each.getMovie().getPriceCode() == Movie.NEW_RELEASE)
            && each.getDaysRented() > 1) frequentRenterPoints ++;

        //show figures for this rental
        result += "\t" + each.getMovie().getTitle()+ "\t" + String.valueOf(each.getCharge())
+ "\n";
        totalAmount += each.getCharge();

    }
    //add footer lines
    result +=  "Amount owed is " + String.valueOf(totalAmount) + "\n";
    result += "You earned " + String.valueOf(frequentRenterPoints)
        + " frequent renter points";
    return result;

}
}
```

Again we look at the use of locally scoped variables. Again each is used and can be passed in as a parameter. The other temp used is frequentRenterPoints. In this case frequentRenterPoints does have a value beforehand. The body of the extracted method doesn't read the value, however, so we don't need to pass it in as a parameter as long as we use an appending assignment.

I did the extraction, compiled, and tested and then did a move and compiled and tested again. With refactoring, small steps are the best; that way less tends to go wrong.

```
class Customer...
    public String statement() {
        double totalAmount = 0;
        int frequentRenterPoints = 0;
        Enumeration rentals = _rentals.elements();
        String result = "Rental Record for " + getName() + "\n";
        while (rentals.hasMoreElements()) {
            Rental each = (Rental) rentals.nextElement();
            frequentRenterPoints += each.getFrequentRenterPoints();

            //show figures for this rental
            result += "\t" + each.getMovie().getTitle()+ "\t" +
                String.valueOf(each.getCharge()) + "\n";
            totalAmount += each.getCharge();
        }

        //add footer lines
        result +=  "Amount owed is " + String.valueOf(totalAmount) + "\n";
        result += "You earned " + String.valueOf(frequentRenterPoints) +
            " frequent renter points";
        return result;
    }

class Rental...
    int getFrequentRenterPoints() {
        if ((getMovie().getPriceCode() == Movie.NEW_RELEASE) && getDaysRented() > 1)
            return 2;
        else
            return 1;
    }
```

I'll summarize the changes I just made with some before-and-after Unified Modeling Language (UML) diagrams (Figures 1.4 through 1.7). Again the diagrams on the left are before the change; those on the right are after the change.

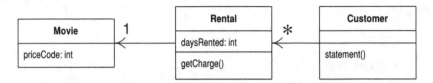

Figure 1.4 *Class diagram before extraction and movement of the frequent renter points calculation*

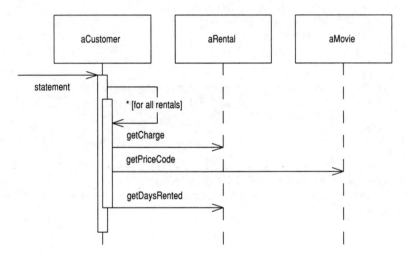

Figure 1.5 *Sequence diagrams before extraction and movement of the frequent renter points calculation*

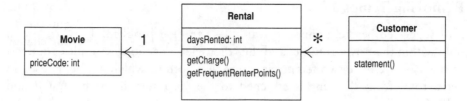

Figure 1.6 *Class diagram after extraction and movement of the frequent renter points calculation*

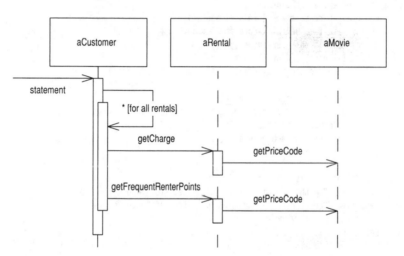

Figure 1.7 *Sequence diagram after extraction and movement of the frequent renter points calculation*

Removing Temps

As I suggested before, temporary variables can be a problem. They are useful only within their own routine, and thus they encourage long, complex routines. In this case we have two temporary variables, both of which are being used to get a total from the rentals attached to the customer. Both the ASCII and HTML versions require these totals. I like to use *Replace Temp with Query (120)* to replace totalAmount and frequentRentalPoints with query methods. Queries are accessible to any method in the class and thus encourage a cleaner design without long, complex methods:

```
class Customer...
    public String statement() {
        double totalAmount = 0;
        int frequentRenterPoints = 0;
        Enumeration rentals = _rentals.elements();
        String result = "Rental Record for " + getName() + "\n";
        while (rentals.hasMoreElements()) {
            Rental each = (Rental) rentals.nextElement();
            frequentRenterPoints += each.getFrequentRenterPoints();

            //show figures for this rental
            result += "\t" + each.getMovie().getTitle()+ "\t" +
                String.valueOf(each.getCharge()) + "\n";
            totalAmount += each.getCharge();
        }

        //add footer lines
        result +=  "Amount owed is " + String.valueOf(totalAmount) + "\n";
        result += "You earned " + String.valueOf(frequentRenterPoints) +
          " frequent renter points";
        return result;
    }
```

I began by replacing totalAmount with a charge method on customer:

```
class Customer...

    public String statement() {
        int frequentRenterPoints = 0;
        Enumeration rentals = _rentals.elements();
        String result = "Rental Record for " + getName() + "\n";
        while (rentals.hasMoreElements()) {
            Rental each = (Rental) rentals.nextElement();
            frequentRenterPoints += each.getFrequentRenterPoints();

            //show figures for this rental
            result += "\t" + each.getMovie().getTitle()+ "\t" +
                String.valueOf(each.getCharge()) + "\n";
        }

        //add footer lines
        result +=  "Amount owed is " + String.valueOf(getTotalCharge()) + "\n";
        result += "You earned " + String.valueOf(frequentRenterPoints) +
           " frequent renter points";
        return result;
    }

    private double getTotalCharge() {
        double result = 0;
        Enumeration rentals = _rentals.elements();
        while (rentals.hasMoreElements()) {
            Rental each = (Rental) rentals.nextElement();
            result += each.getCharge();
        }
        return result;
    }
```

This isn't the simplest case of *Replace Temp with Query (120)*, totalAmount was assigned to within the loop, so I have to copy the loop into the query method.

After compiling and testing that refactoring, I did the same for frequentRenterPoints:

```
class Customer...
    public String statement() {
        int frequentRenterPoints = 0;
        Enumeration rentals = _rentals.elements();
        String result = "Rental Record for " + getName() + "\n";
        while (rentals.hasMoreElements()) {
            Rental each = (Rental) rentals.nextElement();
            frequentRenterPoints += each.getFrequentRenterPoints();

            //show figures for this rental
            result += "\t" + each.getMovie().getTitle()+ "\t" +
                String.valueOf(each.getCharge()) + "\n";
        }

        //add footer lines
        result +=  "Amount owed is " + String.valueOf(getTotalCharge()) + "\n";
        result += "You earned " + String.valueOf(frequentRenterPoints) +
            " frequent renter points";
        return result;
    }
```

```java
public String statement() {
    Enumeration rentals = _rentals.elements();
    String result = "Rental Record for " + getName() + "\n";
    while (rentals.hasMoreElements()) {
        Rental each = (Rental) rentals.nextElement();

        //show figures for this rental
        result += "\t" + each.getMovie().getTitle()+ "\t" +
            String.valueOf(each.getCharge()) + "\n";
    }

    //add footer lines
    result +=  "Amount owed is " + String.valueOf(getTotalCharge()) + "\n";
    result += "You earned " + String.valueOf(getTotalFrequentRenterPoints()) +
            " frequent renter points";
    return result;
}

private int getTotalFrequentRenterPoints(){
    int result = 0;
    Enumeration rentals = _rentals.elements();
    while (rentals.hasMoreElements()) {
        Rental each = (Rental) rentals.nextElement();
        result += each.getFrequentRenterPoints();
    }
    return result;
}
```

Figures 1.8 through 1.11 show the change for these refactorings in the class diagrams and the interaction diagram for the statement method.

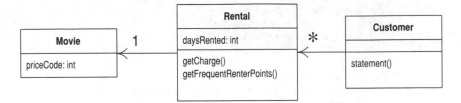

Figure 1.8 *Class diagram before extraction of the totals*

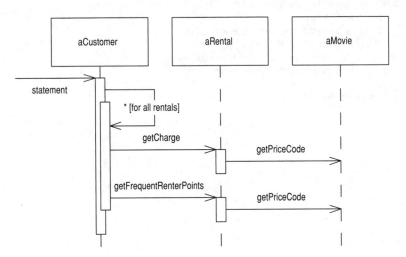

Figure 1.9 *Sequence diagram before extraction of the totals*

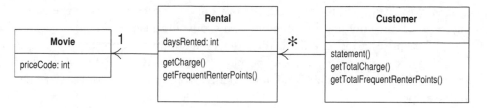

Figure 1.10 *Class diagram after extraction of the totals*

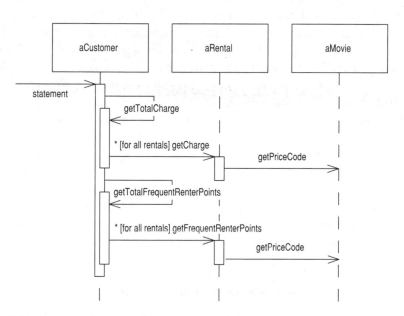

Figure 1.11 *Sequence diagram after extraction of the totals*

It is worth stopping to think a bit about the last refactoring. Most refactorings reduce the amount of code, but this one increases it. That's because Java 1.1 requires a lot of statements to set up a summing loop. Even a simple summing loop with one line of code per element needs six lines of support around it. It's an idiom that is obvious to any programmer but is a lot of lines all the same.

The other concern with this refactoring lies in performance. The old code executed the "while" loop once, the new code executes it three times. A while loop that takes a long time might impair performance. Many programmers would not do this refactoring simply for this reason. But note the words *if* and *might*. Until I profile I cannot tell how much time is needed for the loop to calculate or whether the loop is called often enough for it to affect the overall performance of the system. Don't worry about this while refactoring. When you optimize you will have to worry about it, but you will then be in a much better position to do something about it, and you will have more options to optimize effectively (see the discussion on page 69).

These queries are now available for any code written in the customer class. They can easily be added to the interface of the class should other parts of the system need this information. Without queries like these, other methods have to deal with knowing about the rentals and building the loops. In a complex system, that will lead to much more code to write and maintain.

You can see the difference immediately with the htmlStatement. I am now at the point where I take off my refactoring hat and put on my adding function hat. I can write htmlStatement as follows and add appropriate tests:

```java
public String htmlStatement() {
    Enumeration rentals = _rentals.elements();
    String result = "<H1>Rentals for <EM>" + getName() + "</EM></H1><P>\n";
    while (rentals.hasMoreElements()) {
        Rental each = (Rental) rentals.nextElement();
        //show figures for each rental
        result += each.getMovie().getTitle()+ ": " +
                    String.valueOf(each.getCharge()) + "<BR>\n";
    }
    //add footer lines
    result +=  "<P>You owe <EM>" + String.valueOf(getTotalCharge()) + "</EM><P>\n";
    result += "On this rental you earned <EM>" +
        String.valueOf(getTotalFrequentRenterPoints()) +
        "</EM> frequent renter points<P>";
    return result;
}
```

By extracting the calculations I can create the `htmlStatement` method and reuse all of the calculation code that was in the original statement method. I didn't copy and paste, so if the calculation rules change I have only one place in the code to go to. Any other kind of statement will be really quick and easy to prepare. The refactoring did not take long. I spent most of the time figuring out what the code did, and I would have had to do that anyway.

Some code is copied from the ASCII version, mainly due to setting up the loop. Further refactoring could clean that up. Extracting methods for header, footer, and detail line are one route I could take. You can see how to do this in the example for *Form Template Method (345)*. But now the users are clamoring again. They are getting ready to change the classification of the movies in the store. It's still not clear what changes they want to make, but it sounds like new classifications will be introduced, and the existing ones could well be changed. The charges and frequent renter point allocations for these classifications are to be decided. At the moment, making these kind of changes is awkward. I have to get into the charge and frequent renter point methods and alter the conditional code to make changes to film classifications. Back on with the refactoring hat.

Replacing the Conditional Logic on Price Code with Polymorphism

The first part of this problem is that switch statement. It is a bad idea to do a switch based on an attribute of another object. If you must use a switch statement, it should be on your own data, not on someone else's.

```
class Rental...
  double getCharge() {
      double result = 0;
      switch (getMovie().getPriceCode()) {
          case Movie.REGULAR:
              result += 2;
              if (getDaysRented() > 2)
                  result += (getDaysRented() - 2) * 1.5;
              break;
          case Movie.NEW_RELEASE:
              result += getDaysRented() * 3;
              break;
          case Movie.CHILDRENS:
              result += 1.5;
              if (getDaysRented() > 3)
                  result += (getDaysRented() - 3) * 1.5;
              break;
      }
      return result;
  }
```

This implies that getCharge should move onto movie:

```
class Movie...
  double getCharge(int daysRented) {
      double result = 0;
      switch (getPriceCode()) {
          case Movie.REGULAR:
              result += 2;
              if (daysRented > 2)
                  result += (daysRented - 2) * 1.5;
              break;
          case Movie.NEW_RELEASE:
              result += daysRented * 3;
              break;
          case Movie.CHILDRENS:
              result += 1.5;
              if (daysRented > 3)
                  result += (daysRented - 3) * 1.5;
              break;
      }
      return result;
  }
```

For this to work I had to pass in the length of the rental, which of course is data from the rental. The method effectively uses two pieces of data, the length of the rental and the type of the movie. Why do I prefer to pass the length of rental to the movie rather than the movie type to the rental? It's because the proposed changes are all about adding new types. Type information generally tends to be more volatile. If I change the movie type, I want the least ripple effect, so I prefer to calculate the charge within the movie.

I compiled the method into movie and then changed the getCharge on rental to use the new method (Figures 1.12 and 1.13):

```
class Rental...
  double getCharge() {
      return _movie.getCharge(_daysRented);
  }
```

Once I've moved the getCharge method, I'll do the same with the frequent renter point calculation. That keeps both things that vary with the type together on the class that has the type:

```
class Rental...
  int getFrequentRenterPoints() {
      if ((getMovie().getPriceCode() == Movie.NEW_RELEASE) && getDaysRented() > 1)
          return 2;
      else
          return 1;
  }
```

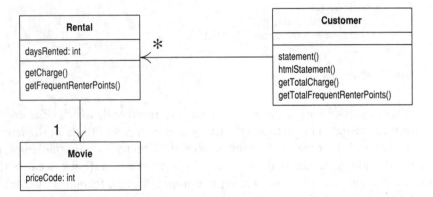

Figure 1.12 *Class diagram before moving methods to movie*

```
class Rental...
  int getFrequentRenterPoints() {
      return _movie.getFrequentRenterPoints(_daysRented);
  }



class Movie...
  int getFrequentRenterPoints(int daysRented) {
      if ((getPriceCode() == Movie.NEW_RELEASE) && daysRented > 1)
          return 2;
      else
          return 1;
  }
```

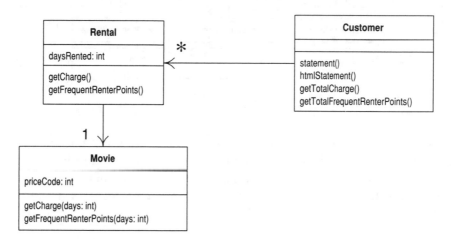

Figure 1.13 *Class diagram after moving methods to movie*

At last . . . Inheritance

We have several types of movie that have different ways of answering the same question. This sounds like a job for subclasses. We can have three subclasses of movie, each of which can have its own version of charge (Figure 1.14).

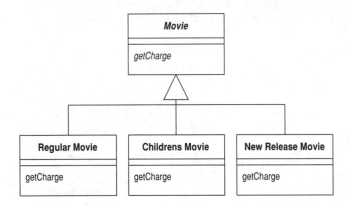

Figure 1.14 *Using inheritance on movie*

This allows me to replace the switch statement by using polymorphism. Sadly it has one slight flaw—it doesn't work. A movie can change its classification during its lifetime. An object cannot change its class during its lifetime. There is a solution, however, the State pattern [Gang of Four]. With the State pattern the classes look like Figure 1.15.

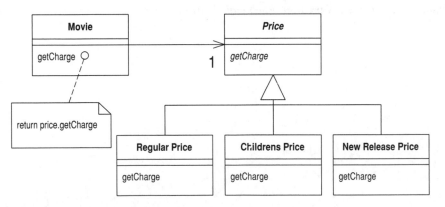

Figure 1.15 *Using the State pattern on movie*

By adding the indirection we can do the subclassing from the price code object and change the price whenever we need to.

If you are familiar with the Gang of Four patterns, you may wonder, "Is this a state, or is it a strategy?" Does the price class represent an algorithm for calculating the price (in which case I prefer to call it Pricer or PricingStrategy), or does it represent a state of the movie (*Star Trek X* is a new release). At this stage the choice of pattern (and name) reflects how you want to think about the structure. At the moment I'm thinking about this as a state of movie. If I later decide a strategy communicates my intention better, I will refactor to do this by changing the names.

To introduce the state pattern I will use three refactorings. First I'll move the type code behavior into the state pattern with *Replace Type Code with State/ Strategy (227)*. Then I can use *Move Method (142)* to move the switch statement into the price class. Finally I'll use *Replace Conditional with Polymorphism (255)* to eliminate the switch statement.

I begin with *Replace Type Code with State/Strategy (227)*. This first step is to use *Self Encapsulate Field (171)* on the type code to ensure that all uses of the type code go through getting and setting methods. Because most of the code came from other classes, most methods already use the getting method. However, the constructors do access the price code:

```
class Movie...
    public Movie(String name, int priceCode) {
      _title = name;
      _priceCode = priceCode;
    }
```

I can use the setting method instead.

```
class Movie
    public Movie(String name, int priceCode) {
      _title = name;
      setPriceCode(priceCode);
    }
```

I compile and test to make sure I didn't break anything. Now I add the new classes. I provide the type code behavior in the price object. I do this with an abstract method on price and concrete methods in the subclasses:

```
abstract class Price {
  abstract int getPriceCode();
}
class ChildrensPrice extends Price {
  int getPriceCode() {
      return Movie.CHILDRENS;
  }
}
class NewReleasePrice extends Price {
  int getPriceCode() {
      return Movie.NEW_RELEASE;
  }
}
class RegularPrice extends Price {
  int getPriceCode() {
      return Movie.REGULAR;
  }
}
```

I can compile the new classes at this point.

Now I need to change movie's accessors for the price code to use the new class:

```
public int getPriceCode() {
    return _priceCode;
}
public setPriceCode (int arg) {
    _priceCode = arg;
}
private int _priceCode;
```

This means replacing the price code field with a price field, and changing the accessors:

```
class Movie...
  public int getPriceCode() {
      return _price.getPriceCode();
  }
  public void setPriceCode(int arg) {
      switch (arg) {
          case REGULAR:
              _price = new RegularPrice();
              break;
          case CHILDRENS:
              _price = new ChildrensPrice();
              break;
          case NEW_RELEASE:
              _price = new NewReleasePrice();
              break;
          default:
              throw new IllegalArgumentException("Incorrect Price Code");
      }
  }
  private Price _price;
```

I can now compile and test, and the more complex methods don't realize the world has changed.

Now I apply *Move Method (142)* to getCharge:

```
class Movie...
  double getCharge(int daysRented) {
      double result = 0;
      switch (getPriceCode()) {
          case Movie.REGULAR:
              result += 2;
              if (daysRented > 2)
                  result += (daysRented - 2) * 1.5;
              break;
          case Movie.NEW_RELEASE:
              result += daysRented * 3;
              break;
          case Movie.CHILDRENS:
              result += 1.5;
              if (daysRented > 3)
                  result += (daysRented - 3) * 1.5;
              break;
      }
      return result;
  }
```

It is simple to move:

```
class Movie...
  double getCharge(int daysRented) {
      return _price.getCharge(daysRented);
  }

class Price...
  double getCharge(int daysRented) {
      double result = 0;
      switch (getPriceCode()) {
          case Movie.REGULAR:
              result += 2;
              if (daysRented > 2)
                  result += (daysRented - 2) * 1.5;
              break;
          case Movie.NEW_RELEASE:
              result += daysRented * 3;
              break;
          case Movie.CHILDRENS:
              result += 1.5;
              if (daysRented > 3)
                  result += (daysRented - 3) * 1.5;
              break;
      }
      return result;
  }
```

Once it is moved I can start using *Replace Conditional with Polymorphism
(255)*:

```
class Price...
  double getCharge(int daysRented) {
      double result = 0;
      switch (getPriceCode()) {
          case Movie.REGULAR:
              result += 2;
              if (daysRented > 2)
                  result += (daysRented - 2) * 1.5;
              break;
          case Movie.NEW_RELEASE:
              result += daysRented * 3;
              break;
          case Movie.CHILDRENS:
              result += 1.5;
              if (daysRented > 3)
                  result += (daysRented - 3) * 1.5;
              break;
      }
      return result;
  }
```

I do this by taking one leg of the case statement at a time and creating an overriding method. I start with RegularPrice:

```
class RegularPrice...
    double getCharge(int daysRented){
        double result = 2;
        if (daysRented > 2)
            result += (daysRented - 2) * 1.5;
        return result;
    }
```

This overrides the parent case statement, which I just leave as it is. I compile and test for this case then take the next leg, compile and test. (To make sure I'm executing the subclass code, I like to throw in a deliberate bug and run it to ensure the tests blow up. Not that I'm paranoid or anything.)

```
class ChildrensPrice
    double getCharge(int daysRented){
        double result = 1.5;
        if (daysRented > 3)
            result += (daysRented - 3) * 1.5;
        return result;
    }

class NewReleasePrice...
    double getCharge(int daysRented){
        return daysRented * 3;
    }
```

When I've done that with all the legs, I declare the Price.getCharge method abstract:

```
class Price...
    abstract double getCharge(int daysRented);
```

I can now do the same procedure with getFrequentRenterPoints:

```
class Movie...
    int getFrequentRenterPoints(int daysRented) {
        if ((getPriceCode() == Movie.NEW_RELEASE) && daysRented > 1)
            return 2;
        else
            return 1;
    }
```

First I move the method over to Price:

```
Class Movie...
  int getFrequentRenterPoints(int daysRented) {
      return _price.getFrequentRenterPoints(daysRented);
  }
Class Price...
  int getFrequentRenterPoints(int daysRented) {
     if ((getPriceCode() == Movie.NEW_RELEASE) && daysRented > 1)
         return 2;
     else
         return 1;
  }
```

In this case, however, I don't make the superclass method abstract. Instead I create an overriding method for new releases and leave a defined method (as the default) on the superclass:

```
Class NewReleasePrice
  int getFrequentRenterPoints(int daysRented) {
      return (daysRented > 1) ? 2: 1;
  }

Class Price...
   int getFrequentRenterPoints(int daysRented){
       return 1;
   }
```

Putting in the state pattern was quite an effort. Was it worth it? The gain is that if I change any of price's behavior, add new prices, or add extra price-dependent behavior, the change will be much easier to make. The rest of the application does not know about the use of the state pattern. For the tiny amount of behavior I currently have, it is not a big deal. In a more complex system with a dozen or so price-dependent methods, this would make a big difference. All these changes were small steps. It seems slow to write it this way, but not once did I have to open the debugger, so the process actually flowed quite quickly. It took me much longer to write this section of the book than it did to change the code.

I've now completed the second major refactoring. It is going to be much easier to change the classification structure of movies, and to alter the rules for charging and the frequent renter point system. Figures 1.16 and 1.17 show how the state pattern works with price information.

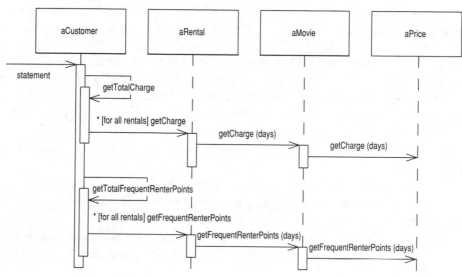

Figure 1.16 *Interactions using the state pattern*

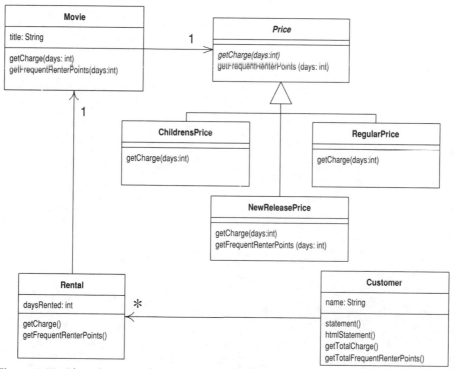

Figure 1.17 *Class diagram after addition of the state pattern*

Final Thoughts

This is a simple example, yet I hope it gives you the feeling of what refactoring is like. I've used several refactorings, including *Extract Method (110)*, *Move Method (142)*, and *Replace Conditional with Polymorphism (255)*. All these lead to better-distributed responsibilities and code that is easier to maintain. It does look rather different from procedural style code, and that takes some getting used to. But once you are used to it, it is hard to go back to procedural programs.

The most important lesson from this example is the rhythm of refactoring: test, small change, test, small change, test, small change. It is that rhythm that allows refactoring to move quickly and safely.

If you're with me this far, you should now understand what refactoring is all about. We can now move on to some background, principles, and theory (although not too much!)

Chapter 2

Principles in Refactoring

The preceding example should have given you a good feel for what refactoring is all about. Now it's time to step back and look at the key principles of refactoring and at some of the issues you need to think about in using refactoring.

Defining Refactoring

I'm always a little leery of definitions because everyone has his or her own, but when you write a book you get to choose your own definitions. In this case I'm basing my definitions on the work done by Ralph Johnson's group and assorted associates.

The first thing to say about this is that the word *Refactoring* has two definitions depending on context. You might find this annoying (I certainly do), but it serves as yet another example of the realities of working with natural language.

The first definition is the noun form.

> *Refactoring (noun): a change made to the internal structure of software to make it easier to understand and cheaper to modify without changing its observable behavior.*

You can find examples of refactorings in the catalog, such as *Extract Method (110)* and *Pull Up Field (320)*. As such, a refactoring is usually a small change to the software, although one refactoring can involve others. For example, *Extract Class (149)* usually involves *Move Method (142)* and *Move Field (146)*.

The other usage of *refactoring* is the verb form

 Refactor *(verb): to restructure software by applying a series of refactorings without changing its observable behavior.*

So you might spend a few hours refactoring, during which you might apply a couple of dozen individual refactorings.

I've been asked, "Is refactoring just cleaning up code?" In a way the answer is yes, but I think refactoring goes further because it provides a technique for cleaning up code in a more efficient and controlled manner. Since I've been using refactoring, I've noticed that I clean code far more effectively than I did before. This is because I know which refactorings to use, I know how to use them in a manner that minimizes bugs, and I test at every possible opportunity.

I should amplify a couple of points in my definitions. First, the purpose of refactoring is to make the software easier to understand and modify. You can make many changes in software that make little or no change in the observable behavior. Only changes made to make the software easier to understand are refactorings. A good contrast is performance optimization. Like refactoring, performance optimization does not usually change the behavior of a component (other than its speed); it only alters the internal structure. However, the purpose is different. Performance optimization often makes code harder to understand, but you need to do it to get the performance you need.

The second thing I want to highlight is that refactoring does not change the observable behavior of the software. The software still carries out the same function that it did before. Any user, whether an end user or another programmer, cannot tell that things have changed.

The Two Hats

This second point leads to Kent Beck's metaphor of two hats. When you use refactoring to develop software, you divide your time between two distinct activities: adding function and refactoring. When you add function, you shouldn't be changing existing code; you are just adding new capabilities. You can measure your progress by adding tests and getting the tests to work. When you refactor, you make a point of not adding function; you only restructure the code. You don't add any tests (unless you find a case you missed earlier); you only change tests when you absolutely need to in order to cope with a change in an interface.

As you develop software, you probably find yourself swapping hats frequently. You start by trying to add a new function, and you realize this would be much easier if the code were structured differently. So you swap hats and refactor for a while. Once the code is better structured, you swap hats and add the new function. Once you get the new function working, you realize you coded it in a way that's awkward to understand, so you swap hats again and refactor. All this might take only ten minutes, but during this time you should always be aware of which hat you're wearing.

Why Should You Refactor?

I don't want to proclaim refactoring as the cure for all software ills. It is no "silver bullet." Yet it is a valuable tool, a pair of silver pliers that helps you keep a good grip on your code. Refactoring is a tool that can, and should, be used for several purposes.

Refactoring Improves the Design of Software

Without refactoring, the design of the program will decay. As people change code—changes to realize short-term goals or changes made without a full comprehension of the design of the code—the code loses its structure. It becomes harder to see the design by reading the code. Refactoring is rather like tidying up the code. Work is done to remove bits that aren't really in the right place. Loss of the structure of code has a cumulative effect. The harder it is to see the design in the code, the harder it is to preserve it, and the more rapidly it decays. Regular refactoring helps code retain its shape.

Poorly designed code usually takes more code to do the same things, often because the code quite literally does the same thing in several places. Thus an important aspect of improving design is to eliminate duplicate code. The importance of this lies in future modifications to the code. Reducing the amount of code won't make the system run any faster, because the effect on the footprint of the programs rarely is significant. Reducing the amount of code does, however, make a big difference in modification of the code. The more code there is, the harder it is to modify correctly. There's more code to understand. You change this bit of code here, but the system doesn't do what you expect because you didn't change that bit over there that does much the same thing in a slightly different context. By eliminating the duplicates, you ensure that the code says everything once and only once, which is the essence of good design.

Refactoring Makes Software Easier to Understand

Programming is in many ways a conversation with a computer. You write code that tells the computer what to do, and it responds by doing exactly what you tell it. In time you close the gap between what you want it to do and what you tell it to do. Programming in this mode is all about saying exactly what you want. But there is another user of your source code. Someone will try to read your code in a few months' time to make some changes. We easily forget that extra user of the code, yet that user is actually the most important. Who cares if the computer takes a few more cycles to compile something? It does matter if it takes a programmer a week to make a change that would have taken only an hour if she had understood your code.

The trouble is that when you are trying to get the program to work, you are not thinking about that future developer. It takes a change of rhythm to make changes that make the code easier to understand. Refactoring helps you to make your code more readable. When refactoring you have code that works but is not ideally structured. A little time spent refactoring can make the code better communicate its purpose. Programming in this mode is all about saying exactly what you mean.

I'm not necessarily being altruistic about this. Often this future developer is me. Here refactoring is particularly important. I'm a very lazy programmer. One of my forms of laziness is that I never remember things about the code I write. Indeed, I deliberately try not remember anything I can look up, because I'm afraid my brain will get full. I make a point of trying to put everything I should remember into the code so I don't have to remember it. That way I'm less worried about Old Peculier [Jackson] killing off my brain cells.

This understandability works another way, too. I use refactoring to help me understand unfamiliar code. When I look at unfamiliar code, I have to try to understand what it does. I look at a couple of lines and say to myself, oh yes, that's what this bit of code is doing. With refactoring I don't stop at the mental note. I actually change the code to better reflect my understanding, and then I test that understanding by rerunning the code to see if it still works.

Early on I do refactoring like this on little details. As the code gets clearer, I find I can see things about the design that I could not see before. Had I not changed the code, I probably never would have seen these things, because I'm just not clever enough to visualize all this in my head. Ralph Johnson describes these early refactorings as wiping the dirt off a window so you can see beyond.

When I'm studying code I find refactoring leads me to higher levels of understanding that otherwise I would miss.

Refactoring Helps You Find Bugs

Help in understanding the code also helps me spot bugs. I admit I'm not terribly good at finding bugs. Some people can read a lump of code and see bugs, I cannot. However, I find that if I refactor code, I work deeply on understanding what the code does, and I put that new understanding right back into the code. By clarifying the structure of the program, I clarify certain assumptions I've made, to the point at which even I can't avoid spotting the bugs.

It reminds me of a statement Kent Beck often makes about himself, "I'm not a great programmer; I'm just a good programmer with great habits." Refactoring helps me be much more effective at writing robust code.

Refactoring Helps You Program Faster

In the end, all the earlier points come down to this: Refactoring helps you develop code more quickly.

This sounds counterintuitive. When I talk about refactoring, people can easily see that it improves quality. Improving design, improving readability, reducing bugs, all these improve quality. But doesn't all this reduce the speed of development?

I strongly believe that a good design is essential for rapid software development. Indeed, the whole point of having a good design is to allow rapid development. Without a good design, you can progress quickly for a while, but soon the poor design starts to slow you down. You spend time finding and fixing bugs instead of adding new function. Changes take longer as you try to understand the system and find the duplicate code. New features need more coding as you patch over a patch that patches a patch on the original code base.

A good design is essential to maintaining speed in software development. Refactoring helps you develop software more rapidly, because it stops the design of the system from decaying. It can even improve a design.

When Should You Refactor?

When I talk about refactoring, I'm often asked about how it should be scheduled. Should we allocate two weeks every couple of months to refactoring?

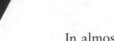

In almost all cases, I'm opposed to setting aside time for refactoring. In my view refactoring is not an activity you set aside time to do. Refactoring is something you do all the time in little bursts. You don't decide to refactor, you refactor because you want to do something else, and refactoring helps you do that other thing.

The Rule of Three

Here's a guideline Don Roberts gave me: The first time you do something, you just do it. The second time you do something similar, you wince at the duplication, but you do the duplicate thing anyway. The third time you do something similar, you refactor.

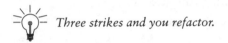 *Three strikes and you refactor.*

Refactor When You Add Function

The most common time to refactor is when I want to add a new feature to some software. Often the first reason to refactor here is to help me understand some code I need to modify. This code may have been written by someone else, or I may have written it. Whenever I have to think to understand what the code is doing, I ask myself if I can refactor the code to make that understanding more immediately apparent. Then I refactor it. This is partly for the next time I pass by here, but mostly it's because I can understand more things if I clarify the code as I'm going along.

The other driver of refactoring here is a design that does not help me add a feature easily. I look at the design and say to myself, "If only I'd designed the code this way, adding this feature would be easy." In this case I don't fret over my past misdeeds—I fix them by refactoring. I do this partly to make future enhancements easy, but mostly I do it because I've found it's the fastest way. Refactoring is a quick and smooth process. Once I've refactored, adding the feature can go much more quickly and smoothly.

Refactor When You Need to Fix a Bug

In fixing bugs much of the use of refactoring comes from making code more understandable. As I look at the code trying to understand it, I refactor to help improve my understanding. Often I find that this active process of working with the code helps in finding the bug. One way to look at it is that if you do get a bug report, it's a sign you need refactoring, because the code was not clear enough for you to see there was a bug.

Refactor As You Do a Code Review

Some organizations do regular code reviews; those that don't would do better if they did. Code reviews help spread knowledge through a development team. Reviews help more experienced developers pass knowledge to less experienced people. They help more people understand more aspects of a large software system. They are also very important in writing clear code. My code may look clear to me but not to my team. That's inevitable—it's very hard for people to put themselves in the shoes of someone unfamiliar with the things they are working on. Reviews also give the opportunity for more people to suggest useful ideas. I can only think of so many good ideas in a week. Having other people contribute makes my life easier, so I always look for many reviews.

I've found that refactoring helps me review someone else's code. Before I started using refactoring, I could read the code, understand some degree of it, and make suggestions. Now when I come up with ideas, I consider whether they can be easily implemented then and there with refactoring. If so, I refactor. When I do it a few times, I can see more clearly what the code looks like with the suggestions in place. I don't have to imagine what it would be like, I can *see* what it is like. As a result, I can come up with a second level of ideas that I would never have realized had I not refactored.

Refactoring also helps the code review have more concrete results. Not only are there suggestions, but also many suggestions are implemented there and then. You end up with much more of a sense of accomplishment from the exercise.

To make this process work, you have to have small review groups. My experience suggests having one reviewer and the original author work on the code together. The reviewer suggests changes, and they both decide whether the changes can be easily refactored in. If so, they make the changes.

With larger design reviews it is often better to obtain several opinions in a larger group. Showing code often is not the best device for this. I prefer UML diagrams and walking through scenarios with CRC cards. So I do design reviews with groups and code reviews with individual reviewers.

This idea of active code review is taken to its limit with the Extreme Programming [Beck, XP] practice of Pair Programming. With this technique all serious development is done with two developers at one machine. In effect it's a continuous code review folded into the development process, and the refactoring that takes place is folded in as well.

Why Refactoring Works

—Kent Beck

Programs have two kinds of value: what they can do for you today and what they can do for you tomorrow. Most times when we are programming, we are focused on what we want the program to do today. Whether we are fixing a bug or adding a feature, we are making today's program more valuable by making it more capable.

You can't program long without realizing that what the system does today is only a part of the story. If you can get today's work done today, but you do it in such a way that you can't possibly get tomorrow's work done tomorrow, then you lose. Notice, though, that you know what you need to do today, but you're not quite sure about tomorrow. Maybe you'll do this, maybe that, maybe something you haven't imagined yet.

I know enough to do today's work. I don't know enough to do tomorrow's. But if I only work for today, I won't be able to work tomorrow at all.

Refactoring is one way out of the bind. When you find that yesterday's decision doesn't make sense today, you change the decision. Now you can do today's work. Tomorrow, some of your understanding as of today will seem naive, so you'll change that, too.

What is it that makes programs hard to work with? Four things I can think of as I am typing this are as follows:

- Programs that are hard to read are hard to modify.

- Programs that have duplicated logic are hard to modify.

- Programs that require additional behavior that requires you to change running code are hard to modify.

- Programs with complex conditional logic are hard to modify.

So, we want programs that are easy to read, that have all logic specified in one and only one place, that do not allow changes to endanger existing behavior, and that allow conditional logic to be expressed as simply as possible.

Refactoring is the process of taking a running program and adding to its value, not by changing its behavior but by giving it more of these qualities that enable us to continue developing at speed.

What Do I Tell My Manager?

How to tell a manager about refactoring is one of the most common questions I've been asked. If the manager is technically savvy, introducing the subject may not be that hard. If the manager is *genuinely* quality oriented, then the thing to stress is the quality aspects. Here using refactoring in the review process is a good way to work things. Tons of studies show that technical reviews are an important way to reduce bugs and thus speed up development. Take a look at any book on reviews, inspections, or the software development process for the latest citations. These should convince most managers of the value of reviews. It is then a short step to introduce refactoring as a way of getting review comments into the code.

Of course, many people say they are driven by quality but are more driven by schedule. In these cases I give my more controversial advice: Don't tell!

Subversive? I don't think so. Software developers are professionals. Our job is to build effective software as rapidly as we can. My experience is that refactoring is a big aid to building software quickly. If I need to add a new function and the design does not suit the change, I find it's quicker to refactor first and then add the function. If I need to fix a bug, I need to understand how the software works—and I find refactoring is the fastest way to do this. A schedule-driven manager wants me to do things the fastest way I can; how I do it is my business. The fastest way is to refactor; therefore I refactor.

▼ ▼

Indirection and Refactoring

—Kent Beck

Computer Science is the discipline that believes all problems can be solved with one more layer of indirection. —Dennis DeBruler

Given software engineers' infatuation with indirection, it may not surprise you to learn that most refactoring introduces more indirection into a program. Refactoring tends to break big objects into several smaller ones and big methods into several smaller ones.

Indirection is a two-edged sword, however. Every time you break one thing into two pieces, you have more things to manage. It also can make a program harder to read as an object delegates to an object delegating to an object. So you'd like to minimize indirection.

Not so fast, buddy. Indirection can pay for itself. Here are some of the ways.

- **To enable sharing of logic.** For example, a submethod invoked in two different places or a method in a superclass shared by all subclasses.

- **To explain intention and implementation separately.** Choosing the name of each class and the name of each method gives you an opportunity to explain what you intend. The internals of the class or method explain how the intention is realized. If the internals also are written in terms of intention in yet smaller pieces, you can write code that communicates most of the important information about its own structure.

- **To isolate change.** I use an object in two different places. I want to change the behavior in one of the two cases. If I change the object, I risk changing both. So I first make a subclass and refer to it in the case that is changing. Now I can modify the subclass without risking an inadvertent change to the other case.

- **To encode conditional logic.** Objects have a fabulous mechanism, polymorphic messages, to flexibly but clearly express conditional logic. By changing explicit conditionals to messages, you can often reduce duplication, add clarity, and increase flexibility all at the same time.

Here is the refactoring game: Maintaining the current behavior of the system, how can you make your system more valuable, either by increasing its quality or by reducing its cost?

The most common variant of the game is to look at your program. Identify a place where it is missing one or more of the benefits of indirection. Put in that indirection without changing the existing behavior. Now you have a more valuable program because it has more qualities that we will appreciate tomorrow.

Contrast this with careful upfront design. Speculative design is an attempt to put all the good qualities into the system before any code is written. Then the code can just be hung on the sturdy skeleton. The problem with this process is that it is too easy to guess wrong. With refactoring, you are never in danger of being completely wrong. The program always behaves at the end as it did at the beginning. In addition, you have the opportunity to add valuable qualities to the code.

There is a second, rarer refactoring game. Identify indirection that isn't paying for itself and take it out. Often this takes the form of intermediate methods that used to serve a purpose but no longer do. Or it could be a component that you expected to be shared or polymorphic but turned out to be used in only one place. When you find parasitic indirection, take it out. Again, you will have a more valuable program, not because there is more of one of the four qualities listed earlier but because it costs less indirection to get the same amount from the qualities.

Problems with Refactoring

When you learn a new technique that greatly improves your productivity, it is hard to see when it does not apply. Usually you learn it within a specific context, often just a single project. It is hard to see what causes the technique to be less effective, even harmful. Ten years ago it was like that with objects. If someone asked me when not to use objects, it was hard to answer. It wasn't that I didn't think objects had limitations—I'm too cynical for that. It was just that I didn't know what those limitations were, although I knew what the benefits were.

Refactoring is like that now. We know the benefits of refactoring. We know they can make a palpable difference to our work. But we haven't had broad enough experience to see where the limitations apply.

This section is shorter than I would like and is more tentative. As more people learn about refactoring, we will learn more. For you this means that while I certainly believe you should try refactoring for the real gains it can provide, you should also monitor its progress. Look out for problems that refactoring may be introducing. Let us know about these problems. As we learn more about refactoring, we will come up with more solutions to problems and learn about what problems are difficult to solve.

Databases

One problem area for refactoring is databases. Most business applications are tightly coupled to the database schema that supports them. That's one reason that the database is difficult to change. Another reason is data migration. Even if you have carefully layered your system to minimize the dependencies between the database schema and the object model, changing the database schema forces you to migrate the data, which can be a long and fraught task.

With nonobject databases a way to deal with this problem is to place a separate layer of software between your object model and your database model. That way you can isolate the changes to the two different models. As you update one model, you don't need to update the other. You just update the intermediate layer. Such a layer adds complexity but gives you a lot of flexibility. Even without refactoring it is very important in situations in which you have multiple databases or a complex database model that you don't have control over.

You don't have to start with a separate layer. You can create the layer as you notice parts of your object model becoming volatile. This way you get the greatest leverage for your changes.

Object databases both help and hinder. Some object-oriented databases provide automatic migration from one version of an object to another. This reduces the effort but still imposes a time penalty while the migration takes place. When migration isn't automatic, you have to do the migration yourself, which is a lot of effort. In this situation you have to be more wary about changes to the data structure of classes. You can still freely move behavior around, but you have to be more cautious about moving fields. You need to use accessors to give the illusion that the data has moved, even when it hasn't. When you are pretty sure you know where the data ought to be, you can move and migrate the data in a single move. Only the accessors need to change, reducing the risk for problems with bugs.

Changing Interfaces

One of the important things about objects is that they allow you to change the implementation of a software module separately from changing the interface. You can safely change the internals of an object without anyone else's worrying about it, but the interface is important—change that and anything can happen.

Something that is disturbing about refactoring is that many of the refactorings do change an interface. Something as simple as *Rename Method (273)* is all about changing an interface. So what does this do to the treasured notion of encapsulation?

There is no problem changing a method name if you have access to all the code that calls that method. Even if the method is public, as long as you can reach and change all the callers, you can rename the method. There is a problem only if the interface is being used by code that you cannot find and change. When this happens, I say that the interface becomes a *published interface* (a step beyond a public interface). Once you publish an interface, you can no longer safely change it and just edit the callers. You need a somewhat more complicated process.

This notion changes the question. Now the problem is: What do you do about refactorings that change published interfaces?

In short, if a refactoring changes a published interface, you have to retain both the old interface and the new one, at least until your users have had a chance to react to the change. Fortunately, this is not too awkward. You can usually arrange things so that the old interface still works. Try to do this so that the old interface calls the new interface. In this way when you change the name of a method, keep the old one, and just let it call the new one. Don't copy the method body—that leads you down the path to damnation by way of duplicated code. You should also use the deprecation facility in Java to mark the code as deprecated. That way your callers will know that something is up.

A good example of this process is the Java collection classes. The new ones present in Java 2 supersede the ones that were originally provided. When the Java 2 ones were released, however, JavaSoft put a lot of effort into providing a migration route.

Protecting interfaces usually is doable, but it is a pain. You have to build and maintain these extra methods, at least for a time. The methods complicate the interface, making it harder to use. There is an alternative: Don't publish the interface. Now I'm not talking about a total ban here, clearly you have to have published interfaces. If you are building APIs for outside consumption, as Sun does, then you have to have published interfaces. I say this because I often see development groups using published interfaces far too much. I've seen a team of three people operate in such a way that each person published interfaces to the other two. This led to all sorts of gyrations to maintain interfaces when it would have been easier to go into the code base and make the edits. Organizations with an overly strong notion of code ownership tend to behave this way. Using published interfaces is useful, but it comes with a cost. So don't publish interfaces unless you really need to. This may mean modifying your code ownership rules to allow people to change other people's code in order to support an interface change. Often it is a good idea to do this with pair programming.

Don't publish interfaces prematurely. Modify your code ownership policies to smooth refactoring.

There is one particular area with problems in changing interfaces in Java: adding an exception to the throws clause. This is not a change in signature, so you cannot use delegation to cover it. The compiler will not let it compile, however. It is tough to deal with this problem. You can choose a new name for the method, let the old method call it, and convert the checked into an unchecked exception. You can also throw an unchecked exception, although then you lose the checking ability. When you do this, you can alert your callers that the exception will become a checked exception at a future date. They then have some time to put the handlers into their code. For this reason I prefer to define a superclass exception for a whole package (such as SQLException for java.sql) and ensure that public methods only declare this exception in their throws clause. That way I can define subclass exceptions if I want to, but this won't affect a caller who knows only about the general case.

Design Changes That Are Difficult to Refactor

Can you refactor your way out of any design mistake, or are some design decisions so central that you cannot count on refactoring to change your mind later? This is an area in which we have very incomplete data. Certainly we have often been surprised by situations in which we can refactor efficiently, but there are places where this is difficult. In one project it was hard, but possible, to refactor a system built with no security requirements into one with good security.

At this stage my approach is to imagine the refactoring. As I consider design alternatives, I ask myself how difficult it would be to refactor from one design into another. If it seems easy, I don't worry too much about the choice, and I pick the simplest design, even if it does not cover all the potential requirements. However, if I cannot see a simple way to refactor, then I put more effort into the design. I do find such situations are in the minority.

When Shouldn't You Refactor?

There are times when you should not refactor at all. The principle example is when you should rewrite from scratch instead. There are times when the existing code is such a mess that although you could refactor it, it would be easier to start from the beginning. This decision is not an easy one to make, and I admit that I don't really have good guidelines for it.

A clear sign of the need to rewrite is when the current code just does not work. You may discover this only by trying to test it and discovering that the code is so full of bugs that you cannot stablilize it. Remember, code has to work mostly correctly before you refactor.

A compromise route is to refactor a large piece of software into components with strong encapsulation. Then you can make a refactor-versus-rebuild decision for one component at a time. This is a promising approach, but I don't have enough data to write good rules for doing that. With a key legacy system, this would certainly be an appealing direction to take.

The other time you should avoid refactoring is when you are close to a deadline. At that point the productivity gain from refactoring would appear after the deadline and thus be too late. Ward Cunningham has a good way to think of this. He describes unfinished refactoring as going into debt. Most companies need some debt in order to function efficiently. However, with debt come interest payments, that is, the extra cost of maintenance and extension caused by overly complex code. You can bear some interest payments, but if the payments become too great, you will be overwhelmed. It is important to manage your debt, paying parts of it off by means of refactoring.

Other than when you are very close to a deadline, however, you should not put off refactoring because you haven't got time. Experience with several projects has shown that a bout of refactoring results in increased productivity. Not having enough time usually is a sign that you need to do some refactoring.

Refactoring and Design

Refactoring has a special role as a complement to design. When I first learned to program, I just wrote the program and muddled my way through it. In time I learned that thinking about the design in advance helped me avoid costly rework. In time I got more into this style of *upfront design*. Many people consider design to be the key piece and programming just mechanics. The analogy is design is an engineering drawing and code is the construction work. But software is very different from physical machines. It is much more malleable, and it is all about thinking. As Alistair Cockburn puts it, "With design I can think very fast, but my thinking is full of little holes."

One argument is that refactoring can be an alternative to upfront design. In this scenario you don't do any design at all. You just code the first approach that comes into your head, get it working, and then refactor it into shape. Actually, this approach can work. I've seen people do this and come out with a very well-designed piece of software. Those who support Extreme Programming [Beck, XP] often are portrayed as advocating this approach.

Although doing only refactoring does work, it is not the most efficient way to work. Even the extreme programmers do some design first. They will try out various ideas with CRC cards or the like until they have a plausible first solution. Only after generating a plausible first shot will they code and then refactor. The point is that refactoring changes the role of upfront design. If you don't refactor, there is a lot of pressure in getting that upfront design right. The sense is that any changes to the design later are going to be expensive. Thus you put more time and effort into the upfront design to avoid the need for such changes.

With refactoring the emphasis changes. You still do upfront design, but now you don't try to find *the* solution. Instead all you want is a reasonable solution. You know that as you build the solution, as you understand more about the problem, you realize that the best solution is different from the one you originally came up with. With refactoring this is not a problem, for it no longer is expensive to make the changes.

An important result of this change in emphasis is a greater movement toward simplicity of design. Before I used refactoring, I always looked for flexible solutions. With any requirement I would wonder how that requirement would change during the life of the system. Because design changes were expensive, I would look to build a design that would stand up to the changes I could foresee. The problem with building a flexible solution is that flexibility costs. Flexible solutions are more complex than simple ones. The resulting software is more difficult to maintain in general, although it is easier to flex in the direction I had in mind. Even there, however, you have to understand how to flex the design. For one or two aspects this is no big deal, but changes occur throughout the system. Building flexibility in all these places makes the overall system a lot more complex and expensive to maintain. The big frustration, of course, is that all this flexibility is not needed. Some of it is, but it's impossible to predict which pieces those are. To gain flexibility, you are forced to put in a lot more flexibility than you actually need.

With refactoring you approach the risks of change differently. You still think about potential changes, you still consider flexible solutions. But instead of implementing these flexible solutions, you ask yourself, "How difficult is it going to be to refactor a simple solution into the flexible solution?" If, as happens most of the time, the answer is "pretty easy," then you just implement the simple solution.

Refactoring can lead to simpler designs without sacrificing flexibility. This makes the design process easier and less stressful. Once you have a broad sense of things that refactor easily, you don't even think of the flexible solutions. You have the confidence to refactor if the time comes. You build the simplest thing that can possibly work. As for the flexible, complex design, most of the time you aren't going to need it.

It Takes Awhile to Create Nothing

—Ron Jeffries

The Chrysler Comprehensive Compensation pay process was running too slowly. Although we were still in development, it began to bother us, because it was slowing down the tests.

Kent Beck, Martin Fowler, and I decided we'd fix it up. While I waited for us to get together, I was speculating, on the basis of my extensive knowledge of the system, about what was probably slowing it down. I thought of several possibilities and chatted with folks about the changes that were probably necessary. We came up with some really good ideas about what would make the system go faster.

Then we measured performance using Kent's profiler. None of the possibilities I had thought of had anything to do with the problem. Instead, we found that the system was spending half its time creating instances of date. Even more interesting was that all the instances had the same couple of values.

When we looked at the date-creation logic, we saw some opportunities for optimizing how these dates were created. They were all going through a string conversion even though no external inputs were involved. The code was just using string conversion for convenience of typing. Maybe we could optimize that.

Then we looked at how these dates were being used. It turned out that the huge bulk of them were all creating instances of date range, an object with a from date and a to date. Looking around little more, we realized that most of these date ranges were empty!

As we worked with date range, we used the convention that any date range that ended before it started was empty. It's a good convention and fits in well with how the class works. Soon after we started using this convention, we realized that just creating a date range that starts after it ends wasn't clear code, so we extracted that behavior into a factory method for empty date ranges.

We had made that change to make the code clearer, but we received an unexpected payoff. We created a constant empty date range and adjusted the factory method to return that object instead of creating it every time. That change doubled the speed of the system, enough for the tests to be bearable. It took us about five minutes.

I had speculated with various members of the team (Kent and Martin deny participating in the speculation) on what was likely wrong with code we knew very well. We had even sketched some designs for improvements without first measuring what was going on.

We were completely wrong. Aside from having a really interesting conversation, we were doing no good at all.

The lesson is: Even if you know exactly what is going on in your system, measure performance, don't speculate. You'll learn something, and nine times out of ten, it won't be that you were right!

Refactoring and Performance

A common concern with refactoring is the effect it has on the performance of a program. To make the software easier to understand, you often make changes that will cause the program to run more slowly. This is an important issue. I'm not one of the school of thought that ignores performance in favor of design purity or in hopes of faster hardware. Software has been rejected for being too slow, and faster machines merely move the goalposts. Refactoring certainly will make software go more slowly, but it also makes the software more amenable to performance tuning. The secret to fast software, in all but hard real-time contexts, is to write tunable software first and then to tune it for sufficient speed.

I've seen three general approaches to writing fast software. The most serious of these is time budgeting, used often in hard real-time systems. In this situation, as you decompose the design you give each component a budget for resources—time and footprint. That component must not exceed its budget, although a mechanism for exchanging budgeted times is allowed. Such a mechanism focuses hard attention on hard performance times. It is essential for systems such as heart pacemakers, in which late data is always bad data. This technique is overkill for other kinds of systems, such as the corporate information systems with which I usually work.

The second approach is the constant attention approach. With this approach every programmer, all the time, does whatever he or she can to keep performance high. This is a common approach and has intuitive attraction, but it does not work very well. Changes that improve performance usually make the program harder to work with. This slows development. This would be a cost worth paying if the resulting software were quicker, but usually it is not. The performance improvements are spread all around the program, and each improvement is made with a narrow perspective of the program's behavior.

The interesting thing about performance is that if you analyze most programs, you find that they waste most of their time in a small fraction of the code. If you optimize all the code equally, you end up with 90 percent of the optimizations wasted, because you are optimizing code that isn't run much. The time spent making the program fast, the time lost because of lack of clarity, is all wasted time.

The third approach to performance improvement takes advantage of this 90 percent statistic. In this approach you build your program in a well-factored manner without paying attention to performance until you begin a performance optimization stage, usually fairly late in development. During the performance optimization stage, you follow a specific process to tune the program.

You begin by running the program under a profiler that monitors the program and tells you where it is consuming time and space. This way you can find that small part of the program where the performance hot spots lie. Then you focus on those performance hot spots and use the same optimizations you would use if you were using the constant attention approach. But because you are focusing your attention on a hot spot, you are having much more effect for less work. Even so you remain cautious. As in refactoring you make the changes in small steps. After each step you compile, test, and rerun the profiler. If you haven't improved performance, you back out the change. You continue the process of finding and removing hot spots until you get the performance that satisfies your users. McConnell [McConnell] gives more information on this technique.

Having a well-factored program helps with this style of optimization in two ways. First, it gives you time to spend on performance tuning. Because you have well-factored code, you can add function more quickly. This gives you more time to focus on performance. (Profiling ensures you focus that time on the right place.) Second, with a well-factored program you have finer granularity for your performance analysis. Your profiler leads you to smaller parts of the code, which are easier to tune. Because the code is clearer, you have a better understanding of your options and of what kind of tuning will work.

I've found that refactoring helps me write fast software. It slows the software in the short term while I'm refactoring, but it makes the software easier to tune during optimization. I end up well ahead.

Where Did Refactoring Come From?

I've not succeeded in pinning down the real birth of the term *refactoring*. Good programmers certainly have spent at least some time cleaning up their code. They do this because they have learned that clean code is easier to change than complex and messy code, and good programmers know that they rarely write clean code the first time around.

Refactoring goes beyond this. In this book I'm advocating refactoring as a key element in the whole process of software development. Two of the first people to recognize the importance of refactoring were Ward Cunningham and Kent Beck, who worked with Smalltalk from the 1980s onward. Smalltalk is an environment that even then was particularly hospitable to refactoring. It is a very dynamic environment that allows you quickly to write highly functional software. Smalltalk has a very short compile-link-execute cycle, which makes it easy to change things quickly. It is also object oriented and thus provides powerful tools for minimizing the impact of change behind well-defined interfaces. Ward and Kent worked hard at developing a software development process geared to working with this kind of environment. (Kent currently refers to this style as *Extreme Programming* [Beck, XP].) They realized that refactoring was important in improving their productivity and ever since have been working with refactoring, applying it to serious software projects and refining the process.

Ward and Kent's ideas have always been a strong influence on the Smalltalk community, and the notion of refactoring has become an important element in the Smalltalk culture. Another leading figure in the Smalltalk community is Ralph Johnson, a professor at the University of Illinois at Urbana-Champaign, who is famous as one of the Gang of Four [Gang of Four]. One of Ralph's biggest interests is in developing software frameworks. He explored how refactoring can help develop an efficient and flexible framework.

Bill Opdyke was one of Ralph's doctoral students and is particularly interested in frameworks. He saw the potential value of refactoring and saw that it could be applied to much more than Smalltalk. His background was in telephone switch development, in which a great deal of complexity accrues over time, and changes are difficult to make. Bill's doctoral research looked at refactoring from a tool builder's perspective. Bill investigated the refactorings that would be useful for C++ framework development and researched the necessary semantics-preserving refactorings, how to prove they were semantics preserving, and how a tool could implement these ideas. Bill's doctoral thesis [Opdyke] is the most substantial work on refactoring to date. He also contributes Chapter 13 to this book.

I remember meeting Bill at the OOPSLA conference in 1992. We sat in a café and discussed some of the work I'd done in building a conceptual framework for healthcare. Bill told me about his research, and I remember thinking, "Interesting, but not really that important." Boy was I wrong!

John Brant and Don Roberts have taken the tool ideas in refactoring much further to produce the Refactoring Browser, a refactoring tool for Smalltalk. They contribute Chapter 14 to this book, which further describes refactoring tools.

And me? I'd always been inclined to clean code, but I'd never considered it to be *that* important. Then I worked on a project with Kent and saw the way he used refactoring. I saw the difference it made in productivity and quality. That experience convinced me that refactoring was a very important technique. I was frustrated, however, because there was no book that I could give to a working programmer, and none of the experts above had any plans to write such a book. So, with their help, I did.

Optimizing a Payroll System

—Rich Garzaniti

We had been developing Chrysler Comprehensive Compensation System for quite a while before we started to move it to GemStone. Naturally, when we did that, we found that the program wasn't fast enough. We brought in Jim Haungs, a master GemSmith, to help us optimize the system.

After a little time with the team to learn how the system worked, Jim used GemStone's ProfMonitor feature to write a profiling tool that plugged into our functional tests. The tool displayed the numbers of objects that were being created and where they were being created.

To our surprise, the biggest offender turned out to be the creation of strings. The biggest of the big was repeated creation of 12,000-byte strings. This was a particular problem because the string was so big that GemStone's usual garbage-collection facilities wouldn't deal with it. Because of the size, GemStone was paging the string to disk every time it was created. It turned out the strings were being built way down in our IO framework, and they were being built three at a time for every output record!

Our first fix was to cache a single 12,000-byte string, which solved most of the problem. Later, we changed the framework to write directly to a file stream, which eliminated the creation of even the one string.

Once the huge string was out of the way, Jim's profiler found similar problems with some smaller strings: 800 bytes, 500 bytes, and so on. Converting these to use the file stream facility solved them as well.

With these techniques we steadily improved the performance of the system. During development it looked like it would take more than 1,000 hours to run the payroll. When we actually got ready to start, it took 40 hours. After a month we got it down to around 18; when we launched we were at 12. After a year of running and enhancing the system for a new group of employees, it was down to 9 hours.

Our biggest improvement was to run the program in multiple threads on a multi-processor machine. The system wasn't designed with threads in mind, but because it was so well factored, it took us only three days to run in multiple threads. Now the payroll takes a couple of hours to run.

Before Jim provided a tool that measured the system in actual operation, we had good ideas about what was wrong. But it was a long time before our good ideas were the ones that needed to be implemented. The real measurements pointed in a different direction and made a much bigger difference.

Chapter 3

Bad Smells in Code

by Kent Beck and Martin Fowler

If it stinks, change it.
— Grandma Beck, discussing child-rearing philosophy

By now you have a good idea of how refactoring works. But just because you know how doesn't mean you know when. Deciding when to start refactoring, and when to stop, is just as important to refactoring as knowing how to operate the mechanics of a refactoring.

Now comes the dilemma. It is easy to explain to you how to delete an instance variable or create a hierarchy. These are simple matters. Trying to explain when you should do these things is not so cut-and-dried. Rather than appealing to some vague notion of programming aesthetics (which frankly is what we consultants usually do), I wanted something a bit more solid.

I was mulling over this tricky issue when I visited Kent Beck in Zurich. Perhaps he was under the influence of the odors of his newborn daughter at the time, but he had come up with the notion describing the "when" of refactoring in terms of smells. "Smells," you say, "and that is supposed to be better than vague aesthetics?" Well, yes. We look at lots of code, written for projects that span the gamut from wildly successful to nearly dead. In doing so, we have learned to look for certain structures in the code that suggest (sometimes they scream for) the possibility of refactoring. (We are switching over to "we" in this chapter to reflect the fact that Kent and I wrote this chapter jointly. You can tell the difference because the funny jokes are mine and the others are his.)

One thing we won't try to do here is give you precise criteria for when a refactoring is overdue. In our experience no set of metrics rivals informed human intuition. What we will do is give you indications that there is trouble that can be solved by a refactoring. You will have to develop your own sense of how many instance variables are too many instance variables and how many lines of code in a method are too many lines.

You should use this chapter and the table on the inside back cover as a way to give you inspiration when you're not sure what refactorings to do. Read the chapter (or skim the table) to try to identify what it is you're smelling, then go to the refactorings we suggest to see whether they will help you. You may not find the exact smell you can detect, but hopefully it should point you in the right direction.

Duplicated Code

Number one in the stink parade is duplicated code. If you see the same code structure in more than one place, you can be sure that your program will be better if you find a way to unify them.

The simplest duplicated code problem is when you have the same expression in two methods of the same class. Then all you have to do is *Extract Method (110)* and invoke the code from both places.

Another common duplication problem is when you have the same expression in two sibling subclasses. You can eliminate this duplication by using *Extract Method (110)* in both classes then *Pull Up Method (322)*. If the code is similar but not the same, you need to use *Extract Method (110)* to separate the similar bits from the different bits. You may then find you can use *Form Template Method (345)*. If the methods do the same thing with a different algorithm, you can choose the clearer of the two algorithms and use *Substitute Algorithm (139)*.

If you have duplicated code in two unrelated classes, consider using *Extract Class (149)* in one class and then use the new component in the other. Another possibility is that the method really belongs only in one of the classes and should be invoked by the other class or that the method belongs in a third class that should be referred to by both of the original classes. You have to decide where the method makes sense and ensure it is there and nowhere else.

Long Method

The object programs that live best and longest are those with short methods. Programmers new to objects often feel that no computation ever takes place, that object programs are endless sequences of delegation. When you have lived with such a program for a few years, however, you learn just how valuable all those little methods are. All of the payoffs of indirection—explanation, sharing, and choosing—are supported by little methods (see Indirection and Refactoring on page 61).

Since the early days of programming people have realized that the longer a procedure is, the more difficult it is to understand. Older languages carried an overhead in subroutine calls, which deterred people from small methods. Modern OO languages have pretty much eliminated that overhead for in-process calls. There is still an overhead to the reader of the code because you have to switch context to see what the subprocedure does. Development environments that allow you to see two methods at once help to eliminate this step, but the real key to making it easy to understand small methods is good naming. If you have a good name for a method you don't need to look at the body.

The net effect is that you should be much more aggressive about decomposing methods. A heuristic we follow is that whenever we feel the need to comment something, we write a method instead. Such a method contains the code that was commented but is named after the intention of the code rather than how it does it. We may do this on a group of lines or on as little as a single line of code. We do this even if the method call is longer than the code it replaces, provided the method name explains the purpose of the code. The key here is not method length but the semantic distance between what the method does and how it does it.

Ninety-nine percent of the time, all you have to do to shorten a method is *Extract Method (110)*. Find parts of the method that seem to go nicely together and make a new method.

If you have a method with lots of parameters and temporary variables, these elements get in the way of extracting methods. If you try to use *Extract Method,* you end up passing so many of the parameters and temporary variables as parameters to the extracted method that the result is scarcely more readable than the original. You can often use *Replace Temp with Query (120)* to eliminate the temps. Long lists of parameters can be slimmed down with *Introduce Parameter Object (295)* and *Preserve Whole Object (288)*.

If you've tried that, and you still have too many temps and parameters, it's time to get out the heavy artillery: *Replace Method with Method Object (135)*.

How do you identify the clumps of code to extract? A good technique is to look for comments. They often signal this kind of semantic distance. A block of code with a comment that tells you what it is doing can be replaced by a method whose name is based on the comment. Even a single line is worth extracting if it needs explanation.

Conditionals and loops also give signs for extractions. Use *Decompose Conditional (238)* to deal with conditional expressions. With loops, extract the loop and the code within the loop into its own method.

Large Class

When a class is trying to do too much, it often shows up as too many instance variables. When a class has too many instance variables, duplicated code cannot be far behind.

You can *Extract Class (149)* to bundle a number of the variables. Choose variables to go together in the component that makes sense for each. For example, "depositAmount" and "depositCurrency" are likely to belong together in a component. More generally, common prefixes or suffixes for some subset of the variables in a class suggest the opportunity for a component. If the component makes sense as a subclass, you'll find *Extract Subclass (330)* often is easier.

Sometimes a class does not use all of its instance variables all of the time. If so, you may be able to *Extract Class (149)* or *Extract Subclass (330)* many times.

As with a class with too many instance variables, a class with too much code is prime breeding ground for duplicated code, chaos, and death. The simplest solution (have we mentioned that we like simple solutions?) is to eliminate redundancy in the class itself. If you have five hundred-line methods with lots of code in common, you may be able to turn them into five ten-line methods with another ten two-line methods extracted from the original.

As with a class with a huge wad of variables, the usual solution for a class with too much code is either to *Extract Class (149)* or *Extract Subclass (330)*. A useful trick is to determine how clients use the class and to use *Extract Interface (341)* for each of these uses. That may give you ideas on how you can further break up the class.

If your large class is a GUI class, you may need to move data and behavior to a separate domain object. This may require keeping some duplicate data in both places and keeping the data in sync. *Duplicate Observed Data (189)* suggests how to do this. In this case, especially if you are using older Abstract Windows Toolkit (AWT) components, you might follow this by removing the GUI class and replacing it with Swing components.

Long Parameter List

In our early programming days we were taught to pass in as parameters everything needed by a routine. This was understandable because the alternative was global data, and global data is evil and usually painful. Objects change this situation because if you don't have something you need, you can always ask another object to get it for you. Thus with objects you don't pass in everything the method needs; instead you pass enough so that the method can get to everything it needs. A lot of what a method needs is available on the method's host class. In object-oriented programs parameter lists tend to be much smaller than in traditional programs.

This is good because long parameter lists are hard to understand, because they become inconsistent and difficult to use, and because you are forever changing them as you need more data. Most changes are removed by passing objects because you are much more likely to need to make only a couple of requests to get at a new piece of data.

Use *Replace Parameter with Method (292)* when you can get the data in one parameter by making a request of an object you already know about. This object might be a field or it might be another parameter. Use *Preserve Whole Object (288)* to take a bunch of data gleaned from an object and replace it with the object itself. If you have several data items with no logical object, use *Introduce Parameter Object (295)*.

There is one important exception to making these changes. This is when you explicitly do not want to create a dependency from the called object to the larger object. In those cases unpacking data and sending it along as parameters is reasonable, but pay attention to the pain involved. If the parameter list is too long or changes too often, you need to rethink your dependency structure.

Divergent Change

We structure our software to make change easier; after all, software is meant to be soft. When we make a change we want to be able to jump to a single clear point in the system and make the change. When you can't do this you are smelling one of two closely related pungencies.

Divergent change occurs when one class is commonly changed in different ways for different reasons. If you look at a class and say, "Well, I will have to change these three methods every time I get a new database; I have to change these four methods every time there is a new financial instrument," you likely have a situation in which two objects are better than one. That way each object is changed only as a result of one kind of change. Of course, you often discover this only after you've added a few databases or financial instruments. Any change to handle a variation should change a single class, and all the typing in the new class should express the variation. To clean this up you identify everything that changes for a particular cause and use *Extract Class (149)* to put them all together.

Shotgun Surgery

Shotgun surgery is similar to divergent change but is the opposite. You whiff this when every time you make a kind of change, you have to make a lot of little changes to a lot of different classes. When the changes are all over the place, they are hard to find, and it's easy to miss an important change.

In this case you want to use *Move Method (142)* and *Move Field (146)* to put all the changes into a single class. If no current class looks like a good candidate, create one. Often you can use *Inline Class (154)* to bring a whole bunch of behavior together. You get a small dose of divergent change, but you can easily deal with that.

Divergent change is one class that suffers many kinds of changes, and shotgun surgery is one change that alters many classes. Either way you want to arrange things so that, ideally, there is a one-to-one link between common changes and classes.

Feature Envy

The whole point of objects is that they are a technique to package data with the processes used on that data. A classic smell is a method that seems more interested in a class other than the one it actually is in. The most common focus of the envy is the data. We've lost count of the times we've seen a method that invokes half-a-dozen getting methods on another object to calculate some value. Fortunately the cure is obvious, the method clearly wants to be elsewhere, so you use *Move Method (142)* to get it there. Sometimes only part of the method suffers from envy; in that case use *Extract Method (110)* on the jealous bit and *Move Method (142)* to give it a dream home.

Of course not all cases are cut-and-dried. Often a method uses features of several classes, so which one should it live with? The heuristic we use is to determine which class has most of the data and put the method with that data. This step is often made easier if *Extract Method (110)* is used to break the method into pieces that go into different places.

Of course there are several sophisticated patterns that break this rule. From the Gang of Four [Gang of Four] Strategy and Visitor immediately leap to mind. Kent Beck's Self Delegation [Beck] is another. You use these to combat the divergent change smell. The fundamental rule of thumb is to put things together that change together. Data and the behavior that references that data usually change together, but there are exceptions. When the exceptions occur, we move the behavior to keep changes in one place. Strategy and Visitor allow you to change behavior easily, because they isolate the small amount of behavior that needs to be overridden, at the cost of further indirection.

Data Clumps

Data items tend to be like children; they enjoy hanging around in groups together. Often you'll see the same three or four data items together in lots of places: fields in a couple of classes, parameters in many method signatures. Bunches of data that hang around together really ought to be made into their own object. The first step is to look for where the clumps appear as fields. Use *Extract Class (149)* on the fields to turn the clumps into an object. Then turn your attention to method signatures using *Introduce Parameter Object (295)* or *Preserve Whole Object (288)* to slim them down. The immediate benefit is that you can shrink a lot of parameter lists and simplify method calling. Don't worry about data clumps that use only some of the fields of the new object. As long as you are replacing two or more fields with the new object, you'll come out ahead.

A good test is to consider deleting one of the data values: if you did this, would the others make any sense? If they don't, it's a sure sign that you have an object that's dying to be born.

Reducing field lists and parameter lists will certainly remove a few bad smells, but once you have the objects, you get the opportunity to make a nice perfume. You can now look for cases of feature envy, which will suggest behavior that can be moved into your new classes. Before long these classes will be productive members of society.

Primitive Obsession

Most programming environments have two kinds of data. Record types allow you to structure data into meaningful groups. Primitive types are your building blocks. Records always carry a certain amount of overhead. They may mean tables in a database, or they may be awkward to create when you want them for only one or two things.

One of the valuable things about objects is that they blur or even break the line between primitive and larger classes. You can easily write little classes that are indistinguishable from the built-in types of the language. Java does have primitives for numbers, but strings and dates, which are primitives in many other environments, are classes.

People new to objects usually are reluctant to use small objects for small tasks, such as money classes that combine number and currency, ranges with an upper and a lower, and special strings such as telephone numbers and ZIP codes. You can move out of the cave into the centrally heated world of objects by using *Replace Data Value with Object (175)* on individual data values. If the data value is a type code, use *Replace Type Code with Class (218)* if the value does not affect behavior. If you have conditionals that depend on the type code, use *Replace Type Code with Subclasses (223)* or *Replace Type Code with State/ Strategy (227)*.

If you have a group of fields that should go together, use *Extract Class (149)*. If you see these primitives in parameter lists, try a civilizing dose of *Introduce Parameter Object (295)*. If you find yourself picking apart an array, use *Replace Array with Object (186)*.

Switch Statements

One of the most obvious symptoms of object-oriented code is its comparative lack of switch (or case) statements. The problem with switch statements is essentially that of duplication. Often you find the same switch statement scattered about a program in different places. If you add a new clause to the switch, you have to find all these switch statements and change them. The object-oriented notion of polymorphism gives you an elegant way to deal with this problem.

Most times you see a switch statement you should consider polymorphism. The issue is where the polymorphism should occur. Often the switch statement switches on a type code. You want the method or class that hosts the type code value. So use *Extract Method (110)* to extract the switch statement and then *Move Method (142)* to get it onto the class where the polymorphism is needed. At that point you have to decide whether to *Replace Type Code with Subclasses (223)* or *Replace Type Code with State/Strategy (227)*. When you have set up the inheritance structure, you can use *Replace Conditional with Polymorphism (255)*.

If you only have a few cases that affect a single method, and you don't expect them to change, then polymorphism is overkill. In this case *Replace Parameter with Explicit Methods (285)* is a good option. If one of your conditional cases is a null, try *Introduce Null Object (260)*.

Parallel Inheritance Hierarchies

Parallel inheritance hierarchies is really a special case of shotgun surgery. In this case, every time you make a subclass of one class, you also have to make a subclass of another. You can recognize this smell because the prefixes of the class names in one hierarchy are the same as the prefixes in another hierarchy.

The general strategy for eliminating the duplication is to make sure that instances of one hierarchy refer to instances of the other. If you use *Move Method (142)* and *Move Field (146)*, the hierarchy on the referring class disappears.

Lazy Class

Each class you create costs money to maintain and understand. A class that isn't doing enough to pay for itself should be eliminated. Often this might be a class that used to pay its way but has been downsized with refactoring. Or it might be a class that was added because of changes that were planned but not made. Either way, you let the class die with dignity. If you have subclasses that aren't doing enough, try to use *Collapse Hierarchy (344)*. Nearly useless components should be subjected to *Inline Class (154)*.

Speculative Generality

Brian Foote suggested this name for a smell to which we are very sensitive. You get it when people say, "Oh, I think we need the ability to do this kind of thing someday" and thus want all sorts of hooks and special cases to handle things that aren't required. The result often is harder to understand and maintain. If all this machinery were being used, it would be worth it. But if it isn't, it isn't. The machinery just gets in the way, so get rid of it.

If you have abstract classes that aren't doing much, use *Collapse Hierarchy (344)*. Unnecessary delegation can be removed with *Inline Class (154)*. Methods with unused parameters should be subject to *Remove Parameter (277)*. Methods named with odd abstract names should be brought down to earth with *Rename Method (273)*.

Speculative generality can be spotted when the only users of a method or class are test cases. If you find such a method or class, delete it and the test case that exercises it. If you have a method or class that is a helper for a test case that exercises legitimate functionality, you have to leave it in, of course.

Temporary Field

Sometimes you see an object in which an instance variable is set only in certain circumstances. Such code is difficult to understand, because you expect an object to need all of its variables. Trying to understand why a variable is there when it doesn't seem to be used can drive you nuts.

Use *Extract Class (149)* to create a home for the poor orphan variables. Put all the code that concerns the variables into the component. You may also be able to eliminate conditional code by using *Introduce Null Object (260)* to create an alternative component for when the variables aren't valid.

A common case of temporary field occurs when a complicated algorithm needs several variables. Because the implementer didn't want to pass around a huge parameter list (who does?), he put them in fields. But the fields are valid only during the algorithm; in other contexts they are just plain confusing. In this case you can use *Extract Class* with these variables and the methods that require them. The new object is a method object [Beck].

Message Chains

You see message chains when a client asks one object for another object, which the client then asks for yet another object, which the client then asks for yet another another object, and so on. You may see these as a long line of getThis methods, or as a sequence of temps. Navigating this way means the client is coupled to the structure of the navigation. Any change to the intermediate relationships causes the client to have to change.

The move to use here is *Hide Delegate (157)*. You can do this at various points in the chain. In principle you can do this to every object in the chain, but doing this often turns every intermediate object into a middle man. Often a better alternative is to see what the resulting object is used for. See whether you can use *Extract Method (110)* to take a piece of the code that uses it and then *Move Method (142)* to push it down the chain. If several clients of one of the objects in the chain want to navigate the rest of the way, add a method to do that.

Some people consider any method chain to be a terrible thing. We are known for our calm, reasoned moderation. Well, at least in this case we are.

Middle Man

One of the prime features of objects is encapsulation—hiding internal details from the rest of the world. Encapsulation often comes with delegation. You ask a director whether she is free for a meeting; she delegates the message to her diary and gives you an answer. All well and good. There is no need to know whether the director uses a diary, an electronic gizmo, or a secretary to keep track of her appointments.

However, this can go too far. You look at a class's interface and find half the methods are delegating to this other class. After a while it is time to use *Remove Middle Man (160)* and talk to the object that really knows what's going on. If only a few methods aren't doing much, use *Inline Method (117)* to inline them into the caller. If there is additional behavior, you can use *Replace Delegation with Inheritance (355)* to turn the middle man into a subclass of the real object. That allows you to extend behavior without chasing all that delegation.

Inappropriate Intimacy

Sometimes classes become far too intimate and spend too much time delving in each others' private parts. We may not be prudes when it comes to people, but we think our classes should follow strict, puritan rules.

Overintimate classes need to be broken up as lovers were in ancient days. Use *Move Method (142)* and *Move Field (146)* to separate the pieces to reduce the intimacy. See whether you can arrange a *Change Bidirectional Association to Unidirectional (200)*. If the classes do have common interests, use *Extract Class (149)* to put the commonality in a safe place and make honest classes of them. Or use *Hide Delegate (157)* to let another class act as go-between.

Inheritance often can lead to overintimacy. Subclasses are always going to know more about their parents than their parents would like them to know. If it's time to leave home, apply *Replace Inheritance with Delegation (352)*.

Alternative Classes with Different Interfaces

Use *Rename Method (273)* on any methods that do the same thing but have different signatures for what they do. Often this doesn't go far enough. In these cases the classes aren't yet doing enough. Keep using *Move Method (142)* to move behavior to the classes until the protocols are the same. If you have to redundantly move code to accomplish this, you may be able to use *Extract Superclass (336)* to atone.

Incomplete Library Class

Reuse is often touted as the purpose of objects. We think reuse is overrated (we just use). However, we can't deny that much of our programming skill is based on library classes so that nobody can tell whether we've forgotten our sort algorithms.

Builders of library classes are rarely omniscient. We don't blame them for that; after all, we can rarely figure out a design until we've mostly built it, so library builders have a really tough job. The trouble is that it is often bad form, and usually impossible, to modify a library class to do something you'd like it to do. This means that tried-and-true tactics such as *Move Method (142)* lie useless.

We have a couple of special-purpose tools for this job. If there are just a couple of methods that you wish the library class had, use *Introduce Foreign Method (162)*. If there is a whole load of extra behavior, you need *Introduce Local Extension (164)*.

Data Class

These are classes that have fields, getting and setting methods for the fields, and nothing else. Such classes are dumb data holders and are almost certainly being manipulated in far too much detail by other classes. In early stages these classes may have public fields. If so, you should immediately apply *Encapsulate Field (206)* before anyone notices. If you have collection fields, check to see whether they are properly encapsulated and apply *Encapsulate Collection (208)* if they aren't. Use *Remove Setting Method (300)* on any field that should not be changed.

Look for where these getting and setting methods are used by other classes. Try to use *Move Method (142)* to move behavior into the data class. If you can't move a whole method, use *Extract Method (110)* to create a method that can be moved. After a while you can start using *Hide Method (303)* on the getters and setters.

Data classes are like children. They are okay as a starting point, but to participate as a grownup object, they need to take some responsibility.

Refused Bequest

Subclasses get to inherit the methods and data of their parents. But what if they don't want or need what they are given? They are given all these great gifts and pick just a few to play with.

The traditional story is that this means the hierarchy is wrong. You need to create a new sibling class and use *Push Down Method (328)* and *Push Down Field (329)* to push all the unused methods to the sibling. That way the parent holds only what is common. Often you'll hear advice that all superclasses should be abstract.

You'll guess from our snide use of *traditional* that we aren't going to advise this, at least not all the time. We do subclassing to reuse a bit of behavior all the time, and we find it a perfectly good way of doing business. There is a smell, we can't deny it, but usually it isn't a strong smell. So we say that if the refused bequest is causing confusion and problems, follow the traditional advice. However, don't feel you have to do it all the time. Nine times out of ten this smell is too faint to be worth cleaning.

The smell of refused bequest is much stronger if the subclass is reusing behavior but does not want to support the interface of the superclass. We don't mind refusing implementations, but refusing interface gets us on our high horses. In this case, however, don't fiddle with the hierarchy; you want to gut it by applying *Replace Inheritance with Delegation (352)*.

Comments

Don't worry, we aren't saying that people shouldn't write comments. In our olfactory analogy, comments aren't a bad smell; indeed they are a sweet smell. The reason we mention comments here is that comments often are used as a deodorant. It's surprising how often you look at thickly commented code and notice that the comments are there because the code is bad.

Comments lead us to bad code that has all the rotten whiffs we've discussed in the rest of this chapter. Our first action is to remove the bad smells by refactoring. When we're finished, we often find that the comments are superfluous.

If you need a comment to explain what a block of code does, try *Extract Method (110)*. If the method is already extracted but you still need a comment to explain what it does, use *Rename Method (273)*. If you need to state some rules about the required state of the system, use *Introduce Assertion (267)*.

When you feel the need to write a comment, first try to refactor the code so that any comment becomes superfluous.

A good time to use a comment is when you don't know what to do. In addition to describing what is going on, comments can indicate areas in which you aren't sure. A comment is a good place to say *why* you did something. This kind of information helps future modifiers, especially forgetful ones.

Chapter 4

Building Tests

If you want to refactor, the essential precondition is having solid tests. Even if you are fortunate enough to have a tool that can automate the refactorings, you still need tests. It will be a long time before all possible refactorings can be automated in a refactoring tool.

I don't see this as a disadvantage. I've found that writing good tests greatly speeds my programming, even if I'm not refactoring. This was a surprise for me, and it is counterintuitive for many programmers, so it's worth explaining why.

The Value of Self-testing Code

If you look at how most programmers spend their time, you'll find that writing code actually is quite a small fraction. Some time is spent figuring out what ought to be going on, some time is spent designing, but most time is spent debugging. I'm sure every reader can remember long hours of debugging, often long into the night. Every programmer can tell a story of a bug that took a whole day (or more) to find. Fixing the bug is usually pretty quick, but finding it is a nightmare. And then when you do fix a bug, there's always a chance that another one will appear and that you might not even notice it till much later. Then you spend ages finding that bug.

The event that started me on the road to self-testing code was a talk at OOPSLA in '92. Someone (I think it was Dave Thomas) said offhandedly, "Classes should contain their own tests." That struck me as a good way to organize tests. I interpreted that as saying that each class should have its own method (called *test*) that can be used to test itself.

At that time I was also into incremental development, so I tried adding test methods to classes as I completed each increment. The project on which I was working at that time was quite small, so we put out increments every week or so. Running the tests became fairly straightforward, but although they were easy to run, the tests were still pretty boring to do. This was because every test produced output to the console that I had to check. Now I'm a pretty lazy person and am prepared to work quite hard in order to avoid work. I realized that instead of looking at the screen to see if it printed out some information from the model, I could get the computer to make that test. All I had to do was put the output I expected in the test code and do a comparison. Now I could run each class' test method, and it would just print "OK" to the screen if all was well. The class was now self-testing.

Make sure all tests are fully automatic and that they check their own results.

Now it was easy to run a test—as easy as compiling. So I started to run tests every time I compiled. Soon I began to notice my productivity had shot upward. I realized that I wasn't spending so much time debugging. If I added a bug that was caught by a previous test, it would show up as soon as I ran that test. Because the test had worked before, I would know that the bug was in the work I had done since I last tested. Because I ran the tests frequently, only a few minutes had elapsed. I thus knew that the source of the bug was the code I had just written. Because that code was fresh in my mind and was a small amount, the bug was easy to find. Bugs that once had taken an hour or more to find now took a couple of minutes at most. Not just had I built self-testing classes, but by running them frequently I had a powerful bug detector.

As I noticed this I became more aggressive about doing the tests. Instead of waiting for the end of increment, I would add the tests immediately after writing a bit of function. Every day I would add a couple of new features and the tests to test them. These days I hardly ever spend more than a few minutes debugging.

A suite of tests is a powerful bug detector that decapitates the time it takes to find bugs.

Of course, it is not so easy to persuade others to follow this route. Writing the tests is a lot of extra code to write. Unless you have actually experienced the way it speeds programming, self-testing does not seem to make sense. This is not helped by the fact that many people have never learned to write tests or even to think about tests. When tests are manual, they are gut-wrenchingly boring. But when they are automatic, tests can actually be quite fun to write.

In fact, one of the most useful times to write tests is before you start programming. When you need to add a feature, begin by writing the test. This isn't as backward as it sounds. By writing the test you are asking yourself what needs to be done to add the function. Writing the test also concentrates on the interface rather than the implementation (always a good thing). It also means you have a clear point at which you are done coding—when the test works.

This notion of frequent testing is an important part of extreme programming [Beck, XP]. The name conjures up notions of programmers who are fast and loose hackers. But extreme programmers are very dedicated testers. They want to develop software as fast as possible, and they know that tests help you to go as fast as you possibly can.

That's enough of the polemic. Although I believe everyone would benefit by writing self-testing code, it is not the point of this book. This book is about refactoring. Refactoring requires tests. If you want to refactor, you have to write tests. This chapter gives you a start in doing this for Java. This is not a testing book, so I'm not going to go into much detail. But with testing I've found that a remarkably small amount can have surprisingly big benefits.

As with everything else in this book, I describe the testing approach using examples. When I develop code, I write the tests as I go. But often when I'm working with people on refactoring, we have a body of non-self-testing code to work on. So first we have to make the code self-testing before we refactor.

The standard Java idiom for testing is the testing main. The idea is that every class should have a main function that tests the class. It's a reasonable convention (although not honored much), but it can become awkward. The problem is that such a convention makes it tricky to run many tests easily. Another approach is to build separate test classes that work in a framework to make testing easier.

The JUnit Testing Framework

The testing framework I use is JUnit, an open-source testing framework developed by Erich Gamma and Kent Beck [JUnit]. The framework is very simple, yet it allows you to do all the key things you need for testing. In this chapter I use this framework to develop tests for some io classes.

To begin I create a FileReaderTester class to test the file reader. Any class that contains tests must subclass the test-case class from the testing framework. The framework uses the composite pattern [Gang of Four] that allows you to group tests into suites (Figure 4.1). These suites can contain the raw test-cases or other

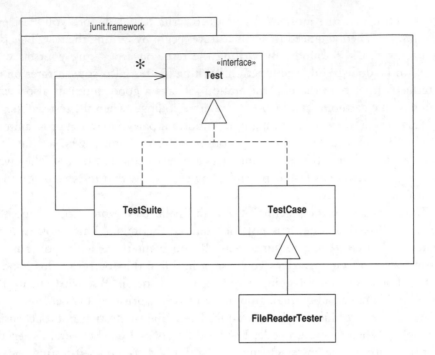

Figure 4.1 *The composite structure of tests*

suites of test-cases. This makes it easy to build a range of large test suites and run the tests automatically.

```
class FileReaderTester extends TestCase {
    public FileReaderTester (String name) {
        super(name);
    }
}
```

The new class has to have a constructor. After this I can start adding some test code. My first job is to set up the test fixture. A test fixture is essentially the objects that act as samples for testing. Because I'm reading a file I need to set up a test file, as follows:

```
Bradman     99.94 52   80   10   6996   334   29
Pollock     60.97 23   41   4    2256   274   7
Headley     60.83 22   40   4    2256   270*  10
Sutcliffe   60.73 54   84   9    4555   194   16
```

To further use the file, I prepare the fixture. The test-case class provides two methods to manipulate the test fixture: setUp creates the objects and tearDown removes them. Both are implemented as null methods on test-case. Most of the time you don't need to do a tear down (the garbage collector can handle it), but it is wise to use it here to close the file, as follows:

```
class FileReaderTester...
    protected void setUp() {
        try {
            _input = new FileReader("data.txt");
        } catch (FileNotFoundException e) {
            throw new RuntimeException ("unable to open test file");
        }
    }

    protected void tearDown() {
        try {
            _input.close();
        } catch (IOException e) {
            throw new RuntimeException ("error on closing test file");
        }
    }
```

Now that I have the test fixture in place, I can start writing tests. The first is to test the read method. To do this I read a few characters and then check that the character I read next is the right one:

```
public void testRead() throws IOException {
    char ch = '&';
    for (int i=0; i < 4; i++)
        ch = (char) _input.read();
    assert('d' == ch);
}
```

The automatic test is the assert method. If the value inside the assert is true, all is well. Otherwise we signal an error. I show how the framework does that later. First I describe how to run the test.

The first step is to create a test suite. To do this, create a method called *suite*:

```
class FileReaderTester...
    public static Test suite() {
        TestSuite suite= new TestSuite();
        suite.addTest(new FileReaderTester("testRead"));
        return suite;
    }
```

This test suite contains only one test-case object, an instance of FileReaderTester. When I create a test case, I give the constructor a string argument, which is the name of the method I'm going to test. This creates one object that tests that one method. The test is bound to the object through Java's reflection capability. You can take a look at the downloaded source code to figure out how it does it. I just treat it as magic.

To run the tests, use a separate TestRunner class. There are two versions of TestRunner: one uses a cool GUI, the other a simple character interface. I can call the character interface version in the main:

```
class FileReaderTester...
    public static void main (String[] args) {
        junit.textui.TestRunner.run (suite());
}
```

The code creates the test runner and tells it to test the FileReaderTester class. When I run it I see

```
.
Time: 0.110

OK (1 tests)
```

JUnit prints a period for each test that runs (so you can see progress). It tells you how long the tests have run. It then says "OK" if nothing goes wrong and tells you how many tests have been run. I can run a thousand tests, and if all goes well, I'll see that OK. This simple feedback is essential to self-testing code. Without it you'll never run the tests often enough. With it you can run masses of tests, go off for lunch (or a meeting), and see the results when you get back.

 Run your tests frequently. Localize tests whenever you compile—every test at least every day.

In refactoring you run only a few tests to exercise the code on which you are working. You can run only a few because they must be fast: otherwise they'll slow you down and you'll be tempted not to run them. Don't give in to that temptation—retribution *will* follow.

What happens if something goes wrong? I'll demonstrate by putting in a deliberate bug, as follows:

```
    public void testRead() throws IOException {
        char ch = '&';
        for (int i=0; i < 4; i++)
            ch = (char) _input.read();
        assert('2' == ch);    //deliberate error
    }
```

The result looks like this:

```
.F
Time: 0.220

!!!FAILURES!!!
```

```
Test Results:
Run: 1 Failures: 1 Errors: 0
There was 1 failure:
1) FileReaderTester.testRead
test.framework.AssertionFailedError
```

The framework alerts me to the failure and tells me which test failed. The error message isn't particularly helpful, though. I can make the error message better by using another form of assert.

```
public void testRead() throws IOException {
    char ch = '&';
    for (int i=0; i < 4; i++)
        ch = (char) _input.read();
    assertEquals('m',ch);
}
```

Most of the asserts you do are comparing two values to see whether they are equal. So the framework includes assertEquals. This is convenient; it uses equals() on objects and == on values, which I often forget to do. It also allows a more meaningful error message:

```
.F
Time: 0.170

!!!FAILURES!!!
Test Results:
Run: 1 Failures: 1 Errors: 0
There was 1 failure:
1) FileReaderTester.testRead "expected:"m"but was:"d""
```

I should mention that often when I'm writing tests, I start by making them fail. With existing code I either change it to make it fail (if I can touch the code) or put an incorrect expected value in the assert. I do this because I like to prove to myself that the test does actually run and the test is actually testing what it's supposed to (which is why I prefer changing the tested code if I can). This may be paranoia, but you can really confuse yourself when tests are testing something other than what you think they are testing.

In addition to catching failures (assertions coming out false), the framework also catches errors (unexpected exceptions). If I close the stream and then try to read from it, I should get an exception. I can test this with

```
public void testRead() throws IOException {
    char ch = '&';
    _input.close();
    for (int i=0; i < 4; i++)
        ch = (char) _input.read();           // will throw exception
    assertEquals('m',ch);
}
```

If I run this I get

```
.E

Time: 0.110

!!!FAILURES!!!
Test Results:
Run: 1 Failures: 0 Errors: 1
There was 1 error:
1) FileReaderTester.testRead
java.io.IOException: Stream closed
```

It is useful to differentiate failures and errors, because they tend to turn up differently and the debugging process is different.

JUnit also includes a nice GUI (Figure 4.2). The progress bar shows green if all tests pass and red if there are any failures. You can leave the GUI up all the time, and the environment automatically links in any changes to your code. This is a very convenient way to run the tests.

Unit and Functional Tests

This framework is used for unit tests, so I should mention the difference between unit tests and functional tests. The tests I'm talking about are *unit tests*. I write them to improve my productivity as a programmer. Making the

Figure 4.2 *The graphical user interface of JUnit*

quality assurance department happy is just a side effect. Unit tests are highly localized. Each test class works within a single package. It tests the interfaces to other packages, but beyond that it assumes the rest just works.

Functional tests are a different animal. They are written to ensure the software as a whole works. They provide quality assurance to the customer and don't care about programmer productivity. They should be developed by a different team, one who delights in finding bugs. This team uses heavyweight tools and techniques to help them do this.

Functional tests typically treat the whole system as a black box as much as possible. In a GUI-based system, they operate through the GUI. In a file or database update program, the tests just look at how the data is changed for certain inputs.

When functional testers, or users, find a bug in the software, at least two things are needed to fix it. Of course you have to change the production code to remove the bug. But you should also add a unit test that exposes the bug. Indeed, when I get a bug report, I begin by writing a unit test that causes the bug to surface. I write more than one test if I need to narrow the scope of the bug, or if there may be related failures. I use the unit tests to help pin down the bug and to ensure that a similar bug doesn't get past my unit tests again.

When you get a bug report, start by writing a unit test that exposes the bug.

The JUnit framework is designed for writing unit tests. Functional tests often are performed with other tools. GUI-based test tools are good examples. Often, however, you'll write your own application-specific test tools that make it easier to manage test-cases than do GUI scripts alone. You can perform functional tests with JUnit, but it's usually not the most efficient way. For refactoring purposes, I count on the unit tests—the programmer's friend.

Adding More Tests

Now we should continue adding more tests. The style I follow is to look at all the things the class should do and test each one of them for any conditions that might cause the class to fail. This is not the same as "test every public method," which some programmers advocate. Testing should be risk driven; remember, you are trying to find bugs now or in the future. So I don't test accessors that just read and write a field. Because they are so simple, I'm not likely to find a bug there.

This is important because trying to write too many tests usually leads to not writing enough. I've often read books on testing, and my reaction has been to shy away from the mountain of stuff I have to do to test. This is counterproductive, because it makes you think that to test you have to do a lot of work. You get many benefits from testing even if you do only a little testing. The key is to test the areas that you are most worried about going wrong. That way you get the most benefit for your testing effort.

It is better to write and run incomplete tests than not to run complete tests.

At the moment I'm looking at the read method. What else should it do? One thing it says is that it returns -1 at the end of the file (not a very nice protocol in my view, but I guess that makes it more natural for C programmers). Let's test it. My text editor tells me there are 141 characters in the file, so here's the test:

```
public
  void testReadAtEnd() throws IOException {
      int ch = -1234;
      for (int i = 0; i < 141; i++)
          ch = _input.read();
      assertEquals("read at end", -1, _input.read());
}
```

To get the test to run, I have to add it to the suite:

```
public static Test suite() {
  TestSuite suite= new TestSuite();
  suite.addTest(new FileReaderTester("testRead"));
  suite.addTest(new FileReaderTester("testReadAtEnd"));
  return suite;
}
```

When this suite is run, it tells each of its component tests (the two test-cases) to run. Each test-case executes setUp, the body of the test code in the testing method, and finally tearDown. It is important to run setUp and tearDown each time so that the tests are isolated from each other. That means we can run them in any order and it doesn't matter.

It's a pain to remember to add the tests to the suite method. Fortunately, Erich Gamma and Kent Beck are just as lazy as I am, so they provided a way to avoid that. A special constructor for the test suite takes a class as a parameter. This constructor builds a test suite that contains a test-case for every method that starts with the word *test*. If I follow that convention, I can replace my main with

```
public static void main (String[] args) {
   junit.textui.TestRunner.run (new TestSuite(FileReaderTester.class));
}
```

That way each test I write is added to the suite.

A key trick with tests is to look for boundary conditions. For the read the boundaries would be the first character, the last character, and the character after the last character:

```
public void testReadBoundaries()throwsIOException {
     assertEquals("read first char",'B', _input.read());
     int ch;
     for (int i = 1;i <140; i++)
        ch =  _input.read();
     assertEquals("read last char",'6',_input.read());
     assertEquals("read at end",-1,_input.read());
  }
```

Notice that you can add a message to the assert that is printed if the test fails.

Think of the boundary conditions under which things might go wrong and concentrate your tests there.

Another part of looking for boundaries is looking for special conditions that can cause the test to fail. For files, empty files are always a good choice:

```
public void testEmptyRead() throws IOException {
   File empty = new File ("empty.txt");
   FileOutputStream out = new FileOutputStream(empty);
   out.close();
   FileReader in = newFileReader (empty);
   assertEquals (-1, in.read());
 }
```

In this case I'm creating a bit of extra fixture just for this test. If I need an empty file for later, I can move it into regular fixture by moving the code to setup.

```
protected void setUp(){
   try {
      _input = new FileReader("data.txt");
      _empty = newEmptyFile();
```

```
  } catch(IOException e){
      throw new RuntimeException(e.toString());
  }
}

private FileReader newEmptyFile() throws IOException {
  File empty = new File ("empty.txt");
  FileOutputStream out = new FileOutputStream(empty);
  out.close();
  return newFileReader(empty);
}

public void testEmptyRead() throws IOException {
  assertEquals (-1, _empty.read());
}
```

What happens if you read after the end of the file? Again -1 should be returned, and I augment one of the other tests to probe that:

```
public void testReadBoundaries()throwsIOException {
  assertEquals("read first char",'B', _input.read());
  int ch;
  for (int i = 1;i <140; i++)
      ch = _input.read();
  assertEquals("read last char",'6',_input.read());
  assertEquals("read at end",-1,_input.read());
  assertEquals ("readpast end", -1, _input.read());
}
```

Notice how I'm playing the part of an enemy to code. I'm actively thinking about how I can break it. I find that state of mind to be both productive and fun. It indulges the mean-spirited part of my psyche.

When you are doing tests, don't forget to check that expected errors occur properly. If you try to read a stream after it is closed, you should get an IOException. This too should be tested:

```
public void testReadAfterClose() throwsIOException{
  _input.close();
  try {
      _input.read();
      fail ("no exception for read past end");
  } catch (IOException io) {}
}
```

Any other exception than the IOException will produce an error in the normal way.

💡 *Don't forget to test that exceptions are raised when things are expected to go wrong.*

Fleshing out the tests continues along these lines. It takes a while to go through the interface to some classes to do this, but in the process you get to really understand the interface of the class. In particular, it helps to think about error conditions and boundary conditions. That's another advantage for writing tests as you write code, or even before you write the production code.

As you add more tester classes, you can create other tester classes that combine suites from multiple classes. This is easy to do because a test suite can contain other test suites. Thus you can have a master test class:

```
class MasterTester extends TestCase {
  public static void main (String[] args) {
      junit.textui.TestRunner.run (suite());
  }
  public static Test suite() {
      TestSuite result = new TestSuite();
      result.addTest(new TestSuite(FileReaderTester.class));
      result.addTest(new TestSuite(FileWriterTester.class));
      // and so on...
      return result;
  }
}
```

When do you stop? I'm sure you have heard many times that you cannot prove a program has no bugs by testing. That's true but does not affect the ability of testing to speed up programming. I've seen various proposals for rules to ensure you have tested every combination of everything. It's worth taking a look at these, but don't let them get to you. There is a point of diminishing returns with testing, and there is the danger that by trying to write too many tests, you become discouraged and end up not writing any. You should concentrate on where the risk is. Look at the code and see where it beomes complex. Look at the function and consider the likely areas of error. Your tests will not find every bug, but as you refactor you will understand the program better and thus find more bugs. Although I always start refactoring with a test suite, I invariably add to it as I go along.

Don't let the fear that testing can't catch all bugs stop you from writing the tests that will catch most bugs.

One of the tricky things about objects is that the inheritance and polymorphism can make testing harder, because there are many combinations to test. If you have three abstract classes that collaborate and each has three subclasses, you have nine alternatives but twenty-seven combinations. I don't always try to test all the combinations possible, but I do try to test each alternative. It boils down to the risk in the combinations. If the alternatives are reasonably independent of each other, I'm not likely to try each combination. There's always a risk that I'll miss something, but it is better to spend a reasonable time to catch most bugs than to spend ages trying to catch them all.

A difference between test code and production code is that it is okay to copy and edit test code. When dealing with combinations and alternatives, I often do that. First take "regular pay event," now take "seniority" and "disabled before the end of the year." Now do it without "seniority" and "disabled before the end of the year," and so on. With simple alternatives like that on top of a reasonable fixture, I can generate tests very quickly. I then can use refactoring to factor out truly common items later.

I hope I have given you a feel for writing tests. I can say a lot more on this topic, but that would obscure the key message. Build a good bug detector and run it frequently. It is a wonderful tool for any development and is a precondition for refactoring.

Chapter 5

Toward a Catalog of Refactorings

Chapters 5 to 12 form an initial catalog of refactorings. They've grown from the notes I've made in refactoring over the last few years. This catalog is by no means comprehensive or watertight, but it should provide a solid starting point for your own refactoring work.

Format of the Refactorings

As I describe the refactorings in this and other chapters, I use a standard format. Each refactoring has five parts, as follows:

- I begin with a **name**. The name is important to building a vocabulary of refactorings. This is the name I use elsewhere in the book.

- I follow the name with a short **summary** of the situation in which you need the refactoring and a summary of what the refactoring does. This helps you find a refactoring more quickly.

- The **motivation** describes why the refactoring should be done and describes circumstances in which it shouldn't be done.

- The **mechanics** are a concise, step-by-step description of how to carry out the refactoring.

- The **examples** show a very simple use of the refactoring to illustrate how it works.

The summary includes a short statement of the problem that the refactoring helps you with, a short description of what you do, and a sketch that shows you a simple before and after example. Sometimes I use code for the sketch and sometimes Unified Modeling Language (UML), depending on which seems to best convey the essence of the refactoring. (All UML diagrams in this book are drawn from the implementation perspective [Fowler, UML].) If you've seen the refactoring before, the sketch should give you a good idea what the refactoring is about. If not you'll probably need to work through the example to get a better idea.

The mechanics come from my own notes to remember how to do the refactoring when I haven't done it for a while. As such they are somewhat terse, usually without explanations of why the steps are done that way. I give more expansive explanations in the example. This way the mechanics are short notes you can refer to easily when you know the refactoring but need to look up the steps (at least this is how I use them). You'll probably need to read the example when you first do the refactoring.

I've written the mechanics in such a way that each step of each refactoring is as small as possible. I emphasize the safe way of doing the refactoring, which is to take very small steps and test after every one. At work I usually take larger steps than some of the baby steps described, but if I run into a bug, I back out the step and take the smaller steps. The steps include a number of references to special cases. The steps thus also function as a checklist; I often forget these things myself.

The examples are of the laughably simple textbook kind. My aim with the example is to help explain the basic refactoring with minimal distractions, so I hope you'll forgive the simplicity. (They are certainly not examples of good business object design.) I'm sure you'll be able to apply them to your rather more complex situations. Some very simple refactorings don't have examples because I didn't think an example would add much.

In particular, remember that the examples are included only to illustrate the one refactoring under discussion. In most cases, there are still problems with the code at the end, but fixing these problems requires other refactorings. In a few cases in which refactorings often go together, I carry examples from one refactoring to another. In most cases I leave the code as it is after the single refactoring. I do this to make each refactoring self-contained, because the primary role of the catalog is as a reference.

Don't take any of these examples as suggestions for how to design employee or order objects. These examples are there only to illustrate the refactorings, nothing more. In particular you'll notice that in the examples I use double to represent monetary values. I've done this only to make the examples simpler, as the representation is not important to the refactoring. I strongly advise against using doubles for money in commercial software. When I represent money I use the Quantity pattern [Fowler, AP].

When I was writing this book, Java 1.1; was the version that was mostly used in commercial work. Hence most of my examples use Java 1.1; this is most noticeable in my use of collections. As I reached the end of the book Java 2 became more available. I don't feel it is necessary to change all the examples, as the collections are secondary to the refactoring. However there are some refactorings, such as *Encapsulate Collection (208)*, that are different in Java 2. In such cases I've explained both the Java 2 and Java 1.1 cases.

I use **boldface code** to highlight changed code where it is buried among code that has not been changed and may be difficult to spot. I do not use boldface type for all changed code, because too much defeats the purpose.

Finding References

Many of the refactorings call for you to find all references to a method, a field, or a class. When you do this, enlist the computer to help you. By using the computer you reduce your chances of missing a reference and can usually do the search much more quickly than you would if you were simply to eyeball the code.

Most languages treat computer programs as text files. Your best help here is a suitable text search. Many programming environments allow you to text search a single file or a group of files. The access control of the feature you are looking for will tell you the range of files you need to look for.

Don't just search and replace blindly. Inspect each reference to ensure it really refers to the thing you are replacing. You can be clever with your search pattern, but I always check mentally to ensure I am making the right replacement. If you can use the same method name on different classes or methods of different signatures on the same class, there are too many chances you will get it wrong.

In a strongly typed language, you can let the compiler help you do the hunting. You can often remove the old feature and let the compiler find the dangling references. The good thing about this is that the compiler will catch every dangling reference. However, there are problems with this technique.

First, the compiler will become confused when a feature is declared more than once in an inheritance hierarchy. This is particularly true when you are looking at a method that is overridden several times. If you are working in a hierarchy, use the text search to see whether any other class declares the method you are manipulating.

The second problem is that the compiler may be too slow to be effective. If so, use a text search first; at least the compiler double-checks your work. This only works when you intend to remove the feature. Often you want to look at all the uses to decide what to do next. In these cases you have to use the text search alternative.

A third problem is that the compiler can't catch uses of the reflection API. This is one reason to be wary of using reflection. If your system uses reflection you will have to use text searches to find things and put additional weight on your testing. In a number of places I suggest compiling without testing in situations in which the compiler usually catches errors. If you use reflection, all such bets are off, and you should test with many of these compiles.

Some Java environments, notably IBM's VisualAge, are following the example of the Smalltalk browser. With these you use menu options to find references rather than using text searches. These environments do not use text files to hold the code; they use an in-memory database. Get used to using these menu items and you will find them often superior to the unavailable text search.

How Mature Are These Refactorings?

Any technical author has the problem of deciding when to publish. The earlier you publish, the quicker people can take advantage of the ideas. However, people are always learning. If you publish half-baked ideas too early, the ideas can be incomplete and even lead to problems for those who try to use them.

The basic technique of refactoring, taking small steps and testing often, has been well tested over many years, especially in the Smalltalk community. So I'm confident that the basic idea of refactoring is very stable.

The refactorings in this book are my notes about the refactorings I use. I have used them all. However, there is a difference between using a refactoring and boiling it down into the mechanical steps I give herein. In particular, you occasionally see problems that crop up only in very specific circumstances. I cannot say that I have had a lot of people work from these steps to spot many of these kinds of problems. As you use the refactorings, be aware of what you are doing. Remember that like working with a recipe, you have to adapt the refactorings to your circumstances. If you run into an interesting problem, drop me an e-mail, and I'll try to pass on these circumstances for others.

Another aspect to remember about these refactorings is that they are described with single-process software in mind. In time, I hope to see refactorings described for use with concurrent and distributed programming. Such refactorings will be different. For example, in single-process software you never need to worry how often you call a method; method calls are cheap. With distributed software, however, round trips have to be minimized. There are different refactorings for those flavors of programming, but those are topics for another book.

Many of the refactorings, such as *Replace Type Code with State/Strategy (227)* and *Form Template Method (345)* are about introducing patterns into a system. As the essential Gang of Four book says, "Design Patterns . . . provide targets for your refactorings." There is a natural relation between patterns and refactorings. Patterns are where you want to be; refactorings are ways to get there from somewhere else. I don't have refactorings for all known patterns in this book, not even for all the Gang of Four patterns [Gang of Four]. This is another aspect of the incompleteness of this catalog. I hope someday the gap will be closed.

As you use the refactorings bear in mind that they are a starting point. You will doubtless find gaps in them. I'm publishing them now because although they are not perfect, I do believe they are useful. I believe they will give you a starting point that will improve your ability to refactor efficiently. That is what they do for me.

As you use more refactorings, I hope you will start developing your own. I hope the examples herein will motivate you and give you a starting point as to how to do that. I'm conscious of the fact that there are many more refactorings than the ones I described. If you do come up with some, please drop me an e-mail.

Chapter 6

Composing Methods

A large part of my refactoring is composing methods to package code properly. Almost all the time the problems come from methods that are too long. Long methods are troublesome because they often contain lots of information, which gets buried by the complex logic that usually gets dragged in. The key refactoring is *Extract Method (110)*, which takes a clump of code and turns it into its own method. *Inline Method (117)* is essentially the opposite. You take a method call and replace it with the body of the code. I need *Inline Method (117)* when I've done multiple extractions and realize some of the resulting methods are no longer pulling their weight or if I need to reorganize the way I've broken down methods.

The biggest problem with *Extract Method (110)* is dealing with local variables, and temps are one of the main sources of this issue. When I'm working on a method, I like *Replace Temp with Query (120)* to get rid of any temporary variables that I can remove. If the temp is used for many things, I use *Split Temporary Variable (128)* first to make the temp easier to replace.

Sometimes, however, the temporary variables are just too tangled to replace. I need *Replace Method with Method Object (135)*. This allows me to break up even the most tangled method, at the cost of introducing a new class for the job.

Parameters are less of a problem than temps, provided you don't assign to them. If you do, you need *Remove Assignments to Parameters (131)*.

Once the method is broken down, I can understand how it works much better. I may also find that the algorithm can be improved to make it clearer. I then use *Substitute Algorithm (139)* to introduce the clearer algorithm.

Extract Method

You have a code fragment that can be grouped together.

*Turn the fragment into a method whose name explains the
purpose of the method.*

```java
void printOwing(double amount) {
    printBanner();

    //print details
    System.out.println ("name:" + _name);
    System.out.println ("amount" + amount);
}
```

⇓

```java
void printOwing(double amount) {
    printBanner();
    printDetails(amount);
}

void printDetails (double amount) {
    System.out.println ("name:" + _name);
    System.out.println ("amount" + amount);
}
```

Motivation

Extract Method is one of the most common refactorings I do. I look at a
method that is too long or look at code that needs a comment to understand its
purpose. I then turn that fragment of code into its own method.

I prefer short, well-named methods for several reasons. First, it increases the
chances that other methods can use a method when the method is finely
grained. Second, it allows the higher-level methods to read more like a series of
comments. Overriding also is easier when the methods are finely grained.

It does take a little getting used to if you are used to seeing larger methods.
And small methods really work only when you have good names, so you need
to pay attention to naming. People sometimes ask me what length I look for in
a method. To me length is not the issue. The key is the semantic distance

between the method name and the method body. If extracting improves clarity, do it, even if the name is longer than the code you have extracted.

Mechanics

- ❑ Create a new method, and name it after the intention of the method (name it by what it does, not by how it does it).

  ⇒ *If the code you want to extract is very simple, such as a single message or function call, you should extract it if the name of the new method will reveal the intention of the code in a better way. If you can't come up with a more meaningful name, don't extract the code.*

- ❑ Copy the extracted code from the source method into the new target method.

- ❑ Scan the extracted code for references to any variables that are local in scope to the source method. These are local variables and parameters to the method.

- ❑ See whether any temporary variables are used only within this extracted code. If so, declare them in the target method as temporary variables.

- ❑ Look to see whether any of these local-scope variables are modified by the extracted code. If one variable is modified, see whether you can treat the extracted code as a query and assign the result to the variable concerned. If this is awkward, or if there is more than one such variable, you can't extract the method as it stands. You may need to use *Split Temporary Variable (128)* and try again. You can eliminate temporary variables with *Replace Temp with Query (120)* (see the discussion in the examples).

- ❑ Pass into the target method as parameters local-scope variables that are read from the extracted code.

- ❑ Compile when you have dealt with all the locally-scoped variables.

- ❑ Replace the extracted code in the source method with a call to the target method.

  ⇒ *If you have moved any temporary variables over to the target method, look to see whether they were declared outside of the extracted code. If so, you can now remove the declaration.*

- ❑ Compile and test.

Example: No Local Variables

In the simplest case, *Extract Method (110)* is trivially easy. Take the following method:

```
void printOwing() {

    Enumeration e = _orders.elements();
    double outstanding = 0.0;

    // print banner
    System.out.println ("**************************");
    System.out.println ("***** Customer Owes ******");
    System.out.println ("**************************");

    // calculate outstanding
    while (e.hasMoreElements()) {
        Order each = (Order) e.nextElement();
        outstanding += each.getAmount();
    }

    //print details
    System.out.println ("name:" + _name);
    System.out.println ("amount" + outstanding);
}
```

It is easy to extract the code that prints the banner. I just cut, paste, and put in a call:

```
void printOwing() {

    Enumeration e = _orders.elements();
    double outstanding = 0.0;

    printBanner();

    // calculate outstanding
    while (e.hasMoreElements()) {
        Order each = (Order) e.nextElement();
        outstanding += each.getAmount();
    }

    //print details
    System.out.println ("name:" + _name);
    System.out.println ("amount" + outstanding);
}

void printBanner() {
    // print banner
    System.out.println ("**************************");
    System.out.println ("***** Customer Owes ******");
    System.out.println ("**************************");
}
```

Example: Using Local Variables

So what's the problem? The problem is local variables: parameters passed into the original method and temporaries declared within the original method. Local variables are only in scope in that method, so when I use *Extract Method (110)*, these variables cause me extra work. In some cases they even prevent me from doing the refactoring at all.

The easiest case with local variables is when the variables are read but not changed. In this case I can just pass them in as a parameter. So if I have the following method:

```
void printOwing() {

    Enumeration e = _orders.elements();
    double outstanding = 0.0;

    printBanner();

    // calculate outstanding
    while (e.hasMoreElements()) {
        Order each = (Order) e.nextElement();
        outstanding += each.getAmount();
    }

    //print details
    System.out.println ("name:" + _name);
    System.out.println ("amount" + outstanding);
}
```

I can extract the printing of details with a method with one parameter:

```
void printOwing() {

    Enumeration e = _orders.elements();
    double outstanding = 0.0;

    printBanner();

    // calculate outstanding
    while (e.hasMoreElements()) {
        Order each = (Order) e.nextElement();
        outstanding += each.getAmount();
    }

    printDetails(outstanding);
}

void printDetails (double outstanding) {
    System.out.println ("name:" + _name);
    System.out.println ("amount" + outstanding);
}
```

You can use this with as many local variables as you need.

The same is true if the local variable is an object and you invoke a modifying method on the variable. Again you can just pass the object in as a parameter. You only have to do something different if you actually assign to the local variable.

Example: Reassigning a Local Variable

It's the assignment to local variables that becomes complicated. In this case we're only talking about temps. If you see an assignment to a parameter, you should immediately use *Remove Assignments to Parameters (131)*.

For temps that are assigned to, there are two cases. The simpler case is that in which the variable is a temporary variable used only within the extracted code. When that happens, you can move the temp into the extracted code. The other case is use of the variable outside the code. If the variable is not used after the code is extracted, you can make the change in just the extracted code. If it is used afterward, you need to make the extracted code return the changed value of the variable. I can illustrate this with the following method:

```
void printOwing() {

    Enumeration e = _orders.elements();
    double outstanding = 0.0;

    printBanner();

    // calculate outstanding
    while (e.hasMoreElements()) {
        Order each = (Order) e.nextElement();
        outstanding += each.getAmount();
    }

    printDetails(outstanding);
}
```

Now I extract the calculation:

```
void printOwing() {
    printBanner();
    double outstanding = getOutstanding();
    printDetails(outstanding);
}

double getOutstanding() {
    Enumeration e = _orders.elements();
    double outstanding = 0.0;
    while (e.hasMoreElements()) {
        Order each = (Order) e.nextElement();
        outstanding += each.getAmount();
    }
    return outstanding;
}
```

The enumeration variable is used only in the extracted code, so I can move it entirely within the new method. The outstanding variable is used in both places, so I need to return it from the extracted method. Once I've compiled and tested for the extraction, I rename the returned value to follow my usual convention:

```
double getOutstanding() {
    Enumeration e = _orders.elements();
    double result = 0.0;
    while (e.hasMoreElements()) {
        Order each = (Order) e.nextElement();
        result += each.getAmount();
    }
    return result;
}
```

In this case the outstanding variable is initialized only to an obvious initial value, so I can initialize it only within the extracted method. If something more involved happens to the variable, I have to pass in the previous value as a parameter. The initial code for this variation might look like this:

```
void printOwing(double previousAmount) {

    Enumeration e = _orders.elements();
    double outstanding = previousAmount * 1.2;

    printBanner();

    // calculate outstanding
    while (e.hasMoreElements()) {
        Order each = (Order) e.nextElement();
        outstanding += each.getAmount();
    }

    printDetails(outstanding);
}
```

In this case the extraction would look like this:

```
void printOwing(double previousAmount) {
    double outstanding = previousAmount * 1.2;
    printBanner();
    outstanding = getOutstanding(outstanding);
    printDetails(outstanding);
}

double getOutstanding(double initialValue) {
    double result = initialValue;
    Enumeration e = _orders.elements();
    while (e.hasMoreElements()) {
        Order each = (Order) e.nextElement();
        result += each.getAmount();
    }
    return result;
}
```

After I compile and test this, I clear up the way the outstanding variable is initialized:

```
void printOwing(double previousAmount) {
    printBanner();
    double outstanding = getOutstanding(previousAmount * 1.2);
    printDetails(outstanding);
}
```

At this point you may be wondering, "What happens if more than one variable needs to be returned?"

Here you have several options. The best option usually is to pick different code to extract. I prefer a method to return one value, so I would try to arrange for multiple methods for the different values. (If your language allows output parameters, you can use those. I prefer to use single return values as much as possible.)

Temporary variables often are so plentiful that they make extraction very awkward. In these cases I try to reduce the temps by using *Replace Temp with Query (120)*. If whatever I do things are still awkward, I resort to *Replace Method with Method Object (135)*. This refactoring doesn't care how many temporaries you have or what you do with them.

Inline Method

A method's body is just as clear as its name.

Put the method's body into the body of its callers and remove the method.

```
int getRating() {
    return (moreThanFiveLateDeliveries()) ? 2 : 1;
}
boolean moreThanFiveLateDeliveries() {
    return _numberOfLateDeliveries > 5;
}
```

⇓

```
int getRating() {
    return (_numberOfLateDeliveries > 5) ? 2 : 1;
}
```

Motivation

A theme of this book is to use short methods named to show their intention, because these methods lead to clearer and easier to read code. But sometimes you do come across a method in which the body is as clear as the name. Or you refactor the body of the code into something that is just as clear as the name. When this happens, you should then get rid of the method. Indirection can be helpful, but needless indirection is irritating.

Another time to use *Inline Method (117)* is when you have a group of methods that seem badly factored. You can inline them all into one big method and then reextract the methods. Kent Beck finds it is often good to do this before using *Replace Method with Method Object (135)*. You inline the various calls made by the method that have behavior you want to have in the method object. It's easier to move one method than to move the method and its called methods.

I commonly use *Inline Method (117)* when someone is using too much indirection and it seems that every method does simple delegation to another method, and I get lost in all the delegation. In these cases some of the indirection is worthwhile, but not all of it. By trying to inline I can flush out the useful ones and eliminate the rest.

Mechanics

❑ Check that the method is not polymorphic.

⇒ *Don't inline if subclasses override the method; they cannot override a method that isn't there.*

❑ Find all calls to the method.

❑ Replace each call with the method body.

❑ Compile and test.

❑ Remove the method definition.

Written this way, *Inline Method (117)* is simple. In general it isn't. I could write pages on how to handle recursion, multiple return points, inlining into another object when you don't have accessors, and the like. The reason I don't is that if you encounter these complexities, you shouldn't do this refactoring.

Inline Temp

You have a temp that is assigned to once with a simple expression, and the temp is getting in the way of other refactorings.

Replace all references to that temp with the expression.

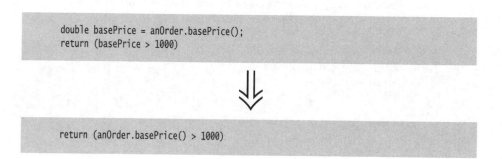

```
double basePrice = anOrder.basePrice();
return (basePrice > 1000)
```

```
return (anOrder.basePrice() > 1000)
```

Motivation

Most of the time *Inline Temp* is used as part of *Replace Temp with Query (120)*, so the real motivation is there. The only time *Inline Temp* is used on its own is when you find a temp that is assigned the value of a method call. Often this temp isn't doing any harm and you can safely leave it there. If the temp is getting in the way of other refactorings, such as *Extract Method (110)*, it's time to inline it.

Mechanics

- ❏ Check that the right hand side of the assignment is free of side-effects.

- ❏ Declare the temp as final if it isn't already, and compile.

  ⇒ *This checks that the temp is really only assigned to once.*

- ❏ Find all references to the temp and replace them with the right-hand side of the assignment.

- ❏ Compile and test after each change.

- ❏ Remove the declaration and the assignment of the temp.

- ❏ Compile and test.

Replace Temp with Query

You are using a temporary variable to hold the result of an expression.

Extract the expression into a method. Replace all references to the temp with the new method. The new method can then be used in other methods.

```
double basePrice = _quantity * _itemPrice;
if (basePrice > 1000)
    return basePrice * 0.95;
else
    return basePrice * 0.98;
```

⇓

```
    if (basePrice() > 1000)
        return basePrice() * 0.95;
    else
        return basePrice() * 0.98;
...
  double basePrice() {
      return _quantity * _itemPrice;
  }
```

Motivation

The problem with temps is that they are temporary and local. Because they can be seen only in the context of the method in which they are used, temps tend to encourage longer methods, because that's the only way you can reach the temp. By replacing the temp with a query method, any method in the class can get at the information. That helps a lot in coming up with cleaner code for the class.

Replace Temp with Query often is a vital step before *Extract Method (110)*. Local variables make it difficult to extract, so replace as many variables as you can with queries.

The straightforward cases of this refactoring are those in which temps are only assigned to once and those in which the expression that generates the assignment is free of side effects. Other cases are trickier but possible. You may need to use *Split Temporary Variable (128)* or *Separate Query from Modifier (279)* first to make things easier. If the temp is used to collect a result (such as summing over a loop), you need to copy some logic into the query method.

Mechanics

Here is the simple case:

- ❑ Look for a temporary variable that is assigned to once.

    ⇒ *If a temp is set more than once consider* Split Temporary Variable (128).

- ❑ Declare the temp as final.

- ❑ Compile.

    ⇒ *This will ensure that the temp is only assigned to once.*

- ❑ Extract the right-hand side of the assignment into a method.

    ⇒ *Initially mark the method as private. You may find more use for it later, but you can easily relax the protection later.*
    ⇒ *Ensure the extracted method is free of side effects, that is, it does not modify any object. If it is not free of side effects, use* Separate Query from Modifier (279).

- ❑ Compile and test.

- ❑ *Inline Temp (119)* on the temp.

Temps often are used to store summary information in loops. The entire loop can be extracted into a method; this removes several lines of noisy code. Sometimes a loop may be used to sum up multiple values, as in the example on page 26. In this case, duplicate the loop for each temp so that you can replace each temp with a query. The loop should be very simple, so there is little danger in duplicating the code.

You may be concerned about performance in this case. As with other performance issues, let it slide for the moment. Nine times out of ten, it won't matter. When it does matter, you will fix the problem during optimization. With your code better factored, you will often find more powerful optimizations, which you would have missed without refactoring. If worse comes to worse, it's very easy to put the temp back.

Example

I start with a simple method:

```
double getPrice() {
    int basePrice = _quantity * _itemPrice;
    double discountFactor;
    if (basePrice > 1000) discountFactor = 0.95;
    else discountFactor = 0.98;
    return basePrice * discountFactor;
}
```

I'm inclined to replace both temps, one at a time.

Although it's pretty clear in this case, I can test that they are assigned only to once by declaring them as final:

```
double getPrice() {
    final int basePrice = _quantity * _itemPrice;
    final double discountFactor;
    if (basePrice > 1000) discountFactor = 0.95;
    else discountFactor = 0.98;
    return basePrice * discountFactor;
}
```

Compiling will then alert me to any problems. I do this first, because if there is a problem, I shouldn't be doing this refactoring. I replace the temps one at a time. First I extract the right-hand side of the assignment:

```
double getPrice() {
    final int basePrice = basePrice();
    final double discountFactor;
    if (basePrice > 1000) discountFactor = 0.95;
    else discountFactor = 0.98;
    return basePrice * discountFactor;
}

private int basePrice() {
    return _quantity * _itemPrice;
}
```

I compile and test, then I begin with *Inline Temp (119)*. First I replace the first reference to the temp:

```
double getPrice() {
    final int basePrice = basePrice();
    final double discountFactor;
    if (basePrice() > 1000) discountFactor = 0.95;
    else discountFactor = 0.98;
    return basePrice * discountFactor;
}
```

Compile and test and do the next (sounds like a caller at a line dance). Because it's the last, I also remove the temp declaration:

```
double getPrice() {
    final double discountFactor;
    if (basePrice() > 1000) discountFactor = 0.95;
    else discountFactor = 0.98;
    return basePrice() * discountFactor;
}
```

With that gone I can extract discountFactor in a similar way:

```
double getPrice() {
    final double discountFactor = discountFactor();
    return basePrice() * discountFactor;
}

private double discountFactor() {
    if (basePrice() > 1000) return 0.95;
    else return 0.98;
}
```

See how it would have been difficult to extract discountFactor if I had not replaced basePrice with a query.

The getPrice method ends up as follows:

```
double getPrice() {
    return basePrice() * discountFactor();
}
```

Introduce Explaining Variable

You have a complicated expression.

Put the result of the expression, or parts of the expression, in a temporary variable with a name that explains the purpose.

```
if ( (platform.toUpperCase().indexOf("MAC") > -1) &&
     (browser.toUpperCase().indexOf("IE") > -1) &&
     wasInitialized() && resize > 0 )
{
  // do something
}
```

⇓

```
final boolean isMacOs    = platform.toUpperCase().indexOf("MAC") > -1;
final boolean isIEBrowser = browser.toUpperCase().indexOf("IE")  > -1;
final boolean wasResized  = resize > 0;

if (isMacOs && isIEBrowser && wasInitialized() && wasResized) {
    // do something
}
```

Motivation

Expressions can become very complex and hard to read. In such situations temporary variables can be helpful to break down the expression into something more manageable.

Introduce Explaining Variable is particularly valuable with conditional logic in which it is useful to take each clause of a condition and explain what the condition means with a well-named temp. Another case is a long algorithm, in which each step in the computation can be explained with a temp.

Introduce Explaining Variable is a very common refactoring, but I confess I don't use it that much. I almost always prefer to use *Extract Method (110)* if I can. A temp is useful only within the context of one method. A method is useable throughout the object and to other objects. There are times, however, when local variables make it difficult to use *Extract Method (110)*. That's when I use *Introduce Explaining Variable (124)*.

Mechanics

- ❑ Declare a final temporary variable, and set it to the result of part of the complex expression.

- ❑ Replace the result part of the expression with the value of the temp.

  ⇒ *If the result part of the expression is repeated, you can replace the repeats one at a time.*

- ❑ Compile and test.

- ❑ Repeat for other parts of the expression.

Example

I start with a simple calculation:

```
double price() {
    // price is base price - quantity discount + shipping
    return _quantity * _itemPrice -
        Math.max(0, _quantity - 500) * _itemPrice * 0.05 +
        Math.min(_quantity * _itemPrice * 0.1, 100.0);
}
```

Simple it may be, but I can make it easier to follow. First I identify the base price as the quantity times the item price. I can turn that part of the calculation into a temp:

```
double price() {
    // price is base price - quantity discount + shipping
    final double basePrice = _quantity * _itemPrice;
    return basePrice -
        Math.max(0, _quantity - 500) * _itemPrice * 0.05 +
        Math.min(_quantity * _itemPrice * 0.1, 100.0);
}
```

Quantity times item price is also used later, so I can substitute with the temp there as well:

```
double price() {
    // price is base price - quantity discount + shipping
    final double basePrice = _quantity * _itemPrice;
    return basePrice -
        Math.max(0, _quantity - 500) * _itemPrice * 0.05 +
        Math.min(basePrice * 0.1, 100.0);
}
```

Introduce
Explaining
Variable

Next I take the quantity discount:

```
double price() {
    // price is base price - quantity discount + shipping
    final double basePrice = _quantity * _itemPrice;
    final double quantityDiscount = Math.max(0, _quantity - 500) * _itemPrice * 0.05;
    return basePrice - quantityDiscount +
        Math.min(basePrice * 0.1, 100.0);
}
```

Finally, I finish with the shipping. As I do that, I can remove the comment, too, because now it doesn't say anything the code doesn't say:

```
double price() {
    final double basePrice = _quantity * _itemPrice;
    final double quantityDiscount = Math.max(0, _quantity - 500) * _itemPrice * 0.05;
    final double shipping = Math.min(basePrice * 0.1, 100.0);
    return basePrice - quantityDiscount + shipping;
}
```

Example with *Extract Method*

For this example I usually wouldn't have done the explaining temps; I would prefer to do that with *Extract Method (110)*. I start again with

```
double price() {
    // price is base price - quantity discount + shipping
    return _quantity * _itemPrice -
        Math.max(0, _quantity - 500) * _itemPrice * 0.05 +
        Math.min(_quantity * _itemPrice * 0.1, 100.0);
}
```

but this time I extract a method for the base price:

```
double price() {
    // price is base price - quantity discount + shipping
    return basePrice() -
        Math.max(0, _quantity - 500) * _itemPrice * 0.05 +
        Math.min(basePrice() * 0.1, 100.0);
}

private double basePrice() {
    return _quantity * _itemPrice;
}
```

I continue one at a time. When I'm finished I get

```
double price() {
    return basePrice() - quantityDiscount() + shipping();
}

private double quantityDiscount() {
    return Math.max(0, _quantity - 500) * _itemPrice * 0.05;
}

private double shipping() {
    return Math.min(basePrice() * 0.1, 100.0);
}

private double basePrice() {
    return _quantity * _itemPrice;
}
```

I prefer to use *Extract Method (110),* because now these methods are available to any other part of the object that needs them. Initially I make them private, but I can always relax that if another object needs them. I find it's usually no more effort to use *Extract Method (110)* than it is to use *Introduce Explaining Variable (124).*

So when do I use *Introduce Explaining Variable (124)?* The answer is when *Extract Method (110) is* more effort. If I'm in an algorithm with a lot of local variables, I may not be able to easily use *Extract Method (110).* In this case I use *Introduce Explaining Variable (124)* to help me understand what is going on. As the logic becomes less tangled, I can always use *Replace Temp with Query (120)* later. The temp also is valuable if I end up having to use *Replace Method with Method Object (135).*

Split Temporary Variable

You have a temporary variable assigned to more than once,
but is not a loop variable nor a collecting temporary variable.

Make a separate temporary variable for each assignment.

```
double temp = 2 * (_height + _width);
System.out.println (temp);
temp = _height * _width;
System.out.println (temp);
```

⇓

```
final double perimeter = 2 * (_height + _width);
System.out.println (perimeter);
final double area = _height * _width;
System.out.println (area);
```

Motivation

Temporary variables are made for various uses. Some of these uses naturally
lead to the temp's being assigned to several times. Loop variables [Beck] change
for each run around a loop (such as the i in for (int i=0; i<10; i++)). Collecting
temporary variables [Beck] collect together some value that is built up during
the method.

Many other temporaries are used to hold the result of a long-winded bit of
code for easy reference later. These kinds of variables should be set only once.
That they are set more than once is a sign that they have more than one responsibility within the method. Any variable with more than one responsibility
should be replaced with a temp for each responsibility. Using a temp for two
different things is very confusing for the reader.

Mechanics

❑ Change the name of a temp at its declaration and its first assignment.

⇒ *If the later assignments are of the form i = i + some expression, that
indicates that it is a collecting temporary variable, so don't split it.
The operator for a collecting temporary variable usually is addition,
string concatenation, writing to a stream, or adding to a collection.*

❑ Declare the new temp as final.

❑ Change all references of the temp up to its second assignment.

❑ Declare the temp at its second assignment.

❑ Compile and test.

❑ Repeat in stages, each stage renaming at the declaration, and changing references until the next assignment.

Example

For this example I compute the distance traveled by a haggis. From a standing start, a haggis experiences an initial force. After a delayed period a secondary force kicks in to further accelerate the haggis. Using the common laws of motion, I can compute the distance traveled as follows:

```
double getDistanceTravelled (int time) {
    double result;
    double acc = _primaryForce / _mass;
    int primaryTime = Math.min(time, _delay);
    result = 0.5 * acc * primaryTime * primaryTime;
    int secondaryTime = time - _delay;
    if (secondaryTime > 0) {
        double primaryVel = acc * _delay;
        acc = (_primaryForce + _secondaryForce) / _mass;
        result += primaryVel * secondaryTime + 0.5 * acc * secondaryTime * secondaryTime;
    }
    return result;
}
```

A nice awkward little function. The interesting thing for our example is the way the variable acc is set twice. It has two responsibilities: one to hold the initial acceleration caused by the first force and another later to hold the acceleration with both forces. This I want to split.

I start at the beginning by changing the name of the temp and declaring the new name as final. Then I change all references to the temp from that point up to the next assignment. At the next assignment I declare it:

```
double getDistanceTravelled (int time) {
    double result;
    final double primaryAcc = _primaryForce / _mass;
    int primaryTime = Math.min(time, _delay);
    result = 0.5 * primaryAcc * primaryTime * primaryTime;
    int secondaryTime = time - _delay;
```

```
    if (secondaryTime > 0) {
        double primaryVel = primaryAcc * _delay;
        double acc = (_primaryForce + _secondaryForce) / _mass;
        result +=  primaryVel * secondaryTime + 0.5 * acc * secondaryTime * secondaryTime;
    }
    return result;
}
```

I choose the new name to represent only the first use of the temp. I make it final to ensure it is only set once. I can then declare the original temp at its second assignment. Now I can compile and test, and all should work.

I continue on the second assignment of the temp. This removes the original temp name completely, replacing it with a new temp named for the second use.

```
double getDistanceTravelled (int time) {
    double result;
    final double primaryAcc = _primaryForce / _mass;
    int primaryTime = Math.min(time, _delay);
    result = 0.5 * primaryAcc * primaryTime * primaryTime;
    int secondaryTime = time - _delay;
    if (secondaryTime > 0) {
        double primaryVel = primaryAcc * _delay;
        final double secondaryAcc = (_primaryForce + _secondaryForce) / _mass;
        result +=  primaryVel * secondaryTime + 0.5 *
                    secondaryAcc * secondaryTime * secondaryTime;
    }
    return result;
}
```

I'm sure you can think of a lot more refactoring to be done here. Enjoy it. (I'm sure it's better than eating the haggis—do you know what they put in those things?)

Remove Assignments to Parameters

The code assigns to a parameter.

Use a temporary variable instead.

```
int discount (int inputVal, int quantity, int yearToDate) {
    if (inputVal > 50) inputVal -= 2;
```

⇓

```
int discount (int inputVal, int quantity, int yearToDate) {
    int result = inputVal;
    if (inputVal > 50) result -= 2;
```

Motivation

First let me make sure we are clear on the phrase "assigns to a parameter." This means that if you pass in an object named *foo,* in the parameter, assigning to the parameter means to change *foo* to refer to a different object. I have no problems with doing something to the object that was passed in; I do that all the time. I just object to changing *foo* to refer to another object entirely:

```
void aMethod(Object foo) {
  foo.modifyInSomeWay();          // that's OK
  foo = anotherObject;            // trouble and despair will follow you
```

The reason I don't like this comes down to lack of clarity and to confusion between *pass by value* and *pass by reference.* Java uses pass by value exclusively (see later), and this discussion is based on that usage.

With pass by value, any change to the parameter is not reflected in the calling routine. Those who have used pass by reference will probably find this confusing.

The other area of confusion is within the body of the code itself. It is much clearer if you use only the parameter to represent what has been passed in, because that is a consistent usage.

In Java, don't assign to parameters, and if you see code that does, apply *Remove Assignments to Parameters.*

Of course this rule does not necessarily apply to other languages that use output parameters, although even with these languages I prefer to use output parameters as little as possible.

Remove Assignments to Parameters

Mechanics

❑ Create a temporary variable for the parameter.

❑ Replace all references to the parameter, made after the assignment, to the temporary variable.

❑ Change the assignment to assign to the temporary variable.

❑ Compile and test.

> ⇒ *If the semantics are call by reference, look in the calling method to see whether the parameter is used again afterward. Also see how many call by reference parameters are assigned to and used afterward in this method. Try to pass a single value back as the return value. If there is more than one, see whether you can turn the data clump into an object, or create separate methods.*

Example

I start with the following simple routine:

```
int discount (int inputVal, int quantity, int yearToDate) {
    if (inputVal > 50) inputVal -= 2;
    if (quantity > 100) inputVal -= 1;
    if (yearToDate > 10000) inputVal -= 4;
    return inputVal;
}
```

Replacing with a temp leads to

```
int discount (int inputVal, int quantity, int yearToDate) {
    int result = inputVal;
    if (inputVal > 50) result -= 2;
    if (quantity > 100) result -= 1;
    if (yearToDate > 10000) result -= 4;
    return result;
}
```

You can enforce this convention with the final keyword:

```
int discount (final int inputVal, final int quantity, final int yearToDate) {
    int result = inputVal;
    if (inputVal > 50) result -= 2;
    if (quantity > 100) result -= 1;
    if (yearToDate > 10000) result -= 4;
    return result;
}
```

I admit that I don't use final much, because I don't find it helps much with clarity for short methods. I use it with a long method to help me see whether anything is changing the parameter.

Pass By Value in Java

Use of pass by value often is a source of confusion in Java. Java strictly uses pass by value in all places, thus the following program:

```java
class Param {
    public static void main(String[] args) {
        int x = 5;
        triple(x);
        System.out.println ("x after triple: " + x);
    }
    private static void triple(int arg) {
        arg = arg * 3;
        System.out.println ("arg in triple: " + arg);
    }
}
```

produces the following output:

```
arg in triple: 15
x after triple: 5
```

The confusion exists with objects. Say I use a date, then this program:

```java
class Param {

    public static void main(String[] args) {
        Date d1 = new Date ("1 Apr 98");
        nextDateUpdate(d1);
        System.out.println ("d1 after nextDay: " + d1);

        Date d2 = new Date ("1 Apr 98");
        nextDateReplace(d2);
        System.out.println ("d2 after nextDay: " + d2);
    }

    private static void nextDateUpdate (Date arg) {
        arg.setDate(arg.getDate() + 1);
        System.out.println ("arg in nextDay: " + arg);
    }

    private static void nextDateReplace (Date arg) {
        arg = new Date (arg.getYear(), arg.getMonth(), arg.getDate() + 1);
        System.out.println ("arg in nextDay: " + arg);
    }
}
```

Remove
Assignments
to Parameters

It produces this output

```
arg in nextDay: Thu Apr 02 00:00:00 EST 1998
d1 after nextDay: Thu Apr 02 00:00:00 EST 1998
arg in nextDay: Thu Apr 02 00:00:00 EST 1998
d2 after nextDay: Wed Apr 01 00:00:00 EST 1998
```

Essentially the object reference is passed by value. This allows me to modify the object but does not take into account the reassigning of the parameter.

Java 1.1 and later versions allow you to mark a parameter as *final*; this prevents assignment to the variable. It still allows you to modify the object the variable refers to. I always treat my parameters as final, but I confess I rarely mark them so in the parameter list.

Replace Method with Method Object

You have a long method that uses local variables in such a way that you cannot apply *Extract Method (110)*.

Turn the method into its own object so that all the local variables become fields on that object. You can then decompose the method into other methods on the same object.

```
class Order...
    double price() {
        double primaryBasePrice;
        double secondaryBasePrice;
        double tertiaryBasePrice;
        // long computation;
        ...
    }
```

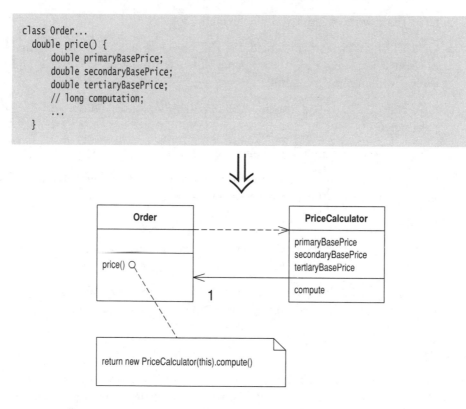

Motivation

In this book I emphasize the beauty of small methods. By extracting pieces out of a large method, you make things much more comprehensible.

The difficulty in decomposing a method lies in local variables. If they are rampant, decomposition can be difficult. Using *Replace Temp with Query (120)* helps to reduce this burden, but occasionally you may find you cannot break down a method that needs breaking. In this case you reach deep into the tool bag and get out your *method object* [Beck].

Applying *Replace Method with Method Object (135)* turns all these local variables into fields on the method object. You can then use *Extract Method (110)* on this new object to create additional methods that break down the original method.

Mechanics

Stolen shamelessly from Beck [Beck].

- ❏ Create a new class, name it after the method.

- ❏ Give the new class a final field for the object that hosted the original method (the source object) and a field for each temporary variable and each parameter in the method.

- ❏ Give the new class a constructor that takes the source object and each parameter.

- ❏ Give the new class a method named "compute."

- ❏ Copy the body of the original method into compute. Use the source object field for any invocations of methods on the original object.

- ❏ Compile.

- ❏ Replace the old method with one that creates the new object and calls compute.

Now comes the fun part. Because all the local variables are now fields, you can freely decompose the method without having to pass any parameters.

Example

A proper example of this requires a long chapter, so I'm showing this refactoring for a method that doesn't need it. (Don't ask what the logic of this method is, I made it up as I went along.)

```
Class Account
  int gamma (int inputVal, int quantity, int yearToDate) {
      int importantValue1 = (inputVal * quantity) + delta();
      int importantValue2 = (inputVal * yearToDate) + 100;
      if ((yearToDate - importantValue1) > 100)
          importantValue2 -= 20;
      int importantValue3 = importantValue2 * 7;
      // and so on.
      return importantValue3 - 2 * importantValue1;
  }
```

To turn this into a method object, I begin by declaring a new class. I provide a final field for the original object and a field for each parameter and temporary variable in the method.

```
class Gamma...
    private final Account _account;
    private int inputVal;
    private int quantity;
    private int yearToDate;
    private int importantValue1;
    private int importantValue2;
    private int importantValue3;
```

I usually use the underscore prefix convention for marking fields. But to keep small steps I'll leave the names as they are for the moment.

I add a constructor:

```
Gamma (Account source, int inputValArg, int quantityArg, int yearToDateArg) {
    _account = source;
    inputVal = inputValArg;
    quantity = quantityArg;
    yearToDate = yearToDateArg;
}
```

Now I can move the original method over. I need to modify any calls of features of account to use the _account field

```
int compute () {
    importantValue1 = (inputVal * quantity) + _account.delta();
    importantValue2 = (inputVal * yearToDate) + 100;
    if ((yearToDate - importantValue1) > 100)
        importantValue2 -= 20;
    int importantValue3 = importantValue2 * 7;
    // and so on.
    return importantValue3 - 2 * importantValue1;
}
```

I then modify the old method to delegate to the method object:

```
int gamma (int inputVal, int quantity, int yearToDate) {
    return new Gamma(this, inputVal, quantity, yearToDate).compute();
}
```

That's the essential refactoring. The benefit is that I can now easily use *Extract Method (110)* on the compute method without ever worrying about the argument's passing:

```
int compute () {
    importantValue1 = (inputVal * quantity) + _account.delta();
    importantValue2 = (inputVal * yearToDate) + 100;
    importantThing();
    int importantValue3 = importantValue2 * 7;
    // and so on.
    return importantValue3 - 2 * importantValue1;
}

void importantThing() {
    if ((yearToDate - importantValue1) > 100)
        importantValue2 -= 20;
}
```

Substitute Algorithm

You want to replace an algorithm with one that is clearer.

Replace the body of the method with the new algorithm.

```java
String foundPerson(String[] people){
    for (int i = 0; i < people.length; i++) {
        if (people[i].equals ("Don")){
            return "Don";
        }
        if (people[i].equals ("John")){
            return "John";
        }
        if (people[i].equals ("Kent")){
            return "Kent";
        }
    }
    return "";
}
```

⇓

```java
String foundPerson(String[] people){
    List candidates = Arrays.asList(new String[] {"Don", "John", "Kent"});
    for (int i=0; i<people.length; i++)
        if (candidates.contains(people[i]))
            return people[i];
    return "";
}
```

Motivation

I've never tried to skin a cat. I'm told there are several ways to do it. I'm sure some are easier than others. So it is with algorithms. If you find a clearer way to do something, you should replace the complicated way with the clearer way. Refactoring can break down something complex into simpler pieces, but sometimes you just reach the point at which you have to remove the whole algorithm and replace it with something simpler. This occurs as you learn more about the problem and realize that there's an easier way to do it. It also happens if you start using a library that supplies features that duplicate your code.

Substitute Algorithm

Sometimes when you want to change the algorithm to do something slightly different, it is easier to subtitute the algorithm first into something easier for the change you need to make.

When you have to take this step, make sure you have decomposed the method as much as you can. Substituting a large, complex algorithm is very difficult; only by making it simple can you make the substitution tractable.

Mechanics

❑ Prepare your alternative algorithm. Get it so that it compiles.

❑ Run the new algorithm against your tests. If the results are the same, you're finished.

❑ If the results aren't the same, use the old algorithm for comparison in testing and debugging.

⇒ *Run each test case with old and new algorithms and watch both results. That will help you see which test cases are causing trouble, and how.*

Chapter 7

Moving Features Between Objects

One of the most fundamental, if not the fundamental, decision in object design is deciding where to put responsibilities. I've been working with objects for more than a decade, but I still never get it right the first time. That used to bother me, but now I realize that I can use refactoring to change my mind in these cases.

Often I can resolve these problems simply by using *Move Method (142)* and *Move Field (146)* to move the behavior around. If I need to use both, I prefer to use *Move Field (146)* first and then *Move Method (142)*.

Often classes become bloated with too many responsibilities. In this case I use *Extract Class (149)* to separate some of these responsibilities. If a class becomes too irresponsible, I use *Inline Class (154)* to merge it into another class. If another class is being used, it often is helpful to hide this fact with *Hide Delegate (157)*. Sometimes hiding the delegate class results in constantly changing the owner's interface, in which case you need to use *Remove Middle Man (160)*

The last two refactorings in this chapter, *Introduce Foreign Method* and *Introduce Local Extension (164)* are special cases. I use these only when I'm not able to access the source code of a class, yet I want to move responsibilities to this unchangeable class. If it is only one or two methods, I use *Introduce Foreign Method (162)*; for more than one or two methods, I use *Introduce Local Extension (164)*.

Move Method

A method is, or will be, using or used by more features of another class than the class on which it is defined.

Create a new method with a similar body in the class it uses most. Either turn the old method into a simple delegation, or remove it altogether.

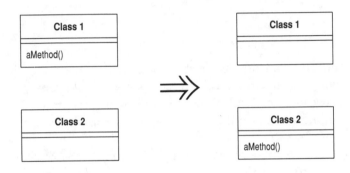

Motivation

Moving methods is the bread and butter of refactoring. I move methods when classes have too much behavior or when classes are collaborating too much and are too highly coupled. By moving methods around, I can make the classes simpler and they end up being a more crisp implementation of a set of responsibilities.

I usually look through the methods on a class to find a method that seems to reference another object more than the object it lives on. A good time to do this is after I have moved some fields. Once I see a likely method to move, I take a look at the methods that call it, the methods it calls, and any redefining methods in the hierarchy. I assess whether to go ahead on the basis of the object with which the method seems to have more interaction.

It's not always an easy decision to make. If I am not sure whether to move a method, I go on to look at other methods. Moving other methods often makes the decision easier. Sometimes the decision still is hard to make. Actually it is then no big deal. If it is difficult to make the decision, it probably does not matter that much. Then I choose according to instinct; after all, I can always change it again later.

Mechanics

- ❏ Examine all features used by the source method that are defined on the source class. Consider whether they also should be moved.

  ⇒ *If a feature is used only by the method you are about to move, you might as well move it, too. If the feature is used by other methods, consider moving them as well. Sometimes it is easier to move a clutch of methods than to move them one at a time.*

- ❏ Check the sub- and superclasses of the source class for other declarations of the method.

  ⇒ *If there are any other declarations, you may not be able to make the move, unless the polymorphism can also be expressed on the target.*

- ❏ Declare the method in the target class.

  ⇒ *You may choose to use a different name, one that makes more sense in the target class.*

- ❏ Copy the code from the source method to the target. Adjust the method to make it work in its new home.

  ⇒ *If the method uses its source, you need to determine how to reference the source object from the target method. If there is no mechanism in the target class, pass the source object reference to the new method as a parameter.*

  ⇒ *If the method includes exception handlers, decide which class should logically handle the exception. If the source class should be responsible, leave the handlers behind.*

- ❏ Compile the target class.

- ❏ Determine how to reference the correct target object from the source.

  ⇒ *There may be an existing field or method that will give you the target. If not, see whether you can easily create a method that will do so. Failing that, you need to create a new field in the source that can store the target. This may be a permanent change, but you can also make it temporarily until you have refactored enough to remove it.*

- ❏ Turn the source method into a delegating method.

- ❏ Compile and test.

- ❏ Decide whether to remove the source method or retain it as a delegating method.

  ⇒ *Leaving the source as a delegating method is easier if you have many references.*

❑ If you remove the source method, replace all the references with references to the target method.

⇒ *You can compile and test after changing each reference, although it is usually easier to change all references with one search and replace.*

❑ Compile and test.

Example

An account class illustrates this refactoring:

```
class Account...
  double overdraftCharge() {
      if (_type.isPremium()) {
          double result = 10;
          if (_daysOverdrawn > 7) result += (_daysOverdrawn - 7) * 0.85;
          return result;
      }
      else return _daysOverdrawn * 1.75;
  }

  double bankCharge() {
      double result = 4.5;
      if (_daysOverdrawn > 0) result += overdraftCharge();
      return result;
  }
  private AccountType _type;
  private int _daysOverdrawn;
```

Let's imagine that there are going to be several new account types, each of which has its own rule for calculating the overdraft charge. So I want to move the overdraft charge method over to the account type.

The first step is to look at the features that the overdraftCharge method uses and consider whether it is worth moving a batch of methods together. In this case I need the _daysOverdrawn field to remain on the account class, because that will vary with individual accounts.

Next I copy the method body over to the account type and get it to fit.

```
class AccountType...
  double overdraftCharge(int daysOverdrawn) {
      if (isPremium()) {
          double result = 10;
          if (daysOverdrawn > 7) result += (daysOverdrawn - 7) * 0.85;
          return result;
      }
      else return daysOverdrawn * 1.75;
  }
```

In this case fitting means removing the _type from uses of features of the account type, and doing something about the features of account that I still need. When I need to use a feature of the source class I can do one of four things: (1) move this feature to the target class as well, (2) create or use a reference from the target class to the source, (3) pass the source object as a parameter to the method, (4) if the feature is a variable, pass it in as a parameter.

In this case I passed the variable as a parameter.

Once the method fits and compiles in the target class, I can replace the source method body with a simple delegation:

```
class Account...
  double overdraftCharge() {
      return _type.overdraftCharge(_daysOverdrawn);
  }
```

At this point I can compile and test.

I can leave things like this, or I can remove the method in the source class. To remove the method I need to find all callers of the method and redirect them to call the method in account type:

```
class Account...
  double bankCharge() {
      double result = 4.5;
      if (_daysOverdrawn > 0) result += _type.overdraftCharge(_daysOverdrawn);
      return result;
  }
```

Once I've replaced all the callers, I can remove the method declaration in account. I can compile and test after each removal, or do them in a batch. If the method isn't private, I need to look for other classes that use this method. In a strongly typed language, the compilation after removal of the source declaration finds anything I missed.

In this case the method referred only to a single field, so I could just pass this field in as a variable. If the method called another method on the account, I wouldn't have been able to do that. In those cases I need to pass in the source object:

```
class AccountType...
  double overdraftCharge(Account account) {
      if (isPremium()) {
          double result = 10;
          if (account.getDaysOverdrawn() > 7)
              result += (account.getDaysOverdrawn() - 7) * 0.85;
          return result;
      }
      else return account.getDaysOverdrawn() * 1.75;
  }
```

I also pass in the source object if I need several features of the class, although if there are too many, further refactoring is needed. Typically I need to decompose and move some pieces back.

Move Field

A field is, or will be, used by another class more than the class on which it is defined.

Create a new field in the target class, and change all its users.

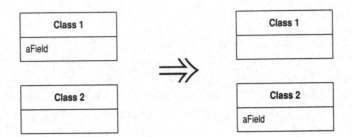

Motivation

Moving state and behavior between classes is the very essence of refactoring. As the system develops, you find the need for new classes and the need to shuffle responsibilities around. A design decision that is reasonable and correct one week can become incorrect in another. That is not a problem; the only problem is not to do something about it.

I consider moving a field if I see more methods on another class using the field than the class itself. This usage may be indirect, through getting and setting methods. I may choose to move the methods; this decision based on interface. But if the methods seem sensible where they are, I move the field.

Another reason for field moving is when doing *Extract Class (149)*. In that case the fields go first and then the methods.

Mechanics

❑ If the field is public, use *Encapsulate Field (206)*.

   ⇒ *If you are likely to be moving the methods that access it frequently or if a lot of methods access the field, you may find it useful to use* Self Encapsulate Field (171)

❑ Compile and test.

❑ Create a field in the target class with getting and setting methods.

❑ Compile the target class.

❑ Determine how to reference the target object from the source.

⇒ *An existing field or method may give you the target. If not, see whether you can easily create a method that will do so. Failing that, you need to create a new field in the source that can store the target. This may be a permanent change, but you can also do it temporarily until you have refactored enough to remove it.*

❑ Remove the field on the source class.

❑ Replace all references to the source field with references to the appropriate method on the target.

⇒ *For accesses to the variable, replace the reference with a call to the target object's getting method; for assignments, replace the reference with a call to the setting method.*
⇒ *If the field is not private, look in all the subclasses of the source for references.*

❑ Compile and test.

Example

Here is part of an account class:

```
class Account...
    private AccountType _type;
    private double _interestRate;

    double interestForAmount_days (double amount, int days) {
        return _interestRate * amount * days / 365;
    }
```

I want to move the interest rate field to the account type. There are several methods with that reference, of which interestForAmount_days is one example.

I next create the field and accessors in the account type:

```
class AccountType...
    private double _interestRate;


    void setInterestRate (double arg) {
        interestRate = arg;
    }

    double getInterestRate () {
        return _interestRate;
    }
```

I can compile the new class at this point.

Now I redirect the methods from the account class to use the account type and remove the interest rate field in the account. I must remove the field to be sure that the redirection is actually happening. This way the compiler helps spot any method I failed to redirect.

Move Field

```
private double _interestRate;

double interestForAmount_days (double amount, int days) {
    return _type.getInterestRate() * amount * days / 365;
}
```

Example: Using Self-Encapsulation

If a lot of methods use the interest rate field, I might start by using *Self Encapsulate Field (171)*:

```
class Account...
  private AccountType _type;
  private double _interestRate;

  double interestForAmount_days (double amount, int days) {
      return getInterestRate() * amount * days / 365;
  }

  private void setInterestRate (double arg) {
      _interestRate = arg;
  }

  private double getInterestRate () {
      return _interestRate;
  }
```

That way I only need to do the redirection for the accessors:

```
double interestForAmountAndDays (double amount, int days) {
    return getInterestRate() * amount * days / 365;
}

private void setInterestRate (double arg) {
    _type.setInterestRate(arg);
}

private double getInterestRate () {
    return _type.getInterestRate();
}
```

I can redirect the clients of the accessors to use the new object later if I want. Using self-encapsulation allows me to take a smaller step. This is useful if I'm doing a lot of things with the class. In particular, it simplifies use *Move Method (142)* to move methods to the target class. If they refer to the accessor, such references don't need to change.

Extract Class

> You have one class doing work that should be done by two.

> *Create a new class and move the relevant fields and methods from the old class into the new class.*

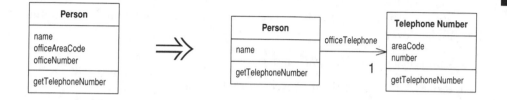

Motivation

You've probably heard that a class should be a crisp abstraction, handle a few clear responsibilities, or some similar guideline. In practice, classes grow. You add some operations here, a bit of data there. You add a responsibility to a class feeling that it's not worth a separate class, but as that responsibility grows and breeds, the class becomes too complicated. Soon your class is as crisp as a microwaved duck.

Such a class is one with many methods and quite a lot of data. A class that is too big to understand easily. You need to consider where it can be split, and you split it. A good sign is that a subset of the data and a subset of the methods seem to go together. Other good signs are subsets of data that usually change together or are particularly dependent on each other. A useful test is to ask yourself what would happen if you removed a piece of data or a method. What other fields and methods would become nonsense?

One sign that often crops up later in development is the way the class is subtyped. You may find that subtyping affects only a few features or that some features need to be subtyped one way and other features a different way.

Mechanics

- ❏ Decide how to split the responsibilities of the class.

- ❏ Create a new class to express the split-off responsibilities.

  ⇒ *If the responsibilities of the old class no longer match its name, rename the old class.*

❑ Make a link from the old to the new class.

⇒ *You may need a two-way link. But don't make the back link until you find you need it.*

❑ Use *Move Field (146)* on each field you wish to move.

❑ Compile and test after each move.

❑ Use *Move Method (142)* to move methods over from old to new. Start with lower-level methods (called rather than calling) and build to the higher level.

❑ Compile and test after each move.

❑ Review and reduce the interfaces of each class.

⇒ *If you did have a two-way link, examine to see whether it can be made one way.*

❑ Decide whether to expose the new class. If you do expose the class, decide whether to expose it as a reference object or as an immutable value object.

Example

I start with a simple person class:

```
class Person...
    public String getName() {
        return _name;
    }
    public String getTelephoneNumber() {
        return ("(" + _officeAreaCode + ") " + _officeNumber);
    }
    String getOfficeAreaCode() {
        return _officeAreaCode;
    }
    void setOfficeAreaCode(String arg) {
        _officeAreaCode = arg;
    }
    String getOfficeNumber() {
        return _officeNumber;
    }
    void setOfficeNumber(String arg) {
        _officeNumber = arg;
    }

    private String _name;
    private String _officeAreaCode;
    private String _officeNumber;
```

In this case I can separate the telephone number behavior into its own class. I start by defining a telephone number class:

```
class TelephoneNumber {
}
```

That was easy! I next make a link from the person to the telephone number:

```
class Person
    private TelephoneNumber _officeTelephone = new TelephoneNumber();
```

Now I use *Move Field (146)* on one of the fields:

```
class TelephoneNumber {
    String getAreaCode() {
        return _areaCode;
    }
    void setAreaCode(String arg) {
        _areaCode = arg;
    }
    private String _areaCode;
}
class Person...
    public String getTelephoneNumber() {
        return ("(" + getOfficeAreaCode() + ") " + _officeNumber);
    }
    String getOfficeAreaCode() {
        return _officeTelephone.getAreaCode();
    }
    void setOfficeAreaCode(String arg) {
        _officeTelephone.setAreaCode(arg);
    }
```

I can then move the other field and use *Move Method (142)* on the telephone number:

```
class Person...
    public String getName() {
        return _name;
    }
    public String getTelephoneNumber(){
        return _officeTelephone.getTelephoneNumber();
    }
    TelephoneNumber getOfficeTelephone() {
        return _officeTelephone;
    }

    private String _name;
    private TelephoneNumber _officeTelephone = new TelephoneNumber();
```

```
class TelephoneNumber...
   public String getTelephoneNumber() {
      return ("(" + _areaCode + ") " + _number);
   }
   String getAreaCode() {
      return _areaCode;
   }
   void setAreaCode(String arg) {
      _areaCode = arg;
   }
   String getNumber() {
      return _number;
   }
   void setNumber(String arg) {
      _number = arg;
   }
   private String _number;
   private String _areaCode;
```

The decision then is how much to expose the new class to my clients. I can completely hide it by providing delegating methods for its interface, or I can expose it. I may choose to expose it to some clients (such as those in my package) but not to others.

If I choose to expose the class, I need to consider the dangers of aliasing. If I expose the telephone number and a client changes the area code in that object, how do I feel about it? It may not be a direct client that makes this change. It might be the client of a client of a client.

I have the following options:

1. I accept that any object may change any part of the telephone number. This makes the telephone number a reference object, and I should consider *Change Value to Reference (179)*. In this case the person would be the access point for the telephone number.

2. I don't want anybody to change the value of the telephone number without going through the person. I can either make the telephone number immutable, or I can provide an immutable interface for the telephone number.

3. Another possibility is to clone the telephone number before passing it out. But this can lead to confusion because people think they can change the value. It also may lead to aliasing problems between clients if the telephone number is passed around a lot.

Extract Class (149) is a common technique for improving the liveness of a concurrent program because it allows you to have separate locks on the two resulting classes. If you don't need to lock both objects you don't have to. For more on this see section 3.3 in Lea [Lea].

However, there is a danger there. If you need to ensure that both objects are locked together, you get into the area of transactions and other kinds of shared locks. As discussed in Lea in section 8.1 [Lea], this is complex territory and requires heavier machinery than it is typically worth. Transactions are very useful when you use them, but writing transaction managers is more than most programmers should attempt.

**Extract
Class**

Inline Class

A class isn't doing very much.

Move all its features into another class and delete it.

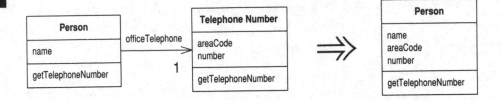

Motivation

Inline Class is the reverse of *Extract Class (149)*. I use *Inline Class* if a class is no longer pulling its weight and shouldn't be around any more. Often this is the result of refactoring that moves other responsibilities out of the class so there is little left. Then I want to fold this class into another class, picking one that seems to use the runt class the most.

Mechanics

❑ Declare the public protocol of the source class onto the absorbing class. Delegate all these methods to the source class.

⇒ *If a separate interface makes sense for the source class methods, use* Extract Interface (341) *before inlining.*

❑ Change all references from the source class to the absorbing class.

⇒ *Declare the source class private to remove out-of-package references. Also change the name of the source class so the compiler catches any dangling references to the source class.*

❑ Compile and test.

❑ Use *Move Method* and *Move Field* to move features from the source class to the absorbing class until there is nothing left.

❑ Hold a short, simple funeral service.

Example

Because I made a class out of telephone number, I now inline it back into person. I start with separate classes:

Inline Class

```
class Person...
    public String getName() {
        return _name;
    }
    public String getTelephoneNumber(){
        return _officeTelephone.getTelephoneNumber();
    }
    TelephoneNumber getOfficeTelephone() {
        return _officeTelephone;
    }

    private String _name;
    private TelephoneNumber _officeTelephone = new TelephoneNumber();

class TelephoneNumber...
    public String getTelephoneNumber() {
        return ("(" + _areaCode + ") " + _number);
    }
    String getAreaCode() {
        return _areaCode;
    }
    void setAreaCode(String arg) {
        _areaCode = arg;
    }
    String getNumber() {
        return _number;
    }
    void setNumber(String arg) {
        _number = arg;
    }
    private String _number;
    private String _areaCode;
```

I begin by declaring all the visible methods on telephone number on person:

```
class Person...
    String getAreaCode() {
        return _officeTelephone.getAreaCode();
    }
    void setAreaCode(String arg) {
        _officeTelephone.setAreaCode(arg);
    }
    String getNumber() {
        return _officeTelephone.getNumber();
```

```
    }
    void setNumber(String arg) {
        _officeTelephone.setNumber(arg);
    }
```

Inline Class

Now I find clients of telephone number and switch them to use the person's interface. So

```
    Person martin = new Person();
    martin.getOfficeTelephone().setAreaCode ("781");
```

becomes

```
    Person martin = new Person();
    martin.setAreaCode ("781");
```

Now I can use *Move Method (142)* and *Move Field (146)* until the telephone class is no more.

Hide Delegate

A client is calling a delegate class of an object.

Create methods on the server to hide the delegate.

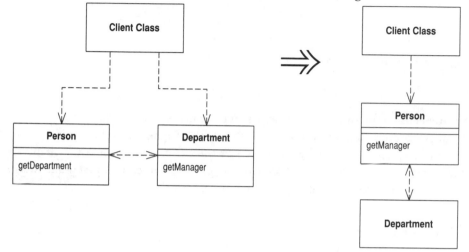

Motivation

One of the keys, if not *the* key, to objects is encapsulation. Encapsulation means that objects need to know less about other parts of the system. Then when things change, fewer objects need to be told about the change—which makes the change easier to make.

Anyone involved in objects knows that you should hide your fields, despite the fact that Java allows fields to be public. As you become more sophisticated, you realize there is more you can encapsulate.

If a client calls a method defined on one of the fields of the server object, the client needs to know about this delegate object. If the delegate changes, the client also may have to change. You can remove this dependency by placing a sim-

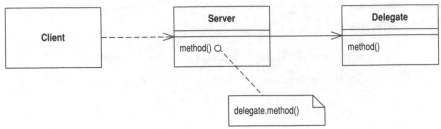

Figure 7.1 *Simple delegation*

ple delegating method on the server, which hides the delegate (Figure 7.1). Changes become limited to the server and don't propagate to the client.

You may find it is worthwhile to use *Extract Class (149)* for some clients of the server or all clients. If you hide from all clients, you can remove all mention of the delegate from the interface of the server.

Mechanics

- ❑ For each method on the delegate, create a simple delegating method on the server.

- ❑ Adjust the client to call the server.

  ⇒ *If the client is not in the same package as the server, consider changing the delegate method's access to package visibility.*

- ❑ Compile and test after adjusting each method.

- ❑ If no client needs to access the delegate anymore, remove the server's accessor for the delegate.

- ❑ Compile and test.

Example

I start with a person and a department:

```
class Person {
  Department _department;

  public Department getDepartment() {
      return _department;
  }
```

```
    public void setDepartment(Department arg) {
        _department = arg;
    }
}

class Department {
    private String _chargeCode;
    private Person _manager;

    public Department (Person manager) {
        _manager = manager;
    }

    public Person getManager() {
        return _manager;
    }
...
```

If a client wants to know a person's manager, it needs to get the department first:

```
manager = john.getDepartment().getManager();
```

This reveals to the client how the department class works and that the department is responsible to tracking the manager. I can reduce this coupling by hiding the department class from the client. I do this by creating a simple delegating method on person:

```
public Person getManager() {
    return _department.getManager();
}
```

I now need to change all clients of person to use this new method:

```
manager = john.getManager();
```

Once I've made the change for all methods of department and for all the clients of person, I can remove the getDepartment accessor on person.

Remove Middle Man

A class is doing too much simple delegation.

Get the client to call the delegate directly.

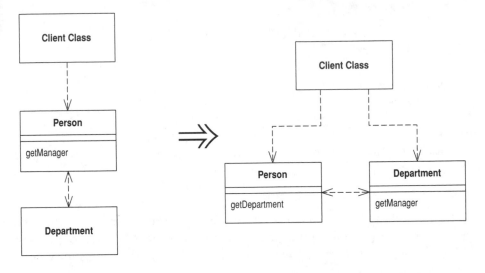

Motivation

In the motivation for *Hide Delegate,* I talked about the advantages of encapsulating the use of a delegated object. There is a price for this. The price is that every time the client wants to use a new feature of the delegate, you have to add a simple delegating method to the server. After adding features for a while, it becomes painful. The server class is just a middle man, and perhaps it's time for the client to call the delegate directly.

It's hard to figure out what the right amount of hiding is. Fortunately, with *Hide Delegate* and *Remove Middle Man (160)* it does not matter so much. You can adjust your system as time goes on. As the system changes, the basis for how much you hide also changes. A good encapsulation six months ago may be awkward now. Refactoring means you never have to say you're sorry—you just fix it.

Mechanics

❑ Create an accessor for the delegate.

❑ For each client use of a delegate method, remove the method from the server and replace the call in the client to call method on the delegate.

❑ Compile and test after each method.

Example

For an example I use person and department flipped the other way. I start with person hiding the department:

```
class Person...
  Department _department;
  public Person getManager() {
      return _department.getManager();
```

```
class Department...
  private Person _manager;
  public Department (Person manager) {
      _manager = manager;
  }
```

To find a person's manager, clients ask:

```
manager = john.getManager();
```

This is simple to use and encapsulates the department. However, if lots of methods are doing this, I end up with too many of these simple delegations on the person. That's when it is good to remove the middle man. First I make an accessor for the delegate:

```
class Person...
  public Department getDepartment() {
      return _department;
  }
```

Then I take each method at a time. I find clients that use the method on person and change it to first get the delegate. Then I use it:

```
manager = john.getDepartment().getManager();
```

I can then remove getManager from person. A compile shows whether I missed anything.

I may want to keep some of these delegations for convenience. I also may want to hide the delegate from some clients but show it to others. That also will leave some of the simple delegations in place.

Introduce Foreign Method

Introduce
Foreign
Method

A server class you are using needs an additional method, but you can't modify the class.

Create a method in the client class with an instance of the server class as its first argument.

```
Date newStart = new Date (previousEnd.getYear(),
                previousEnd.getMonth(), previousEnd.getDate() + 1);
```

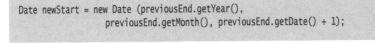

```
Date newStart = nextDay(previousEnd);

private static Date nextDay(Date arg) {
    return new Date (arg.getYear(),arg.getMonth(), arg.getDate() + 1);
}
```

Motivation

It happens often enough. You are using this really nice class that gives you all these great services. Then there is one service it doesn't give you but should. You curse the class, saying, "Why don't you do that?" If you can change the source, you can add in the method. If you can't change the source, you have to code around the lack of the method in the client.

If you use the method only once in the client class then the extra coding is no big deal and probably wasn't needed on the original class anyway. If you use the method several times, however, you have to repeat this coding around. Because repetition is the root of all software evil, this repetitive code should be factored into a single method. When you do this refactoring, you can clearly signal that this method is really a method that should be on the original by making it a foreign method.

If you find yourself creating many foreign methods on a server class, or you find many of your classes need the same foreign method, you should use *Introduce Local Extension (164)* instead.

Don't forget that foreign methods are a work-around. If you can, try to get the methods moved to their proper homes. If code ownership is the issue, send the foreign method to the owner of the server class and ask the owner to implement the method for you.

Mechanics

❑ Create a method in the client class that does what you need.

⇒ *The method should not access any of the features of the client class. If it needs a value, send it in as a parameter.*

❑ Make an instance of the server class the first parameter.

❑ Comment the method as "foreign method; should be in *server.*"

⇒ *This way you can use a text search to find foreign methods later if you get the chance to move the method.*

Example

I have some code that needs to roll over a billing period. The original code looks like this:

```
Date newStart = new Date (previousEnd.getYear(),
    previousEnd.getMonth(), previousEnd.getDate() + 1);
```

I can extract the code on the right-hand side of the assignment into a method. This method is a foreign method for date:

```
Date newStart = nextDay(previousEnd);

private static Date nextDay(Date arg) {
// foreign method, should be on date
    return new Date (arg.getYear(),arg.getMonth(), arg.getDate() + 1);
}
```

Introduce Local Extension

A server class you are using needs several additional methods,
but you can't modify the class.

*Create a new class that contains these extra methods. Make
this extension class a subclass or a wrapper of the original.*

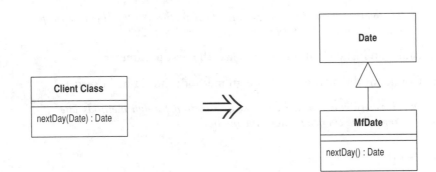

Motivation

Authors of classes sadly are not omniscient, and they fail to provide useful
methods for you. If you can modify the source, often the best thing is to add
that method. However, you often cannot modify the source. If you need one or
two methods, you can use *Introduce Foreign Method (162)*. Once you get
beyond a couple of these methods, however, they get out of hand. So you need
to group the methods together in a sensible place for them. The standard
object-oriented techniques of subclassing and wrapping are an obvious way to
do this. In these circumstances I call the subclass or wrapper a local extension.

A local extension is a separate class, but it is a subtype of the class it is
extending. That means it supports all the things the original can do but also
adds the extra features. Instead of using the original class, you instantiate the
local extension and use it.

By using the local extension you keep to the principle that methods and data
should be packaged into well-formed units. If you keep putting code in other
classes that should lie in the extension, you end up complicating the other
classes, and making it harder to reuse these methods.

In choosing between subclass and wrapper, I usually prefer the subclass because it is less work. The biggest roadblock to a subclass is that it needs to apply at object-creation time. If I can take over the creation process that's no problem. The problem occurs if you apply the local extension later. Subclassing forces me to create a new object of that subclass. If other objects refer to the old one, I have two objects with the original's data. If the original is immutable, there is no problem; I can safely take a copy. But if the original can change, there is a problem, because changes in one object won't change the other and I have to use a wrapper. That way changes made through the local extension affect the original object and vice versa.

Mechanics

❑ Create an extension class either as a subclass or a wrapper of the original.

❑ Add converting constructors to the extension.

⇒ *A constructor takes the original as an argument. The subclass version calls an appropriate superclass constructor; the wrapper version sets the delegate field to the argument.*

❑ Add new features to the extension.

❑ Replace the original with the extension where needed.

❑ Move any foreign methods defined for this class onto the extension.

Examples

I had to do this kind of thing quite a bit with Java 1.0.1 and the date class. The calendar class in 1.1 gave me a lot of the behavior I wanted, but before it arrived, it gave me quite a few opportunities to use extension. I use it as an example here.

The first thing to decide is whether to use a subclass or a wrapper. Subclassing is the more obvious way:

```
class MfDateSub extends Date {
  public MfDateSub nextDay()...
  public int dayOfYear()...
```

A wrapper uses delegation:

```
class mfDateWrap {
  private Date _original;
```

Example: Using a Subclass

First I create the new date as a subclass of the original:

```
class MfDateSub extends Date
```

Next I deal with changing between dates and the extension. The constructors of the original need to be repeated with simple delegation:

```
public MfDateSub (String dateString) {
      super (dateString);
};
```

Now I add a converting constructor, one that takes an original as an argument:

```
public MfDateSub (Date arg) {
    super (arg.getTime());
}
```

I can now add new features to the extension and use *Move Method (142)* to move any foreign methods over to the extension:

```
client class...
  private static Date nextDay(Date arg) {
  // foreign method, should be on date
      return new Date (arg.getYear(),arg.getMonth(), arg.getDate() + 1);
  }
```

becomes

```
class MfDateSub...
  Date nextDay() {
      return new Date (getYear(),getMonth(), getDate() + 1);
}
```

Example: Using a Wrapper

I start by declaring the wrapping class:

```
class mfDateWrap {
  private Date _original;
}
```

With the wrapping approach, I need to set up the constructors differently. The original constructors are implemented with simple delegation:

```
public MfDateWrap (String dateString) {
    _original = new Date(dateString);
};
```

The converting constructor now just sets the instance variable:

```
public MfDateWrap (Date arg) {
    _original = arg;
}
```

Then there is the tedious task of delegating all the methods of the original class. I show only a couple.

```
public int getYear() {
    return _original.getYear();
}

public boolean equals(Object arg) {
    if (this == arg) return true;
    if (! (arg instanceof MfDateWrap)) return false;
    MfDateWrap other = ((MfDateWrap) arg);
    return  (_original.equals(other._original));
}
```

Once I've done this I can use *Move Method (142)* to put date-specific behavior onto the new class:

```
client class...
  private static Date nextDay(Date arg) {
  // foreign method, should be on date
      return new Date (arg.getYear(),arg.getMonth(), arg.getDate() + 1);
  }
```

becomes

```
class MfDateWrap...
  Date nextDay() {
      return new Date (getYear(),getMonth(), getDate() + 1);
}
```

A particular problem with using wrappers is how to deal with methods that take an original as an argument, such as

```
public boolean after (Date arg)
```

Because I can't alter the original, I can only do after in one direction:

```
aWrapper.after(aDate)                 // can be made to work
aWrapper.after(anotherWrapper)        // can be made to work
aDate.after(aWrapper)                 // will not work
```

The purpose of this kind of overriding is to hide the fact I'm using a wrapper from the user of the class. This is good policy because the user of wrapper really shouldn't care about the wrapper and should be able to treat the two equally. However, I can't completely hide this information. The problem lies in certain system methods, such as `equals`. Ideally you would think that you could override equals on `MfDateWrap` like this

Introduce Local Extension

```
public boolean equals (Date arg)          // causes problems
```

This is dangerous because although I can make it work for my own purposes, other parts of the java system assume that equals is symmetric: that if `a.equals(b)` then `b.equals(a)`. If I violate this rule I'll run into a bevy of strange bugs. The only way to avoid that would be to modify Date, and if I could do that I wouldn't be using this refactoring. So in situations like this I just have to expose the fact that I'm wrapping. For equality tests this means a new method name.

```
public boolean equalsDate (Date arg)
```

I can avoid testing the type of unknown objects by providing versions of this method for both Date and MfDateWrap.

```
public boolean equalsDate (MfDateWrap arg)
```

The same problem is not an issue with subclassing, if I don't override the operation. If I do override, I become completely confused with the method lookup. I usually don't do override methods with extensions; I usually just add methods.

Chapter 8

Organizing Data

In this chapter I discuss several refactorings that make working with data easier. For many people *Self Encapsulate Field (171)* seems unnecessary. It's long been a matter of good-natured debate about whether an object should access its own data directly or through accessors. Sometimes you do need the accessors, and then you can get them with *Self Encapsulate Field (171)*. I generally use direct access because I find it simple to do this refactoring when I need it.

One of the useful things about object languages is that they allow you to define new types that go beyond what can be done with the simple data types of traditional languages. It takes a while to get used to how to do this, however. Often you start with a simple data value and then realize that an object would be more useful. *Replace Data Value with Object (175)* allows you to turn dumb data into articulate objects. When you realize that these objects are instances that will be needed in many parts of the program, you can use *Change Value to Reference (179)* to make them into reference objects.

If you see an array acting as a data structure, you can make the data structure clearer with *Replace Array with Object (186)*. In all these cases the object is but the first step. The real advantage comes when you use *Move Method (142)* to add behavior to the new objects.

Magic numbers, numbers with special meaning, have long been a problem. I remember being told in my earliest programming days not to use them. They do keep appearing, however, and I use *Replace Magic Number with Symbolic Constant (204)* to get rid of magic numbers whenever I figure out what they are doing.

Links between objects can be one way or two way. One-way links are easier, but sometimes you need to *Change Unidirectional Association to Bidirectional (197)* to support a new function. *Change Bidirectional Association to Unidirectional (200)* removes unnecessary complexity should you find you no longer need the two-way link anymore.

I've often run into cases in which GUI classes are doing business logic that they shouldn't. To move the behavior into proper domain classes, you need to have the data in the domain class and support the GUI by using *Duplicate Observed Data (189)*. I normally don't like duplicating data, but this is an exception that is usually impossible to avoid.

One of the key tenets of object-oriented programming is encapsulation. If any public data is streaking around, you can use *Encapsulate Field (206)* to decorously cover it up. If that data is a collection, use *Encapsulate Collection (208)* instead, because that has special protocol. If an entire record is naked, use *Replace Record with Data Class (217)*.

One form of data that requires particular treatment is the type code: a special value that indicates something particular about a type of instance. These often show up as enumerations, often implemented as static final integers. If the codes are for information and do not alter the behavior of the class, you can use *Replace Type Code with Class (218)*, which gives you better type checking and a platform for moving behavior later. If the behavior of a class is affected by a type code, use *Replace Type Code with Subclasses (223)* if possible. If you can't do that, use the more complicated (but more flexible) *Replace Type Code with State/Strategy (227)*.

Self Encapsulate Field

You are accessing a field directly, but the coupling to the field is becoming awkward.

Create getting and setting methods for the field and use only those to access the field.

```
private int _low, _high;
boolean includes (int arg) {
    return arg >= _low && arg <= _high;
}
```

⇓

```
private int _low, _high;
boolean includes (int arg) {
    return arg >= getLow() && arg <= getHigh();
}
int getLow() {return _low;}
int getHigh() {return _high;}
```

Motivation

When it comes to accessing fields, there are two schools of thought. One is that within the class where the variable is defined, you should access the variable freely (direct variable access). The other school is that even within the class, you should always use accessors (indirect variable access). Debates between the two can be heated. (See also the discussion in Auer [Auer] on page 413 and Beck [Beck].)

Essentially the advantages of *indirect variable access* are that it allows a subclass to override how to get that information with a method and that it supports more flexibility in managing the data, such as lazy initialization, which initializes the value only when you need to use it.

The advantage of *direct variable access* is that the code is easier to read. You don't need to stop and say, "This is just a getting method."

I'm always of two minds with this choice. I'm usually happy to do what the rest of the team wants to do. Left to myself, though, I like to use direct variable access as a first resort, until it gets in the way. Once things start becoming awkward, I switch to indirect variable access. Refactoring gives you the freedom to change your mind.

The most important time to use *Self Encapsulate Field* is when you are accessing a field in a superclass but you want to override this variable access with a computed value in the subclass. Self-encapsulating the field is the first step. After that you can override the getting and setting methods as you need to.

Mechanics

- ❑ Create a getting and setting method for the field.
- ❑ Find all references to the field and replace them with a getting or setting method.
  - ⇛ *Replace accesses to the field with a call to the getting method; replace assignments with a call to the setting method.*
  - ⇛ *You can get the compiler to help you check by temporarily renaming the field.*
- ❑ Make the field private.
- ❑ Double check that you have caught all references.
- ❑ Compile and test.

Example

This seems almost too simple for an example, but, hey, at least it is quick to write:

```
class IntRange {

  private int _low, _high;

  boolean includes (int arg) {
      return arg >= _low && arg <= _high;
  }

  void grow(int factor) {
      _high = _high * factor;
  }
```

```
IntRange (int low, int high) {
    _low = low;
    _high = high;
}
```

To self-encapsulate I define getting and setting methods (if they don't already exist) and use those:

```
class IntRange {

    boolean includes (int arg) {
        return arg >= getLow() && arg <= getHigh();
    }

    void grow(int factor) {
        setHigh (getHigh() * factor);
    }

    private int _low, _high;

    int getLow() {
        return _low;
    }

    int getHigh() {
        return _high;
    }

    void setLow(int arg) {
        _low = arg;
    }

    void setHigh(int arg) {
        _high = arg;
    }
```

When you are using self-encapsulation you have to be careful about using the setting method in the constructor. Often it is assumed that you use the setting method for changes after the object is created, so you may have different behavior in the setter than you have when initializing. In cases like this I prefer using either direct access from the constructor or a separate initialization method:

```
IntRange (int low, int high) {
    initialize (low, high);
}

private void initialize (int low, int high) {
    _low = low;
    _high = high;
}
```

The value in doing all this comes when you have a subclass, as follows:

```
class CappedRange extends IntRange {

    CappedRange (int low, int high, int cap) {
        super (low, high);
        _cap = cap;
    }

    private int _cap;

    int getCap() {
        return _cap;
    }

    int getHigh() {
        return Math.min(super.getHigh(), getCap());
    }
}
```

I can override all of the behavior of IntRange to take into account the cap without changing any of that behavior.

Self Encapsulate Field

Replace Data Value with Object

You have a data item that needs additional data or behavior.

Turn the data item into an object.

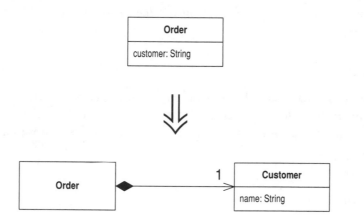

Motivation

Often in early stages of development you make decisions about representing simple facts as simple data items. As development proceeds you realize that those simple items aren't so simple anymore. A telephone number may be represented as a string for a while, but later you realize that the telephone needs special behavior for formatting, extracting the area code, and the like. For one or two items you may put the methods in the owning object, but quickly the code smells of duplication and feature envy. When the smell begins, turn the data value into an object.

Mechanics

- ❏ Create the class for the value. Give it a final field of the same type as the value in the source class. Add a getter and a constructor that takes the field as an argument.

- ❏ Compile.

- ❏ Change the type of the field in the source class to the new class.

- ❏ Change the getter in the source class to call the getter in the new class.

- ❏ If the field is mentioned in the source class constructor, assign the field using the constructor of the new class.

- ❏ Change the setting method to create a new instance of the new class.

- ❏ Compile and test.

- ❏ You may now need to use *Change Value to Reference (179)* on the new object.

Example

I start with an order class that has stored the customer of the order as a string and wants to turn the customer into an object. This way I have somewhere to store data, such as an address or credit rating, and useful behavior that uses this information.

```
class Order...
  public Order (String customer) {
      _customer = customer;
  }
  public String getCustomer() {
      return _customer;
  }
  public void setCustomer(String arg) {
      _customer = arg;
  }
  private String _customer;
```

Some client code that uses this looks like

```
private static int numberOfOrdersFor(Collection orders, String customer) {
    int result = 0;
    Iterator iter = orders.iterator();
    while (iter.hasNext()) {
        Order each = (Order) iter.next();
        if (each.getCustomer().equals(customer)) result++;
    }
    return result;
}
```

First I create the new customer class. I give it a final field for a string attribute, because that is what the order currently uses. I call it *name,* because that seems to be what the string is used for. I also add a getting method and provide a constructor that uses the attribute:

```
class Customer {
  public Customer (String name) {
      _name = name;
  }
```

```
    public String getName() {
        return _name;
    }
    private final String _name;
}
```

Now I change the type of the customer field and change methods that reference it to use the appropriate references on the customer class. The getter and constructor are obvious. For the setter I create a new customer:

```
class Order...
    public Order (String customer) {
        _customer = new Customer(customer);
    }
    public String getCustomer() {
        return _customer.getName();
    }
    private Customer _customer;

    public void setCustomer(String arg) {
        _customer = new Customer(arg);
    }
```

Replace Data
Value with
Object

The setter creates a new customer because the old string attribute was a value object, and thus the customer currently also is a value object. This means that each order has its own customer object. As a rule value objects should be immutable; this avoids some nasty aliasing bugs. Later on I will want customer to be a reference object, but that's another refactoring. At this point I can compile and test.

Now I look at the methods on order that manipulate customer and make some changes to make the new state of affairs clearer. With the getter I use *Rename Method (273)* to make it clear that it is the name not the object that is returned:

```
    public String getCustomerName() {
        return _customer.getName();
    }
```

On the constructor and setter, I don't need to change the signature, but the name of the arguments should change:

```
    public Order (String customerName) {
        _customer = new Customer(customerName);
    }
    public void setCustomer(String customerName) {
        _customer = new Customer(customerName);
    }
```

Further refactoring may well cause me to add a new constructor and setter that takes an existing customer.

This finishes this refactoring, but in this case, as in many others, there is another step. If I want to add such things as credit ratings and addresses to our customer, I cannot do so now. This is because the customer is treated as a value object. Each order has its own customer object. To give a customer these attributes I need to apply *Change Value to Reference (179)* to the customer so that all orders for the same customer share the same customer object. You'll find this example continued there.

Replace Data
Value with
Object

Change Value to Reference

You have a class with many equal instances that you want to replace with a single object.

Turn the object into a reference object.

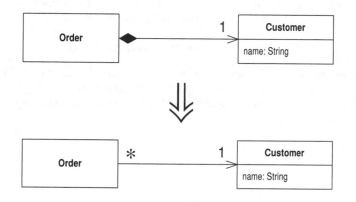

Motivation

You can make a useful classification of objects in many systems: reference objects and value objects. *Reference object*s are things like customer or account. Each object stands for one object in the real world, and you use the object identity to test whether they are equal. *Value objects* are things like date or money. They are defined entirely through their data values. You don't mind that copies exist; you may have hundreds of "1/1/2000" objects around your system. You do need to tell whether two of the objects are equal, so you need to override the equals method (and the hashCode method too).

The decision between reference and value is not always clear. Sometimes you start with a simple value with a small amount of immutable data. Then you want to give it some changeable data and ensure that the changes ripple to everyone referring to the object. At this point you need to turn it into a reference object.

Mechanics

- ❏ Use *Replace Constructor with Factory Method (304)*.

- ❏ Compile and test.

❏ Decide what object is responsible for providing access to the objects.

⇒ *This may be a static dictionary or a registry object.*
⇒ *You may have more than one object that acts as an access point for the new object.*

❏ Decide whether the objects are precreated or created on the fly.

⇒ *If the objects are precreated and you are retrieving them from memory, you need to ensure they are loaded before they are needed.*

❏ Alter the factory method to return the reference object.

⇒ *If the objects are precomputed, you need to decide how to handle errors if someone asks for an object that does not exist.*
⇒ *You may want to use* Rename Method (273) *on the factory to convey that it returns an existing object.*

❏ Compile and test.

Example

I start where I left off in the example for *Replace Data Value with Object (175)*. I have the following customer class:

```
class Customer {
  public Customer (String name) {
      _name = name;
  }
  public String getName() {
      return _name;
  }
  private final String _name;
}
```

It is used by an order class:

```
class Order...
  public Order (String customerName) {
      _customer = new Customer(customerName);
  }
  public void setCustomer(String customerName) {
      _customer = new Customer(customerName);
  }
  public String getCustomerName() {
      return _customer.getName();
  }
  private Customer _customer;
```

and some client code:

```
private static int numberOfOrdersFor(Collection orders, String customer) {
    int result = 0;
    Iterator iter = orders.iterator();
    while (iter.hasNext()) {
        Order each = (Order) iter.next();
        if (each.getCustomerName().equals(customer)) result++;
    }
    return result;
}
```

Change Value to Reference

At the moment it is a value. Each order has its own customer object even if they are for the same conceptual customer. I want to change this so that if we have several orders for the same conceptual customer, they share a single customer object. For this case this means that there should be only one customer object for each customer name.

I begin by using *Replace Constructor with Factory Method (304)*. This allows me to take control of the creation process, which will become important later. I define the factory method on customer:

```
class Customer {
  public static Customer create (String name) {
      return new Customer(name);
  }
```

Then I replace the calls to the constructor with calls to the factory:

```
class Order {
  public Order (String customer) {
      _customer = Customer.create(customer);
  }
```

Then I make the constructor private:

```
class Customer {
  private Customer (String name) {
      _name = name;
  }
```

Now I have to decide how to access the customers. My preference is to use another object. Such a situation works well with something like the line items on an order. The order is responsible for providing access to the line items. However, in this situation there isn't such an obvious object. In this situation I usually create a registry object to be the access point. For simplicity in this example, however, I store them using a static field on customer, making the customer class the access point:

```
private static Dictionary _instances = new Hashtable();
```

Then I decide whether to create customers on the fly when asked or to create them in advance. I'll use the latter. In my application start-up code I load the customers that are in use. These could come from a database or from a file. For simplicity I use explicit code. I can always use *Substitute Algorithm (139)* to change it later.

Change Value to Reference

```
class Customer...
  static void loadCustomers() {
      new Customer ("Lemon Car Hire").store();
      new Customer ("Associated Coffee Machines").store();
      new Customer ("Bilston Gasworks").store();
  }
  private void store() {
      _instances.put(this.getName(), this);
  }
```

Now I alter the factory method to return the precreated customer:

```
public static Customer create (String name) {
    return (Customer) _instances.get(name);
}
```

Because the create method always returns an existing customer, I should make this clear by using *Rename Method (273)*.

```
class Customer...
  public static Customer getNamed (String name) {
      return (Customer) _instances.get(name);
  }
```

Change Reference to Value

You have a reference object that is small, immutable, and awkward to manage.

Turn it into a value object.

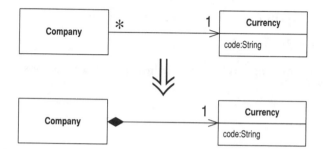

Motivation

As with *Change Value to Reference (179)*, the decision between a reference and a value object is not always clear. It is a decision that often needs reversing.

The trigger for going from a reference to a value is that working with the reference object becomes awkward. Reference objects have to be controlled in some way. You always need to ask the controller for the appropriate object. The memory links also can be awkward. Value objects are particularly useful for distributed and concurrent systems.

An important property of value objects is that they should be immutable. Any time you invoke a query on one, you should get the same result. If this is true, there is no problem having many objects represent the same thing. If the value is mutable, you have to ensure that changing any object also updates all the other objects that represent the same thing. That's so much of a pain that the easiest thing to do is to make it a reference object.

It's important to be clear on what *immutable* means. If you have a money class with a currency and a value, that's usually an immutable value object. That does not mean your salary cannot change. It means that to change your salary, you need to replace the existing money object with a new money object rather than changing the amount on an exisiting money object. Your relationship can change, but the money object itself does not.

Mechanics

❏ Check that the candidate object is immutable or can become immutable.

⇛ *If the object isn't currently immutable, use* Remove Setting Method (300) *until it is.*

⇛ *If the candidate cannot become immutable, you should abandon this refactoring.*

❏ Create an equals method and a hash method.

❏ Compile and test.

❏ Consider removing any factory method and making a constructor public.

Change
Reference to
Value

Example

I begin with a currency class:

```
class Currency...
  private String _code;

  public String getCode() {
      return _code;
  }
  private Currency (String code) {
      _code = code;
  }
```

All this class does is hold and return a code. It is a reference object, so to get an instance I need to use

```
Currency usd = Currency.get("USD");
```

The currency class maintains a list of instances. I can't just use a constructor (which is why it's private).

```
new Currency("USD").equals(new Currency("USD")) // returns false
```

To convert this to a value object, the key thing to do is verify that the object is immutable. If it isn't, I don't try to make this change, as a mutable value causes no end of painful aliasing.

In this case the object is immutable, so the next step is to define an equals method:

```
public boolean equals(Object arg) {
    if (! (arg instanceof Currency)) return false;
    Currency other = (Currency) arg;
    return (_code.equals(other._code));
}
```

If I define equals, I also need to define hashCode. The simple way to do this is to take the hash codes of all the fields used in the equals method and do a bitwise xor (^) on them. Here it's easy because there's only one:

```
public int hashCode() {
    return _code.hashCode();
}
```

With both methods replaced, I can compile and test. I need to do both; otherwise any collection that relies on hashing, such as Hashtable, HashSet or HashMap, may act strangely.

Now I can create as many equal currencies as I like. I can get rid of all the controller behavior on the class and the factory method and just use the constructor, which I can now make public.

```
new Currency("USD").equals(new Currency("USD")) // now returns true
```

Change
Reference to
Value

Replace Array with Object

You have an array in which certain elements mean different things.

Replace the array with an object that has a field for each element.

Replace Array
with Object

```
String[] row = new String[3];
row [0] = "Liverpool";
row [1] = "15";
```

⇓

```
Performance row = new Performance();
row.setName("Liverpool");
row.setWins("15");
```

Motivation

Arrays are a common structure for organizing data. However, they should be used only to contain a collection of similar objects in some order. Sometimes, however, you see them used to contain a number of different things. Conventions such as "the first element on the array is the person's name" are hard to remember. With an object you can use names of fields and methods to convey this information so you don't have to remember it or hope the comments are up to date. You can also encapsulate the information and use *Move Method (142)* to add behavior to it.

Mechanics

- ❏ Create a new class to represent the information in the array. Give it a public field for the array.

- ❏ Change all users of the array to use the new class.

- ❏ Compile and test.

- ❏ One by one, add getters and setters for each element of the array. Name the accessors after the purpose of the array element. Change the clients to use the accessors. Compile and test after each change.

- When all array accesses are replaced by methods, make the array private.

- Compile.

- For each element of the array, create a field in the class and change the accessors to use the field.

- Compile and test after each element is changed.

- When all elements have been replaced with fields, delete the array.

Replace Array
with Object

Example

I start with an array that's used to hold the name, wins, and losses of a sports team. It would be declared as follows:

```
String[] row = new String[3];
```

It would be used with code such as the following:

```
row [0] = "Liverpool";
row [1] = "15";

String name = row[0];
int wins = Integer.parseInt(row[1]);
```

To turn this into an object, I begin by creating a class:

```
class Performance {}
```

For my first step I give the new class a public data member. (I know this is evil and wicked, but I'll reform in due course.)

```
    public String[] _data = new String[3];
```

Now I find the spots that create and access the array. When the array is created I use

```
Performance row = new Performance();
```

When it is used, I change to

```
row._data [0] = "Liverpool";
row._data [1] = "15";

String name = row._data[0];
int wins = Integer.parseInt(row._data[1]);
```

One by one, I add more meaningful getters and setters. I start with the name:

```
class Performance...
    public String getName() {
        return _data[0];
```

```
    }
    public void setName(String arg) {
        _data[0] = arg;
    }
```

I alter the users of that row to use the getters and setters instead:

```
row.setName("Liverpool");
row._data  [1] = "15";

String name = row.getName();
int wins = Integer.parseInt(row._data[1]);
```

Replace Array
with Object

I can do the same with the second element. To make matters easier, I can encapsulate the data type conversion:

```
class Performance...
    public int getWins() {
        return Integer.parseInt(_data[1]);
    }
    public void setWins(String arg) {
        _data[1] = arg;
    }

....
client code...
    row.setName("Liverpool");
    row.setWins("15");

    String name = row.getName();
    int wins = row.getWins();
```

Once I've done this for each element, I can make the array private.

```
private String[] _data = new String[3];
```

The most important part of this refactoring, changing the interface, is now done. It is also useful, however, to replace the array internally. I can do this by adding a field for each array element and changing the accessors to use it:

```
class Performance...
    public String getName() {
        return _name;
    }
    public void setName(String arg) {
        _name = arg;
    }
    private String _name;
```

I do this for each element in the array. When I've done them all, I delete the array.

Duplicate Observed Data

You have domain data available only in a GUI control, and
domain methods need access.

*Copy the data to a domain object. Set up an observer to
synchronize the two pieces of data.*

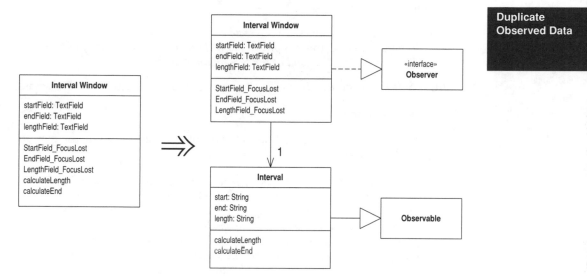

Motivation

A well-layered system separates code that handles the user interface from code
that handles the business logic. It does this for several reasons. You may want several interfaces for similar business logic; the user interface becomes too complicated if it does both; it is easier to maintain and evolve domain objects separate
from the GUI; or you may have different developers handling the different pieces.

Although the behavior can be separated easily, the data often cannot. Data
needs to be embedded in GUI control that has the same meaning as data that
lives in the domain model. User interface frameworks, from model-view-con-
troller (MVC) onward, used a multitiered system to provide mechanisms to
allow you to provide this data and keep everything in sync.

If you come across code that has been developed with a two-tiered approach in
which business logic is embedded into the user interface, you need to separate the

behaviors. Much of this is about decomposing and moving methods. For the data, however, you cannot just move the data, you have to duplicate it and provide the synchronization mechanism.

Mechanics

❑ Make the presentation class an observer of the domain class [Gang of Four].

 ⇒ *If there is no domain class yet, create one.*
 ⇒ *If there is no link from the presentation class to the domain class, put the domain class in a field of the presentation class.*

❑ Use *Self Encapsulate Field (171)* on the domain data within the GUI class.

❑ Compile and test.

❑ Add a call to the setting method in the event handler to update the component with its current value using direct access.

 ⇒ *Put a method in the event handler that updates the value of the component on the basis of its current value. Of course this is completely unnecessary; you are just setting the value to its current value, but by using the setting method, you allow any behavior there to execute.*
 ⇒ *When you make this change, don't use the getting method for the component; use direct access to the component. Later the getting method will pull the value from the domain, which does not change until the setting method executes.*
 ⇒ *Make sure the event-handling mechanism is triggered by the test code.*

❑ Compile and test.

❑ Define the data and accessor methods in the domain class.

 ⇒ *Make sure the setting method on the domain triggers the notify mechanism in the observer pattern.*
 ⇒ *Use the same data type in the domain as is on the presentation (usually a string). Convert the data type in a later refactoring.*

❑ Redirect the accessors to write to the domain field.

❑ Modify the observer's update method to copy the data from the domain field to the GUI control.

❑ Compile and test.

Example

I start with the window in Figure 8.1. The behavior is very simple. Whenever you change the value in one of the text fields, the other ones update. If you change the start or end fields, the length is calculated; if you change the length field, the end is calculated.

All the methods are on a single `IntervalWindow` class. The fields are set to respond to the loss of focus from the field.

```
public class IntervalWindow extends Frame...
  java.awt.TextField _startField;
  java.awt.TextField _endField;
  java.awt.TextField _lengthField;

  class SymFocus extends java.awt.event.FocusAdapter
  {
      public void focusLost(java.awt.event.FocusEvent event)
      {
          Object object = event.getSource();
          if (object == _startField)
             StartField_FocusLost(event);
          else if (object == _endField)
             EndField_FocusLost(event);
          else if (object == _lengthField)
             LengthField_FocusLost(event);
      }
  }
```

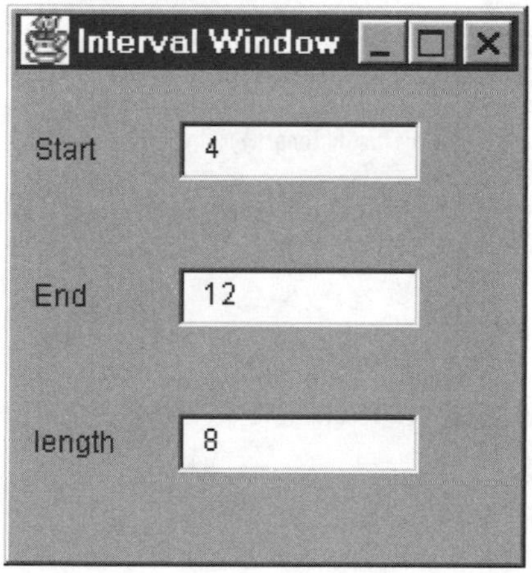

Figure 8.1 *A simple GUI window*

The listener reacts by calling StartField_FocusLost when focus is lost on the start field and EndField_FocusLost and LengthField_FocusLost for the other fields. These event-handling methods look like this:

```
void StartField_FocusLost(java.awt.event.FocusEvent event) {
    if (isNotInteger(_startField.getText()))
        _startField.setText("0");
    calculateLength();
}
```

Duplicate Observed Data

```
void EndField_FocusLost(java.awt.event.FocusEvent event) {
    if (isNotInteger(_endField.getText()))
        _endField.setText("0");
    calculateLength();
}

void LengthField_FocusLost(java.awt.event.FocusEvent event) {
    if (isNotInteger(_lengthField.getText()))
        _lengthField.setText("0");
    calculateEnd();
}
```

If you are wondering why I did the window this way, I just did it the easiest way my IDE (Cafe) encouraged me to.

All fields insert a zero if any noninteger characters appear and call the relevant calculation routine:

```
void calculateLength(){
    try {
        int start = Integer.parseInt(_startField.getText());
        int end = Integer.parseInt(_endField.getText());
        int length = end - start;
        _lengthField.setText(String.valueOf(length));
    } catch (NumberFormatException e) {
        throw new RuntimeException ("Unexpected Number Format Error");
    }
}
void calculateEnd() {
    try {
        int start = Integer.parseInt(_startField.getText());
        int length = Integer.parseInt(_lengthField.getText());
        int end = start + length;
        _endField.setText(String.valueOf(end));
    } catch (NumberFormatException e) {
        throw new RuntimeException ("Unexpected Number Format Error");
    }
}
```

My overall task, should I choose to accept it, is to separate the non-visual logic from the GUI. Essentially this means moving calculateLength and calculateEnd to a separate domain class. To do this I need to refer to the start, end, and length data *without* referring to the window class. The only way I can do this is to duplicate this data in the domain class and synchronize the data with the GUI. This task is described by *Duplicate Observed Data (189)*.

I don't currently have a domain class, so I create an (empty) one:

```
class Interval extends Observable {}
```

The interval window needs a link to this new domain class.

```
    private Interval _subject;
```

I then need to properly initialize this field and make interval window an observer of the interval. I can do this by putting the following code in interval window's constructor:

```
    _subject = new Interval();
    _subject.addObserver(this);
    update(_subject, null);
```

I like to put this code at the end of construction process. The call to update ensures that as I duplicate the data in the domain class, the GUI is initialized from the domain class. To do this I need to declare that interval window implements Observer:

```
public class IntervalWindow extends Frame implements Observer
```

To implement observer I need to create an update method. For the moment this can be blank:

```
    public void update(Observable observed, Object arg) {
    }
```

I can compile and test at this point. I haven't made any real changes yet, but I can make mistakes in the simplest places.

Now I can turn my attention to moving fields. As usual I make the changes one field at a time. To demonstrate my command of the English language, I'll start with the end field. The first task is to apply *Self Encapsulate Field (171)*. Text fields are updated with getText and setText methods. I create accessors that call these

```
String getEnd() {
    return _endField.getText();
}

void setEnd (String arg) {
    _endField.setText(arg);
}
```

I find every reference to _endField and replace them with the appropriate accessors:

```
void calculateLength(){
  try {
    int start = Integer.parseInt(_startField.getText());
    int end = Integer.parseInt(getEnd());
    int length = end - start;
    _lengthField.setText(String.valueOf(length));
  } catch (NumberFormatException e) {
    throw new RuntimeException ("Unexpected Number Format Error");
  }
}
```

**Duplicate
Observed Data**

```
void calculateEnd() {
  try {
    int start = Integer.parseInt(_startField.getText());
    int length = Integer.parseInt(_lengthField.getText());
    int end = start + length;
    setEnd(String.valueOf(end));
  } catch (NumberFormatException e) {
    throw new RuntimeException ("Unexpected Number Format Error");
  }
}

void EndField_FocusLost(java.awt.event.FocusEvent event) {
    if (isNotInteger(getEnd()))
        setEnd("0");
    calculateLength();
}
```

That's the normal process for *Self Encapsulate Field (171)*. However, when you are working with a GUI, there is a complication. The user can change the field value directly without calling setEnd. So I need to put a call to setEnd into the event handler for the GUI. This call changes the value of the end field to the current value of the end field. Of course this does nothing at the moment, but it does ensure the user input goes through the setting method:

```
void EndField_FocusLost(java.awt.event.FocusEvent event) {
    setEnd(_endField.getText());
    if (isNotInteger(getEnd()))
        setEnd("0");
    calculateLength();
}
```

In this call I don't use getEnd; instead I access the field directly. I do this because later in the refactoring getEnd gets a value from the domain object, not from the field. At that point using it would mean that every time the user were to change the value of the field, this code would change it back again, so here I must use direct access. At this point I can compile and test the encapsulated behavior.

Now I add the end field to the domain class:

```
class Interval...
    private String _end = "0";
```

I initialize it to the same value it is initialized to in the GUI. I now add getting and setting methods:

```
class Interval...

  String getEnd() {
      return _end;
  }
  void setEnd (String arg) {
      _end = arg;
      setChanged();
      notifyObservers();
  }
```

Because I'm using the observer pattern, I have to add the notification code into the setting method. I use a string, not a (more logical) number. This is because I want to make the smallest possible change. Once I've successfully duplicated the data, I can change the internal data type to an integer.

I can now do one more compile and test before I perform the duplication. By doing all this preparatory work, I've minimized the risk in this tricky step.

The first change is updating the accessors on IntervalWindow to use Interval.

```
class IntervalWindow...
  String getEnd() {
      return _subject.getEnd();
  }
  void setEnd (String arg) {
      _subject.setEnd(arg);
  }
```

I also need to update update to ensure the GUI reacts to the notification:

```
class IntervalWindow...
    public void update(Observable observed, Object arg) {
      _endField.setText(_subject.getEnd());
    }
```

This is the other place where I have to use direct access. If I were to call the setting method, I would get into an infinite recursion.

I can now compile and test, and the data is properly duplicated.

I can repeat for the other two fields. Once this is done I can apply *Move Method (142)* to move `calculateEnd` and `calculateLength` over to the interval class. At that point I have a domain class that contains all the domain behavior and data and separates it from the GUI code.

If I've done this, I consider getting rid of the GUI class completely. If my class is an older AWT class, I can get better looks by using Swing, and Swing does a better job with coordination. I can build the Swing GUI on top of the domain class. When I'm happy, I can remove the old GUI class.

Duplicate Observed Data

Using Event Listeners

Duplicate Observed Data also applies if you use event listeners instead of observer/observable. In this case you need to create a listener and event in the domain model (or you can use classes from AWT if you don't mind the dependency). The domain object then needs to register the listeners in the same way that observable does and send an event to them when it changes, as in the update method. The interval window can then use an inner class to implement the listener interface and call the appropriate update methods.

Change Unidirectional Association to Bidirectional

You have two classes that need to use each other's features, but there is only a one-way link.

Add back pointers, and change modifiers to update both sets.

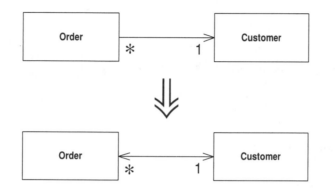

Motivation

You may find that you have initially set up two classes so that one class refers to the other. Over time you may find that a client of the referred class needs to get to the objects that refer to it. This effectively means navigating backward along the pointer. Pointers are one-way links, so you can't do this. Often you can get around this problem by finding another route. This may cost in computation but is reasonable, and you can have a method on the referred class that uses this behavior. Sometimes, however, this is not easy, and you need to set up a two-way reference, sometimes called a *back pointer*. If you aren't used to back pointers, it's easy to become tangled up using them. Once you get used to the idiom, however, it is not too complicated.

The idiom is awkward enough that you should have tests, at least until you are comfortable with the idiom. Because I usually don't bother testing accessors (the risk is not high enough), this is the rare case of a refactoring that adds a test.

This refactoring uses back pointers to implement bidirectionality. Other techniques, such as link objects, require other refactorings.

Mechanics

- ❏ Add a field for the back pointer.

- ❏ Decide which class will control the association.

❑ Create a helper method on the noncontrolling side of the association. Name this method to clearly indicate its restricted use.

❑ If the existing modifier is on the controlling side, modify it to update the back pointers.

❑ If the existing modifier is on the controlled side, create a controlling method on the controlling side and call it from the existing modifier.

Change
Unidirectional
Association to
Bidirectional

Example

A simple program has an order that refers to a customer:

```
class Order...
  Customer getCustomer() {
      return _customer;
  }
  void setCustomer (Customer arg) {
      _customer = arg;
  }
  Customer _customer;
```

The customer class has no reference to the order.

I start the refactoring by adding a field to the customer. As a customer can have several orders, so this field is a collection. Because I don't want a customer to have the same order more than once in its collection, the correct collection is a set:

```
class Customer  {
  private Set _orders = new HashSet();
```

Now I need to decide which class will take charge of the association. I prefer to let one class take charge because it keeps all the logic for manipulating the association in one place. My decision process runs as follows:

1. If both objects are reference objects and the association is one to many, then the object that has the one reference is the controller. (That is, if one customer has many orders, the order controls the association.)

2. If one object is a component of the other, the composite should control the association.

3. If both objects are reference objects and the association is many to many, it doesn't matter whether the order or the customer controls the association.

Because the order will take charge, I need to add a helper method to the customer that allows direct access to the orders collection. The order's modifier will use this to synchronize both sets of pointers. I use the name friendOrders to signal that this method is to be used only in this special case. I also minimize its visibility by making it package visibility if at all possible. I do have to make it public if the other class is in another package:

```
class Customer...
  Set friendOrders() {
  /** should only be used by Order when modifying the association */
      return _orders;
  }
```

Now I update the modifier to update the back pointers:

```
class Order...
  void setCustomer (Customer arg) ...
      if (_customer != null) _customer.friendOrders().remove(this);
      _customer = arg;
      if (_customer != null) _customer.friendOrders().add(this);
  }
```

Change
Unidirectional
Association to
Bidirectional

The exact code in the controlling modifier varies with the multiplicity of the association. If the customer is not allowed to be null, I can forgo the null checks, but I need to check for a null argument. The basic pattern is always the same, however: first tell the other object to remove its pointer to you, set your pointer to the new object, and then tell the new object to add a pointer to you.

If you want to modify the link through the customer, let it call the controlling method:

```
class Customer...
  void addOrder(Order arg) {
      arg.setCustomer(this);
  }
```

If an order can have many customers, you have a many-to-many case, and the methods look like this:

```
class Order... //controlling methods
  void addCustomer (Customer arg) {
      arg.friendOrders().add(this);
      _customers.add(arg);
  }
  void removeCustomer (Customer arg) {
      arg.friendOrders().remove(this);
      _customers.remove(arg);
  }

class Customer...
  void addOrder(Order arg) {
      arg.addCustomer(this);
  }
  void removeOrder(Order arg) {
      arg.removeCustomer(this);
  }
```

Change Bidirectional Association to Unidirectional

You have a two-way association but one class no longer needs features from the other.

Drop the unneeded end of the association.

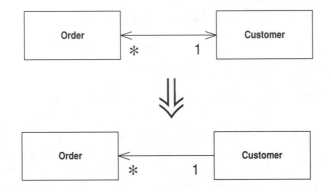

Motivation

Bidirectional associations are useful, but they carry a price. The price is the added complexity of maintaining the two-way links and ensuring that objects are properly created and removed. Bidirectional associations are not natural for many programmers, so they often are a source of errors.

Lots of two-way links also make it easy for mistakes to lead to zombies: objects that should be dead but still hang around because of a reference that was not cleared.

Bidirectional associations force an interdependency between the two classes. Any change to one class may cause a change to another. If the classes are in separate packages, you get an interdependency between the packages. Many interdependencies lead to a highly coupled system, in which any little change leads to lots of unpredictable ramifications.

You should use bidirectional associations when you need to but not when you don't. As soon as you see a bidirectional association is no longer pulling its weight, drop the unnecessary end.

Mechanics

❑ Examine all the readers of the field that holds the pointer that you wish to remove to see whether the removal is feasible.

⇒ *Look at direct readers and further methods that call the methods.*

⇒ *Consider whether it is possible to determine the other object without using the pointer. If so you will be able to use* Substitute Algorithm (139) *on the getter to allow clients to use the getting method even if there is no pointer.*

⇒ *Consider adding the object as an argument to all methods that use the field.*

❑ If clients need to use the getter, use *Self Encapsulate Field (171)*, carry out *Substitute Algorithm (139)* on the getter, compile, and test.

❑ If clients don't need the getter, change each user of the field so that it gets the object in the field another way. Compile and test after each change.

❑ When no reader is left in the field, remove all updates to the field, and remove the field.

⇒ *If there are many places that assign the field, use* Self Encapsulate Field (171) *so that they all use a single setter. Compile and test. Change the setter to have an empty body. Compile and test. If that works, remove the field, the setter, and all calls to the setter.*

❑ Compile and test.

Change
Bidirectional
Association to
Unidirectional

Example

I start from where I ended up from the example in *Change Unidirectional Association to Bidirectional (197)*. I have a customer and order with a bidirectional link:

```
class Order...
  Customer getCustomer() {
      return _customer;
  }
  void setCustomer (Customer arg) {
      if (_customer != null) _customer.friendOrders().remove(this);
      _customer = arg;
      if (_customer != null) _customer.friendOrders().add(this);
  }
  private Customer _customer;

class Customer...
  void addOrder(Order arg) {
      arg.setCustomer(this);
  }
  private Set _orders = new HashSet();
  Set friendOrders() {
      /** should only be used by Order */
      return _orders;
  }
```

I've found that in my application I don't have orders unless I already have a customer, so I want to break the link from order to customer.

The most difficult part of this refactoring is checking that I can do it. Once I know it's safe to do, it's easy. The issue is whether code relies on the customer field's being there. To remove the field, I need to provide an alternative.

My first move is to study all the readers of the field and the methods that use those readers. Can I find another way to provide the customer object? Often this means passing in the customer as an argument for an operation. Here's a simplistic example of this:

```
class Order...
  double getDiscountedPrice() {
      return getGrossPrice() * (1 - _customer.getDiscount());
  }
```

changes to

```
class Order...
  double getDiscountedPrice(Customer customer) {
      return getGrossPrice() * (1 - customer.getDiscount());
  }
```

This works particularly well when the behavior is being called by the customer, because then it's easy to pass itself in as an argument. So

```
class Customer...
  double getPriceFor(Order order) {
      Assert.isTrue(_orders.contains(order)); // see Introduce Assertion (267)
      return order.getDiscountedPrice();
```

becomes

```
class Customer...
  double getPriceFor(Order order) {
      Assert.isTrue(_orders.contains(order));
      return order.getDiscountedPrice(this);
  }
```

Another alternative I consider is changing the getter so that it gets the customer without using the field. If it does, I can use *Substitute Algorithm (139)* on the body of Order.getCustomer. I might do something like this:

```
Customer getCustomer() {
    Iterator iter = Customer.getInstances().iterator();
    while (iter.hasNext()) {
        Customer each = (Customer)iter.next();
        if (each.containsOrder(this)) return each;
    }
    return null;
}
```

Slow, but it works. In a database context it may not even be that slow if I use a database query. If the order class contains methods that use the customer field, I can change them to use getCustomer by using *Self Encapsulate Field (171)*.

If I retain the accessor, the association is still bidirectional in interface but is unidirectional in implementation. I remove the backpointer but retain the interdependencies between the two classes.

If I substitute the getting method, I substitute that and leave the rest till later. Otherwise I change the callers one at a time to use the customer from another source. I compile and test after each change. In practice, this process usually is pretty rapid. If it were complicated, I would give up on this refactoring.

Once I've eliminated the readers of the field, I can work on the writers of the field. This is as simple as removing any assignments to the field and then removing the field. Because nobody is reading it any more, that shouldn't matter.

Replace Magic Number with Symbolic Constant

You have a literal number with a particular meaning.

Create a constant, name it after the meaning, and replace the number with it.

```
double potentialEnergy(double mass, double height) {
    return mass * 9.81 * height;
}
```

⇓

```
double potentialEnergy(double mass, double height) {
    return mass * GRAVITATIONAL_CONSTANT * height;
}
static final double GRAVITATIONAL_CONSTANT = 9.81;
```

Motivation

Magic numbers are one of oldest ills in computing. They are numbers with special values that usually are not obvious. Magic numbers are really nasty when you need to reference the same logical number in more than one place. If the numbers might ever change, making the change is a nightmare. Even if you don't make a change, you have the difficulty of figuring out what is going on.

Many languages allow you to declare a constant. There is no cost in performance and there is a great improvement in readability.

Before you do this refactoring, you should always look for an alternative. Look at how the magic number is used. Often you can find a better way to use it. If the magic number is a type code, consider *Replace Type Code with Class (218).* If the magic number is the length of an array, use anArray.length instead when you are looping through the array.

Mechanics

❑ Declare a constant and set it to the value of the magic number.

❑ Find all occurrences of the magic number.

❑ See whether the magic number matches the usage of the constant; if it does, change the magic number to use the constant.

❑ Compile.

❑ When all magic numbers are changed, compile and test. At this point all should work as if nothing has been changed.

⇒ *A good test is to see whether you can change the constant easily. This may mean altering some expected results to match the new value. This isn't always possible, but it is a good trick when it works.*

Replace Magic
Number with
Symbolic
Constant

Encapsulate Field

There is a public field.

Make it private and provide accessors.

```
public String _name
```

```
private String _name;
public String getName() {return _name;}
public void setName(String arg) {_name = arg;}
```

Motivation

One of the principal tenets of object orientation is encapsulation, or data hiding. This says that you should never make your data public. When you make data public, other objects can change and access data values without the owning object's knowing about it. This separates data from behavior.

This is seen as a bad thing because it reduces the modularity of the program. When the data and behavior that uses it are clustered together, it is easier to change the code, because the changed code is in one place rather than scattered all over the program.

Encapsulate Field begins the process by hiding the data and adding accessors. But this is only the first step. A class with only accessors is a dumb class that doesn't really take advantage of the opportunities of objects, and an object is terrible thing to waste. Once I've done *Encapsulate Field (206)* I look for methods that use the new methods to see whether they fancy packing their bags and moving to the new object with a quick *Move Method (142)*.

Mechanics

❑ Create getting and setting methods for the field.

❑ Find all clients outside the class that reference the field. If the client uses the value, replace the reference with a call to the getting method. If the client changes the value, replace the reference with a call to the setting method.

> ⇒ *If the field is an object and the client invokes a modifier on the object, that is a use. Only use the setting method to replace an assignment.*

❑ Compile and test after each change.

❑ Once all clients are changed, declare the field as private.

❑ Compile and test.

Encapsulate
Field

Encapsulate Collection

A method returns a collection.

*Make it return a read-only view and provide
add/remove methods.*

**Encapsulate
Collection**

Motivation

Often a class contains a collection of instances. This collection might be an array, list, set, or vector. Such cases often have the usual getter and setter for the collection.

However, collections should use a protocol slightly different from that for other kinds of data. The getter should not return the collection object itself, because that allows clients to manipulate the contents of the collection without the owning class's knowing what is going on. It also reveals too much to clients about the object's internal data structures. A getter for a multivalued attribute should return something that prevents manipulation of the collection and hides unnecessary details about its structure. How you do this varies depending on the version of Java you are using.

In addition there should not be a setter for collection: rather there should be operations to add and remove elements. This gives the owning object control over adding and removing elements from the collection.

With this protocol the collection is properly encapsulated, which reduces the coupling of the owning class to its clients.

Mechanics

❑ Add an add and remove method for the collection.

❑ Initialize the field to an empty collection.

❑ Compile.

❏ Find callers of the setting method. Either modify the setting method to use the add and remove operations or have the clients call those operations instead.

⇒ *Setters are used in two cases: when the collection is empty and when the setter is replacing a nonempty collection.*
⇒ *You may wish to use* Rename Method (273) *to rename the setter. Change it from set to initialize or replace.*

❏ Compile and test.

❏ Find all users of the getter that modify the collection. Change them to use the add and remove methods. Compile and test after each change.

❏ When all uses of the getter that modify have been changed, modify the getter to return a read-only view of the collection.

⇒ *In Java 2, this is the appropriate unmodifiable collection view.*
⇒ *In Java 1.1, you should return a copy of the collection.*

❏ Compile and test.

❏ Find the users of the getter. Look for code that should be on the host object. Use *Extract Method (110)* and *Move Method (142)* to move the code to the host object.

For Java 2, you are done with that. For Java 1.1, however, clients may prefer to use an enumeration. To provide the enumeration:

❏ Change the name of the current getter and add a new getter to return an enumeration. Find users of the old getter and change them to use one of the new methods.

⇒ *If this is too big a jump, use* Rename Method (273) *on the old getter, create a new method that returns an enumeration, and change callers to use the new method.*

❏ Compile and test.

Examples

Java 2 added a whole new group of classes to handle collections. It not only added new classes but also altered the style of using collections. As a result the way you encapsulate a collection is different depending on whether you use the Java 2 collections or the Java 1.1 collections. I discuss the Java 2 approach first,

Encapsulate Collection

because I expect the more functional Java 2 collections to displace the Java 1.1 collections during the lifetime of this book.

Example: Java 2

A person is taking courses. Our course is pretty simple:

```
class Course...
    public Course (String name, boolean isAdvanced) {...};
    public boolean isAdvanced() {...};
```

Encapsulate Collection

I'm not going to bother with anything else on the course. The interesting class is the person:

```
class Person...
    public Set getCourses() {
        return _courses;
    }
    public void setCourses(Set arg) {
        _courses = arg;
    }
    private Set _courses;
```

With this interface, clients adds courses with code such as

```
Person kent = new Person();
Set s = new HashSet();
s.add(new Course ("Smalltalk Programming", false));
s.add(new Course ("Appreciating Single Malts", true));
kent.setCourses(s);
Assert.equals (2, kent.getCourses().size());
Course refact = new Course ("Refactoring", true);
kent.getCourses().add(refact);
kent.getCourses().add(new Course ("Brutal Sarcasm", false));
Assert.equals (4, kent.getCourses().size());
kent.getCourses().remove(refact);
Assert.equals (3, kent.getCourses().size());
```

A client that wants to know about advanced courses might do it this way:

```
Iterator iter = person.getCourses().iterator();
int count = 0;
while (iter.hasNext()) {
    Course each = (Course) iter.next();
    if (each.isAdvanced()) count ++;
}
```

The first thing I want to do is to create the proper modifiers for the collection and compile, as follows:

```
class Person
  public void addCourse (Course arg) {
      _courses.add(arg);
  }
  public void removeCourse (Course arg) {
      _courses.remove(arg);
  }
```

Encapsulate Collection

Life will be easier if I initialize the field as well:

```
private Set _courses = new HashSet();
```

I then look at the users of the setter. If there are many clients and the setter is used heavily, I need to replace the body of the setter to use the add and remove operations. The complexity of this process depends on how the setter is used. There are two cases. In the simplest case the client uses the setter to initialize the values, that is, there are no courses before the setter is applied. In this case I replace the body of the setter to use the add method:

```
class Person...
  public void setCourses(Set arg) {
      Assert.isTrue(_courses.isEmpty());
      Iterator iter = arg.iterator();
      while (iter.hasNext()) {
          addCourse((Course) iter.next());
      }
  }
```

After changing the body this way, it is wise to use *Rename Method (273)* to make the intention clearer.

```
public void initializeCourses(Set arg) {
    Assert.isTrue(_courses.isEmpty());
    Iterator iter = arg.iterator();
    while (iter.hasNext()) {
        addCourse((Course) iter.next());
    }
}
```

In the more general case I have to use the remove method to remove every element first and then add the elements. But I find that occurs rarely (as general cases often do).

If I know that I don't have any additional behavior when adding elements as I initialize, I can remove the loop and use addAll.

```
public void initializeCourses(Set arg) {
    Assert.isTrue(_courses.isEmpty());
    _courses.addAll(arg);
}
```

I can't just assign the set, even though the previous set was empty. If the client were to modify the set after passing it in, that would violate encapsulation. I have to make a copy.

If the clients simply create a set and use the setter, I can get them to use the add and remove methods directly and remove the setter completely. Code such as

```
Person kent = new Person();
Set s = new HashSet();
s.add(new Course ("Smalltalk Programming", false));
s.add(new Course ("Appreciating Single Malts", true));
kent.initializeCourses(s);
```

becomes

```
Person kent = new Person();
kent.addCourse(new Course ("Smalltalk Programming", false));
kent.addCourse(new Course ("Appreciating Single Malts", true));
```

Now I start looking at users of the getter. My first concern is cases in which someone uses the getter to modify the underlying collection, for example:

```
kent.getCourses().add(new Course ("Brutal Sarcasm", false));
```

I need to replace this with a call to the new modifier:

```
kent.addCourse(new Course ("Brutal Sarcasm", false));
```

Once I've done this for everyone, I can check that nobody is modifying through the getter by changing the getter body to return an unmodifiable view:

```
public Set getCourses() {
    return Collections.unmodifiableSet(_courses);
}
```

At this point I've encapsulated the collection. No one can change the elements of collection except through methods on the person.

Moving Behavior into the Class

I have the right interface. Now I like to look at the users of the getter to find code that ought to be on person. Code such as

```
Iterator iter = person.getCourses().iterator();
int count = 0;
while (iter.hasNext()) {
    Course each = (Course) iter.next();
    if (each.isAdvanced()) count ++;
}
```

is better moved to person because it uses only person's data. First I use *Extract Method (110)* on the code:

```
int numberOfAdvancedCourses(Person person) {
    Iterator iter = person.getCourses().iterator();
    int count = 0;
    while (iter.hasNext()) {
        Course each = (Course) iter.next();
        if (each.isAdvanced()) count ++;
    }
    return count;
}
```

And then I use *Move Method (142)* to move it to person:

```
class Person...
    int numberOfAdvancedCourses() {
        Iterator iter = getCourses().iterator();
        int count = 0;
        while (iter.hasNext()) {
            Course each = (Course) iter.next();
            if (each.isAdvanced()) count ++;
        }
        return count;
    }
```

A common case is

```
kent.getCourses().size()
```
which can be changed to the more readable

```
kent.numberOfCourses()
```

```
class Person...
    public int numberOfCourses() {
        return _courses.size();
    }
```

Encapsulate
Collection

A few years ago I was concerned that moving this kind of behavior over to person would lead to a bloated person class. In practice, I've found that usually isn't a problem.

Example: Java 1.1

Encapsulate Collection

In many ways the Java 1.1 case is pretty similar to the Java 2. I use the same example but with a vector:

```
class Person...
  public Vector getCourses() {
      return _courses;
  }
  public void setCourses(Vector arg) {
      _courses = arg;
  }
  private Vector _courses;
```

Again I begin by creating modifiers and initializing the field as follows:

```
class Person
  public void addCourse(Course arg) {
      _courses.addElement(arg);
  }
  public void removeCourse(Course arg) {
      _courses.removeElement(arg);
  }
  private Vector _courses = new Vector();
```

I can modify the setCourses to initialize the vector:

```
public void initializeCourses(Vector arg) {
    Assert.isTrue(_courses.isEmpty());
    Enumeration e = arg.elements();
    while (e.hasMoreElements()) {
        addCourse((Course) e.nextElement());
    }
}
```

I change users of the getter to use the modifiers, so

```
kent.getCourses().addElement(new Course ("Brutal Sarcasm", false));
```

becomes

```
kent.addCourse(new Course ("Brutal Sarcasm", false));
```

My final step changes because vectors do not have an unmodifiable version:

```
class Person...
  Vector getCourses() {
      return (Vector) _courses.clone();
  }
```

At this point I've encapsulated the collection. No one can change the elements of collection except through the person.

Example: Encapsulating Arrays

Arrays are commonly used, especially by programmers who are not familiar with collections. I rarely use arrays, because I prefer the more behaviorally rich collections. I often change arrays into collections as I do the encapsulation.

This time I begin with a string array for skills:

```
String[] getSkills() {
    return _skills;
}
void setSkills (String[] arg) {
    _skills = arg;
}
String[] _skills;
```

Again I begin by providing a modifier operation. Because the client is likely to change a value at a particular position, I need a set operation for a particular element:

```
void setSkill(int index, String newSkill) {
    _skills[index] = newSkill;
}
```

If I need to set the whole array, I can do so using the following operation:

```
void setSkills (String[] arg) {
    _skills = new String[arg.length];
    for (int i=0; i < arg.length; i++)
        setSkill(i,arg[i]);
}
```

There are numerous pitfalls here if things have to be done with the removed elements. The situation is complicated by what happens when the argument array is different in length from the original array. That's another reason to prefer a collection.

At this point I can start looking at users of the getter. I can change

```
kent.getSkills()[1] = "Refactoring";
```

to

```
kent.setSkill(1,"Refactoring");
```

When I've made all the changes, I can modify the getter to return a copy:

```
String[] getSkills() {
    String[] result = new String[_skills.length];
    System.arraycopy(_skills, 0, result, 0, _skills.length);
    return result;
}
```

Encapsulate Collection

This is a good point to replace the array with a list:

```
class Person...
  String[] getSkills() {
      return (String[]) _skills.toArray(new String[0]);
  }
  void setSkill(int index, String newSkill) {
      _skills.set(index,newSkill);
  }
  List _skills = new ArrayList();
```

Replace Record with Data Class

> You need to interface with a record structure in a traditional programming environment.

> *Make a dumb data object for the record.*

Motivation

Record structures are a common feature of programming environments. There are various reasons for bringing them into an object-oriented program. You could be copying a legacy program, or you could be communicating a structured record with a traditional programming API, or a database record. In these cases it is useful to create an interfacing class to deal with this external element. It is simplest to make the class look like the external record. You move other fields and methods into the class later. A less obvious but very compelling case is an array in which the element in each index has a special meaning. In this case you use *Replace Array with Object (186)*.

Mechanics

- ❏ Create a class to represent the record.

- ❏ Give the class a private field with a getting method and a setting method for each data item.

You now have a dumb data object. It has no behavior yet but further refactoring will explore that issue.

Replace Type Code with Class

A class has a numeric type code that does not affect its behavior.

Replace the number with a new class.

Motivation

Numeric type codes, or enumerations, are a common feature of C-based languages. With symbolic names they can be quite readable. The problem is that the symbolic name is only an alias; the compiler still sees the underlying number. The compiler type checks using the number not the symbolic name. Any method that takes the type code as an argument expects a number, and there is nothing to force a symbolic name to be used. This can reduce readability and be a source of bugs.

If you replace the number with a class, the compiler can type check on the class. By providing factory methods for the class, you can statically check that only valid instances are created and that those instances are passed on to the correct objects.

Before you do *Replace Type Code with Class,* however, you need to consider the other type code replacements. Replace the type code with a class only if the type code is pure data, that is, it does not cause different behavior inside a switch statement. For a start Java can only switch on an integer, not an arbitrary class, so the replacement will fail. More important than that, any switch has to be removed with *Replace Conditional with Polymorphism (255).* In order for that refactoring, the type code first has to be handled with *Replace*

Type Code with Subclasses (223) or *Replace Type Code with State/Strategy (227)*.

Even if a type code does not cause different behavior depending on its value, there might be behavior that is better placed in the type code class, so be alert to the value of a *Move Method (142)* or two.

Mechanics

❑ Create a new class for the type code.

⇒ *The class needs a code field that matches the type code and a getting method for this value. It should have static variables for the allowable instances of the class and a static method that returns the appropriate instance from an argument based on the original code.*

❑ Modify the implementation of the source class to use the new class.

⇒ *Maintain the old code-based interface, but change the static fields to use new class to generate the codes. Alter the other code-based methods to get the code numbers from the new class.*

❑ Compile and test.

⇒ *At this point the new class can do run-time checking of the codes.*

❑ For each method on the source class that uses the code, create a new method that uses the new class instead.

⇒ *Methods that use the code as an argument need new methods that use an instance of the new class as an argument. Methods that return a code need a new method that returns an instance of the new class. It is often wise to use* Rename Method (273) *on an old accessor before creating a new one to make the program clearer when it is using an old code.*

❑ One by one, change the clients of the source class so that they use the new interface.

❑ Compile and test after each client is updated.

⇒ *You may need to alter several methods before you have enough consistency to compile and test.*

❑ Remove the old interface that uses the codes, and remove the static declarations of the codes.

❑ Compile and test.

Example

A person has a blood group modeled with a type code:

```
class Person {

    public static final int O = 0;
    public static final int A = 1;
    public static final int B = 2;
    public static final int AB = 3;

    private int _bloodGroup;

    public Person (int bloodGroup) {
        _bloodGroup = bloodGroup;
    }

    public void setBloodGroup(int arg) {
        _bloodGroup = arg;
    }

    public int getBloodGroup() {
        return _bloodGroup;
    }
}
```

Replace Type
Code with
Class

I start by creating a new blood group class with instances that contain the type code number:

```
class BloodGroup {
    public static final BloodGroup O = new BloodGroup(0);
    public static final BloodGroup A = new BloodGroup(1);
    public static final BloodGroup B = new BloodGroup(2);
    public static final BloodGroup AB = new BloodGroup(3);
    private static final BloodGroup[] _values = {O, A, B, AB};

    private final int _code;

    private BloodGroup (int code ) {
        _code = code;
    }

    public int getCode() {
        return _code;
    }

    public static BloodGroup code(int arg) {
        return _values[arg];
    }

}
```

I then replace the code in Person with code that uses the new class:

```
class Person {

    public static final int O = BloodGroup.O.getCode();
    public static final int A = BloodGroup.A.getCode();
    public static final int B = BloodGroup.B.getCode();
    public static final int AB = BloodGroup.AB.getCode();

    private BloodGroup _bloodGroup;

    public Person (int bloodGroup) {
        _bloodGroup = BloodGroup.code(bloodGroup);
    }

    public int getBloodGroup() {
        return _bloodGroup.getCode();
    }

    public void setBloodGroup(int arg) {
        _bloodGroup = BloodGroup.code (arg);
    }
}
```

At this point I have run-time checking within the blood group class. To really gain from the change I have to alter the users of the person class to use blood group instead of integers.

To begin I use *Rename Method (273)* on the accessor for the person's blood group to clarify the new state of affairs:

```
class Person...
    public int getBloodGroupCode() {
        return _bloodGroup.getCode();
    }
```

I then add a new getting method that uses the new class:

```
    public BloodGroup getBloodGroup() {
        return _bloodGroup;
    }
```

I also create a new constructor and setting method that uses the class:

```
public Person (BloodGroup bloodGroup ) {
    _bloodGroup = bloodGroup;
}

public void setBloodGroup(BloodGroup arg) {
    _bloodGroup = arg;
}
```

Now I go to work on the clients of Person. The art is to work on one client at a time so that you can take small steps. Each client may need various changes, and that makes it more tricky. Any reference to the static variables needs to be changed. So

```
Person thePerson = new Person(Person.A)
```

becomes

```
Person thePerson = new Person(BloodGroup.A);
```

Replace Type
Code with
Class

References to the getting method need to use the new one, so

```
thePerson.getBloodGroupCode()
```

becomes

```
thePerson.getBloodGroup().getCode()
```

The same is true for setting methods, so

```
thePerson.setBloodGroup(Person.AB)
```

becomes

```
thePerson.setBloodGroup(BloodGroup.AB)
```

Once this is done for all clients of Person, I can remove the getting method, constructor, static definitions, and setting methods that use the integer:

```
class Person ...
    public static final int O = BloodGroup.O.getCode();
    public static final int A = BloodGroup.A.getCode();
    public static final int B = BloodGroup.B.getCode();
    public static final int AB = BloodGroup.AB.getCode();
    public Person (int bloodGroup) {
        _bloodGroup = BloodGroup.code(bloodGroup);
    }
    public int getBloodGroupCode() {
        return _bloodGroup.getCode();
    }
    public void setBloodGroup(int arg) {
        _bloodGroup = BloodGroup.code (arg);
    }
```

If no clients use the numeric code I can also privatize the methods on blood group that use the code:

```
class BloodGroup...
    private int getCode() {
        return _code;
    }

    private static BloodGroup code(int arg) {
        return _values[arg];
    }
```

Replace Type Code with Subclasses

You have an immutable type code that affects the behavior
of a class.

Replace the type code with subclasses.

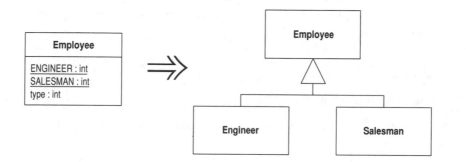

Motivation

If you have a type code that does not affect behavior, you can use *Replace Type Code with Class (218)*. However, if the type code affects behavior, the best thing to do is to use polymorphism to handle the variant behavior.

This situation usually is indicated by the presence of case-like conditional statements. These may be switches or if-then-else constructs. In either case they test the value of the type code and then execute different code depending on the value of the type code. Such conditionals need to be refactored with *Replace Conditional with Polymorphism (255)*. For this refactoring to work, the type code has to be replaced with an inheritance structure that will host the polymorphic behavior. Such an inheritance structure has a class with subclasses for each type code.

The simplest way to establish this structure is *Replace Type Code with Subclasses*. You take the class that has the type code and create a subclass for each type code. However, there are cases in which you can't do this. In the first the value of the type code changes after the object is created. In the second the class with the type code is already subclassed for another reason. In either of these cases you need to use *Replace Type Code with State/Strategy*.

Replace Type Code with Subclasses is primarily a scaffolding move that enables *Replace Conditional with Polymorphism (255)*. The trigger to use *Replace Type Code with Subclasses* is the presence of conditional statements. If there are no conditional statements, *Replace Type Code with Class (218)* is the better and less critical move.

Another reason to *Replace Type Code with Subclasses* is the presence of features that are relevant only to objects with certain type codes. Once you've done this refactoring, you can use *Push Down Method (328)* and *Push Down Field (329)* to clarify that these features are relevant only in certain cases.

The advantage of *Replace Type Code with Subclasses* is that it moves knowledge of the variant behavior from clients of the class to the class itself. If I add new variants, all I need to do is add a subclass. Without polymorphism I have to find all the conditionals and change those. So this refactoring is particularly valuable when variants keep changing.

Mechanics

❑ Self-encapsulate the type code.

⇒ *If the type code is passed into the constructor, you need to* replace the constructor with a factory method.

❑ For each value of the type code, create a subclass. Override the getting method of the type code in the subclass to return the relevant value.

⇒ *This value is hard coded into the return (e.g.,* return 1*). This looks messy, but it is a temporary measure until all case statements have been replaced.*

❑ Compile and test after replacing each type code value with a subclass.

❑ Remove the type code field from the superclass. Declare the accessors for the type code as abstract.

❑ Compile and test.

Example

I use the boring and unrealistic example of employee payment:

```
class Employee...
  private int _type;
  static final int ENGINEER = 0;
  static final int SALESMAN = 1;
  static final int MANAGER = 2;

  Employee (int type) {
      _type = type;
  }
```

The first step is to use *Self Encapsulate Field (171)* on the type code:

```
int getType() {
    return _type;
}
```

Because the employee's constructor uses a type code as a parameter, I need to replace it with a factory method:

```
static Employee create(int type) {
    return new Employee(type);
}

private Employee (int type) {
    _type = type;
}
```

Replace Type
Code with
Subclasses

I can now start with engineer as a subclass. First I create the subclass and the overriding method for the type code:

```
class Engineer extends Employee {

  int getType() {
      return Employee.ENGINEER;
  }

}
```

I also need to alter the factory method to create the appropriate object:

```
class Employee
  static Employee create(int type) {
      if (type == ENGINEER) return new Engineer();
      else return new Employee(type);
  }
```

I continue, one by one, until all the codes are replaced with subclasses. At this point I can get rid of the type code field on employee and make getType an abstract method. At this point the factory method looks like this:

```
abstract int getType();

static Employee create(int type) {
    switch (type) {
        case ENGINEER:
            return new Engineer();
        case SALESMAN:
            return new Salesman();
        case MANAGER:
            return new Manager();
```

```
        default:
            throw new IllegalArgumentException("Incorrect type code value");
    }
}
```

Of course this is the kind of switch statement I would prefer to avoid. But there is only one, and it is only used at creation.

Naturally once you have created the subclasses you should use *Push Down Method (328)* and *Push Down Field (329)* on any methods and fields that are relevant only for particular types of employee.

Replace Type Code with Subclasses

Replace Type Code with State/Strategy

You have a type code that affects the behavior of a class, but you cannot use subclassing.

Replace the type code with a state object.

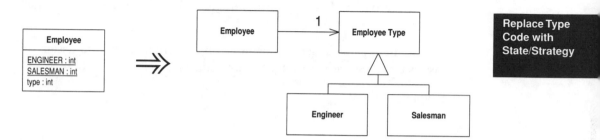

Motivation

This is similar to *Replace Type Code with Subclasses (223)*, but can be used if the type code changes during the life of the object or if another reason prevents subclassing. It uses either the state or strategy pattern [Gang of Four].

State and strategy are very similar, so the refactoring is the same whichever you use, and it doesn't really matter. Choose the pattern that better fits the specific circumstances. If you are trying to simplify a single algorithm with *Replace Conditional with Polymorphism (255)*, strategy is the better term. If you are going to move state-specific data and you think of the object as changing state, use the state pattern.

Mechanics

❑ Self-encapsulate the type code.

❑ Create a new class, and name it after the purpose of the type code. This is the state object.

❑ Add subclasses of the state object, one for each type code.

⇒ *It is easier to add the subclasses all at once, rather than one at a time.*

❑ Create an abstract query in the state object to return the type code. Create overriding queries of each state object subclass to return the correct type code.

❑ Compile.

❑ Create a field in the old class for the new state object.

❑ Adjust the type code query on the original class to delegate to the state object.

❑ Adjust the type code setting methods on the original class to assign an instance of the appropriate state object subclass.

❑ Compile and test.

Example

I again use the tiresome and brainless example of employee payment:

```
class Employee {

    private int _type;
    static final int ENGINEER = 0;
    static final int SALESMAN = 1;
    static final int MANAGER = 2;

    Employee (int type) {
        _type = type;
    }
}
```

Here's an example of the kind of conditional behavior that would use these codes:

```
int payAmount() {
    switch (_type) {
        case ENGINEER:
            return _monthlySalary;
        case SALESMAN:
            return _monthlySalary + _commission;
        case MANAGER:
            return _monthlySalary + _bonus;
        default:
            throw new RuntimeException("Incorrect Employee");
    }
}
```

I assume this is an exciting and go-ahead company that allows promotion of managers to engineers. Thus the type code is mutable, and I can't use subclassing. My first step, as ever, is to self-encapsulate the type code:

```
Employee (int type) {
    setType (type);
}

int getType() {
    return _type;
}

void setType(int arg) {
    _type = arg;
}

int payAmount() {
    switch (getType()) {
        case ENGINEER:
            return _monthlySalary;
        case SALESMAN:
            return _monthlySalary + _commission;
        case MANAGER:
            return _monthlySalary + _bonus;
        default:
            throw new RuntimeException("Incorrect Employee");
    }
}
```

Now I declare the state class. I declare this as an abstract class and provide an abstract method for returning the type code:

```
abstract class EmployeeType {
    abstract int getTypeCode();
}
```

I now create the subclasses:

```
class Engineer extends EmployeeType {

    int getTypeCode () {
        return Employee.ENGINEER;
    }
}

class Manager extends EmployeeType {
```

Replace Type
Code with
State/Strategy

```
    int getTypeCode () {
        return Employee.MANAGER;
    }
}

class Salesman extends EmployeeType {

    int getTypeCode () {
        return Employee.SALESMAN;
    }
}
```

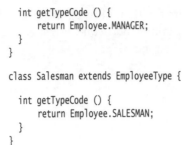

Replace Type
Code with
State/Strategy

I compile so far, and it is all so trivial that even for me it compiles easily. Now I actually hook the subclasses into the employee by modifying the accessors for the type code:

```
class Employee...
    private EmployeeType _type;

    int getType() {
        return _type.getTypeCode();
    }

    void setType(int arg) {
        switch (arg) {
            case ENGINEER:
                _type = new Engineer();
                break;
            case SALESMAN:
                _type = new Salesman();
                break;
            case MANAGER:
                _type = new Manager();
                break;
            default:
                throw new IllegalArgumentException("Incorrect Employee Code");
        }
    }
```

This means I now have a switch statement here. Once I'm finished refactoring, it will be the only one anywhere in the code, and it will be executed only when the type is changed. I can also use *Replace Constructor with Factory Method (304)* to create factory methods for different cases. I can eliminate all the other case statements with a swift thrust of *Replace Conditional with Polymorphism (255)*.

I like to finish *Replace Type Code with State/Strategy (227)* by moving all knowledge of the type codes and subclasses over to the new class. First I copy the type code definitions into the employee type, create a factory method for employee types, and adjust the setting method on employee:

```
class Employee...
  void setType(int arg) {
      _type = EmployeeType.newType(arg);
  }

class EmployeeType...
  static EmployeeType newType(int code) {
      switch (code) {
          case ENGINEER:
              return new Engineer();
          case SALESMAN:
              return new Salesman();
          case MANAGER:
              return new Manager();
          default:
              throw new IllegalArgumentException("Incorrect Employee Code");
      }
  }
  static final int ENGINEER = 0;
  static final int SALESMAN = 1;
  static final int MANAGER = 2;
```

Replace Type Code with State/Strategy

Then I remove the type code definitions from the employee and replace them with references to the employee type:

```
class Employee...
  int payAmount() {
      switch (getType()) {
          case EmployeeType.ENGINEER:
              return _monthlySalary;
          case EmployeeType.SALESMAN:
              return _monthlySalary + _commission;
          case EmployeeType.MANAGER:
              return _monthlySalary + _bonus;
          default:
              throw new RuntimeException("Incorrect Employee");
      }
  }
```

I'm now ready to use *Replace Conditional with Polymorphism (255)* on payAmount.

Replace Subclass with Fields

You have subclasses that vary only in methods that return constant data.

Change the methods to superclass fields and eliminate the subclasses.

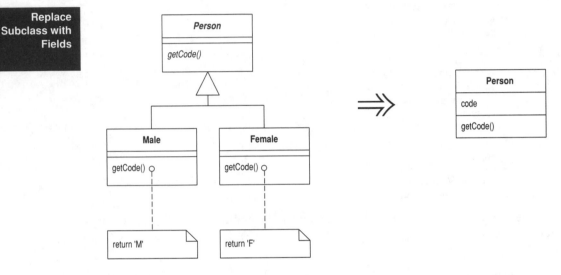

Motivation

You create subclasses to add features or allow behavior to vary. One form of variant behavior is the constant method [Beck]. A constant method is one that returns a hard-coded value. This can be very useful on subclasses that return different values for an accessor. You define the accessor in the superclass and implement it with different values on the subclass.

Although constant methods are useful, a subclass that consists only of constant methods is not doing enough to be worth existing. You can remove such subclasses completely by putting fields in the superclass. By doing that you remove the extra complexity of the subclasses.

Mechanics

- ❑ Use *Replace Constructor with Factory Method (304)* on the subclasses.

- ❑ If any code refers to the subclasses, replace the reference with one to the superclass.

- Declare final fields for each constant method on the superclass.

- Declare a protected superclass constructor to initialize the fields.

- Add or modify subclass constructors to call the new superclass constructor.

- Compile and test.

- Implement each constant method in the superclass to return the field and remove the method from the subclasses.

- Compile and test after each removal.

- When all the subclass methods have been removed, use *Inline Method (117)* to inline the constructor into the factory method of the superclass.

- Compile and test.

- Remove the subclass.

- Compile and test.

- Repeat inlining the constructor and eliminating each subclass until they are all gone.

Example

I begin with a person and sex-oriented subclasses:

```
abstract class Person {

  abstract boolean isMale();
  abstract char getCode();
...

class Male extends Person {
  boolean isMale() {
      return true;
  }
  char getCode() {
      return 'M';
  }
}

class Female extends Person {
  boolean isMale() {
      return false;
  }
  char getCode() {
      return 'F';
  }
}
```

Here the only difference between the subclasses is that they have implementations of abstract methods that return a hard-coded constant method [Beck]. I remove these lazy subclasses.

First I need to use *Replace Constructor with Factory Method (304)*. In this case I want a factory method for each subclass:

```
class Person...
  static Person createMale(){
      return new Male();
  }
  static Person createFemale() {
      return new Female();
  }
```

I then replace calls of the form

```
Person kent = new Male();
```

with

```
Person kent = Person.createMale();
```

Once I've replaced all of these calls I shouldn't have any references to the subclasses. I can check this with a text search and check that at least nothing accesses them outside the package by making the classes private.

Now I declare fields for each constant method on the superclass:

```
class Person...
  private final boolean _isMale;
  private final char _code;
```

I add a protected constructor on the superclass:

```
class Person...
  protected Person (boolean isMale, char code) {
      _isMale = isMale;
      _code = code;
  }
```

I add constructors that call this new constructor:

```
class Male...
  Male() {
      super (true, 'M');
  }
class Female...
  Female() {
      super (false, 'F');
  }
```

Replace Subclass with Fields

With that done I can compile and test. The fields are created and initialized, but so far they aren't being used. I can now start bringing the fields into play by putting accessors on the superclass and eliminating the subclass methods:

```
class Person...
  boolean isMale() {
      return _isMale;
  }
class Male...
  boolean isMale() {
      return true;
  }
```

I can do this one field and one subclass at a time or all in one go if I'm feeling lucky.

After all the subclasses are empty, so I remove the abstract marker from the person class and use *Inline Method (117)* to inline the subclass constructor into the superclass:

```
class Person
  static Person createMale(){
      return new Person(true, 'M');
  }
```

After compiling and testing I delete the male class and repeat the process for the female class.

Replace
Subclass with
Fields

Chapter 9

Simplifying Conditional Expressions

Conditional logic has a way of getting tricky, so here are a number of refactorings you can use to simplify it. The core refactoring here is *Decompose Conditional (238)*, which entails breaking a conditional into pieces. It is important because it separates the switching logic from the details of what happens.

The other refactorings in this chapter involve other important cases. Use *Consolidate Conditional Expression (240)* when you have several tests and all have the same effect. Use *Consolidate Duplicate Conditional Fragments (243)* to remove any duplication within the conditional code.

If you are working with code developed in a one exit point mentality, you often find control flags that allow the conditions to work with this rule. I don't follow the rule about one exit point from a method. Hence I use *Replace Nested Conditional with Guard Clauses (250)* to clarify special case conditionals and *Remove Control Flag (245)* to get rid of the awkward control flags.

Object-oriented programs often have less conditional behavior than procedural programs because much of the conditional behavior is handled by polymorphism. Polymorphism is better because the caller does not need to know about the conditional behavior, and it is thus easier to extend the conditions. As a result, object-oriented programs rarely have switch (case) statements. Any that show up are prime candidates for *Replace Conditional with Polymorphism (255)*.

One of the most useful, but less obvious, uses of polymorphism is to use *Introduce Null Object (260)* to remove checks for a null value.

Decompose Conditional

You have a complicated conditional (if-then-else) statement.

Extract methods from the condition, then part, and else parts.

```
if (date.before (SUMMER_START) || date.after(SUMMER_END))
    charge = quantity * _winterRate + _winterServiceCharge;
else charge = quantity * _summerRate;
```

⇓

```
if (notSummer(date))
    charge = winterCharge(quantity);
else charge = summerCharge (quantity);
```

Motivation

One of the most common areas of complexity in a program lies in complex conditional logic. As you write code to test conditions and to do various things depending on various conditions, you quickly end up with a pretty long method. Length of a method is in itself a factor that makes it harder to read, but conditions increase the difficulty. The problem usually lies in the fact that the code, both in the condition checks and in the actions, tells you what happens but can easily obscure why it happens.

As with any large block of code, you can make your intention clearer by decomposing it and replacing chunks of code with a method call named after the intention of that block of code. With conditions you can receive further benefit by doing this for the conditional part and each of the alternatives. This way you highlight the condition and make it clearly what you are branching on. You also highlight the reason for the branching.

Mechanics

❑ Extract the condition into its own method.

❑ Extract the then part and the else part into their own methods.

If I find a nested conditional, I usually first look to see whether I should use *Replace Nested Conditional with Guard Clauses (250)*. If that does not make sense, I decompose each of the conditionals.

Example

Suppose I'm calculating the charge for something that has separate rates for winter and summer:

```
if (date.before (SUMMER_START) || date.after(SUMMER_END))
    charge = quantity * _winterRate + _winterServiceCharge;
else charge = quantity * _summerRate;
```

I extract the conditional and each leg as follows:

Decompose
Conditional

```
if (notSummer(date))
    charge = winterCharge(quantity);
else charge = summerCharge (quantity);

private boolean notSummer(Date date) {
    return date.before (SUMMER_START) || date.after(SUMMER_END);
}

private double summerCharge(int quantity) {
    return quantity * _summerRate;
}

private double winterCharge(int quantity) {
    return quantity * _winterRate + _winterServiceCharge;
}
```

Here I show the result of the complete refactoring for clarity. In practice, however, I do each extraction separately and compile and test after each one.

Many programmers don't extract the condition parts in situations such as this. The conditions often are quite short, so it hardly seems worth it. Although the condition is often short, there often is a big gap between the intention of the code and its body. Even in this little case, reading notSummer(date) conveys a clearer message to me than does the original code. With the original I have to look at the code and figure out what it is doing. It's not difficult to do that here, but even so the extracted method reads more like a comment.

Consolidate Conditional Expression

You have a sequence of conditional tests with the same result.

Combine them into a single conditional expression and extract it.

```
double disabilityAmount() {
    if (_seniority < 2) return 0;
    if (_monthsDisabled > 12) return 0;
    if (_isPartTime) return 0;
    // compute the disability amount
```

**Consolidate
Conditional
Expression**

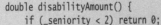

```
double disabilityAmount() {
    if (isNotEligibleForDisability()) return 0;
    // compute the disability amount
```

Motivation

Sometimes you see a series of conditional checks in which each check is different yet the resulting action is the same. When you see this, you should use ands and ors to consolidate them into a single conditional check with a single result.

Consolidating the conditional code is important for two reasons. First, it makes the check clearer by showing that you are really making a single check that's oring the other checks together. The sequence has the same effect, but it communicates carrying out a sequence of separate checks that just happen to be done together. The second reason for this refactoring is that it often sets you up for *Extract Method (110)*. Extracting a condition is one of the most useful things you can do to clarify your code. It replaces a statement of what you are doing with why you are doing it.

The reasons in favor of consolidating conditionals also point to reasons for not doing it. If you think the checks are really independent and shouldn't be thought of as a single check, don't do the refactoring. Your code already communicates your intention.

Mechanics

- ❏ Check that none of the conditionals has side effects.

  ⇒ *If there are side effects, you won't be able to do this refactoring.*

- ❏ Replace the string of conditionals with a single conditional statement using logical operators.

- ❏ Compile and test.

- ❏ Consider using *Extract Method (110)* on the condition.

Example: Ors

The state of the code is along the lines of the following:

```
double disabilityAmount() {
    if (_seniority < 2) return 0;
    if (_monthsDisabled > 12) return 0;
    if (_isPartTime) return 0;
    // compute the disability amount
    ...
```

Here we see a sequence of conditional checks that all result in the same thing. With sequential code like this, the checks are the equivalent of an or statement:

```
double disabilityAmount() {
    if ((_seniority < 2) || (_monthsDisabled > 12) || (_isPartTime)) return 0;
    // compute the disability amount
    ...
```

Now I can look at the condition and use *Extract Method (110)* to communicate what the condition is looking for:

```
double disabilityAmount() {
    if (isNotEligibleForDisability()) return 0;
    // compute the disability amount
    ...
}

boolean isNotEligibleForDisability() {
    return ((_seniority < 2) || (_monthsDisabled > 12) || (_isPartTime));
}
```

Consolidate
Conditional
Expression

Example: Ands

That example showed ors, but I can do the same with ands. Here the set up is something like the following:

```
if (onVacation())
    if (lengthOfService() > 10)
        return 1;
return 0.5;
```

This would be changed to

```
if (onVacation() && lengthOfService() > 10) return 1;
else return 0.5;
```

Consolidate
Conditional
Expression

You may well find you get a combination of these that yields an expression with ands, ors, and nots. In these cases the conditions may be messy, so I try to use *Extract Method (110)* on parts of the expression to make it simpler.

If the routine I'm looking at tests only the condition and returns a value, I can turn the routine into a single return statement using the ternary operator. So

```
if (onVacation() && lengthOfService() > 10) return 1;
else return 0.5;
```

becomes

```
return (onVacation() && lengthOfService() > 10) ? 1 : 0.5;
```

Consolidate Duplicate Conditional Fragments

The same fragment of code is in all branches of a conditional expression.

Move it outside of the expression.

```
if (isSpecialDeal()) {
    total = price * 0.95;
    send();
}
else {
    total = price * 0.98;
    send();
}
```

Consolidate
Duplicate
Conditional
Fragments

⇓

```
if (isSpecialDeal())
    total = price * 0.95;
else
    total - price * 0.98;
send();
```

Motivation

Sometimes you find the same code executed in all legs of a conditional. In that case you should move the code to outside the conditional. This makes clearer what varies and what stays the same.

Mechanics

- ❏ Identify code that is executed the same way regardless of the condition.

- ❏ If the common code is at the beginning, move it to before the conditional.

- ❏ If the common code is at the end, move it to after the conditional.

❑ If the common code is in the middle, look to see whether the code before or after it changes anything. If it does, you can move the common code forward or backward to the ends. You can then move it as described for code at the end or the beginning.

❑ If there is more than a single statement, you should extract that code into a method.

Example

You find this situation with code such as the following:

```
if (isSpecialDeal()) {
    total = price * 0.95;
    send();
}
else {
    total = price * 0.98;
    send();
}
```

Because the send method is executed in either case, I should move it out of the conditional:

```
if (isSpecialDeal())
    total = price * 0.95;
else
    total = price * 0.98;
send();
```

The same situation can apply to exceptions. If code is repeated after an exception-causing statement in the try block and all the catch blocks, I can move it to the final block.

Consolidate
Duplicate
Conditional
Fragments

Remove Control Flag

> You have a variable that is acting as a control flag for a series
> of boolean expressions.

> *Use a break or return instead.*

Motivation

When you have a series of conditional expressions, you often see a control flag
used to determine when to stop looking:

```
set done to false
while not done
  if (condition)
      do something
      set done to true
  next step of loop
```

Such control flags are more trouble than they are worth. They come from
rules of structured programming that call for routines with one entry and one
exit point. I agree with (and modern languages enforce) one entry point, but the
one exit point rule leads you to very convoluted conditionals with these awkward flags in the code. This is why languages have break and continue statements to get out of a complex conditional. It is often surprising what you can
do when you get rid of a control flag. The real purpose of the conditional
becomes so much more clear.

Mechanics

The obvious way to deal with control flags is to use the break or continue
statements present in Java.

- ❑ Find the value of the control flag that gets you out of the logic statement.

- ❑ Replace assignments of the break-out value with a break or continue
  statement.

- ❑ Compile and test after each replacement.

Another approach, also usable in languages without break and continue, is as follows:

- ❏ Extract the logic into a method.

- ❏ Find the value of the control flag that gets you out of the logic statement.

- ❏ Replace assignments of the break-out value with a return.

- ❏ Compile and test after each replacement.

Even in languages with a break or continue, I usually prefer use of an extraction and of a return. The return clearly signals that no more code in the method is executed. If you have that kind of code, you often need to extract that piece anyway.

Keep an eye on whether the control flag also indicates result information. If it does, you still need the control flag if you use the break, or you can return the value if you have extracted a method.

Example: Simple Control Flag Replaced with Break

The following function checks to see whether a list of people contains a couple of hard-coded suspicious characters:

```
void checkSecurity(String[] people) {
    boolean found = false;
    for (int i = 0; i < people.length; i++) {
        if (! found) {
            if (people[i].equals ("Don")){
                sendAlert();
                found = true;
            }
            if (people[i].equals ("John")){
                sendAlert();
                found = true;
            }
        }
    }
}
```

In a case like this, it is easy to see the control flag. It's the piece that sets the found variable to true. I can introduce the breaks one at a time:

```
void checkSecurity(String[] people) {
    boolean found = false;
    for (int i = 0; i < people.length; i++) {
        if (! found) {
            if (people[i].equals ("Don")){
                sendAlert();
                break;
            }
            if (people[i].equals ("John")){
                sendAlert();
                found = true;
            }
        }
    }
}
```

until I have them all:

```
void checkSecurity(String[] people) {
    boolean found = false;
    for (int i = 0; i < people.length; i++) {
        if (! found) {
            if (people[i].equals ("Don")){
                sendAlert();
                break;
            }
            if (people[i].equals ("John")){
                sendAlert();
                break;
            }
        }
    }
}
```

Then I can remove all references to the control flag:

```
void checkSecurity(String[] people) {
    for (int i = 0; i < people.length; i++) {
        if (people[i].equals ("Don")){
            sendAlert();
            break;
        }
        if (people[i].equals ("John")){
            sendAlert();
            break;
        }
    }
}
```

Example: Using Return with a Control Flag Result

The other style of this refactoring uses a return. I illustrate this with a variant that uses the control flag as a result value:

```
void checkSecurity(String[] people) {
    String found = "";
    for (int i = 0; i < people.length; i++) {
        if (found.equals("")) {
            if (people[i].equals ("Don")){
                sendAlert();
                found = "Don";
            }
            if (people[i].equals ("John")){
                sendAlert();
                found = "John";
            }
        }
    }
    someLaterCode(found);
}
```

Remove Control Flag

Here found is doing two things. It is indicating a result and acting as a control flag. When I see this, I like to extract the code that is determining found into its own method:

```
void checkSecurity(String[] people) {
    String found = foundMiscreant(people);
    someLaterCode(found);
}

String foundMiscreant(String[] people){
    String found = "";
    for (int i = 0; i < people.length; i++) {
        if (found.equals("")) {
            if (people[i].equals ("Don")){
                sendAlert();
                found = "Don";
            }
            if (people[i].equals ("John")){
                sendAlert();
                found = "John";
            }
        }
    }
    return found;
}
```

Then I can replace the control flag with a return:

```java
String foundMiscreant(String[] people){
    String found = "";
    for (int i = 0; i < people.length; i++) {
        if (found.equals("")) {
            if (people[i].equals ("Don")){
                sendAlert();
                return "Don";
            }
            if (people[i].equals ("John")){
                sendAlert();
                found = "John";
            }
        }
    }
    return found;
}
```

Remove
Control Flag

until I have removed the control flag:

```java
String foundMiscreant(String[] people){
    for (int i = 0; i < people.length; i++) {
        if (people[i].equals ("Don")){
            sendAlert();
            return "Don";
        }
        if (people[i].equals ("John")){
            sendAlert();
            return "John";
        }
    }
    return "";
}
```

You can also use the return style when you're not returning a value. Just use return without the argument.

Of course this has the problem of a function with side effects. So I want to use *Separate Query from Modifier (279)*. You'll find this example continued there.

Replace Nested Conditional with Guard Clauses

A method has conditional behavior that does not make clear
the normal path of execution.

Use guard clauses for all the special cases.

Replace Nested Conditional with Guard Clauses

```
double getPayAmount() {
  double result;
  if (_isDead) result = deadAmount();
  else {
      if (_isSeparated) result = separatedAmount();
      else {
          if (_isRetired) result = retiredAmount();
          else result = normalPayAmount();
      };
  }
  return result;
};
```

⇓

```
double getPayAmount() {
  if (_isDead) return deadAmount();
  if (_isSeparated) return separatedAmount();
  if (_isRetired) return retiredAmount();
  return normalPayAmount();
};
```

Motivation

I often find that conditional expressions come in two forms. The first form is a
check whether either course is part of the normal behavior. The second form is
a situation in which one answer from the conditional indicates normal behavior
and the other indicates an unusual condition.

These kinds of conditionals have different intentions, and these intentions
should come through in the code. If both are part of normal behavior, use a
condition with an if and an else leg. If the condition is an unusual condition,
check the condition and return if the condition is true. This kind of check is
often called a *guard clause* [Beck].

The key point about *Replace Nested Conditional with Guard Clauses* is one of emphasis. If you are using an if-then-else construct you are giving equal weight to the if leg and the else leg. This communicates to the reader that the legs are equally likely and important. Instead the guard clause says, "This is rare, and if it happens, do something and get out."

I often find I use *Replace Nested Conditional with Guard Clauses* when I'm working with a programmer who has been taught to have only one entry point and one exit point from a method. One entry point is enforced by modern languages, and one exit point is really not a useful rule. Clarity is the key principle: if the method is clearer with one exit point, use one exit point; otherwise don't.

Mechanics

Replace Nested
Conditional
with Guard
Clauses

❑ For each check put in the guard clause.

   ⇒ *The guard clause either returns, or throws an exception.*

❑ Compile and test after each check is replaced with a guard clause.

   ⇒ *If all guard clauses yield the same result, use* Consolidate Conditional Expressions.

Example

Imagine a run of a payroll system in which you have special rules for dead, separated, and retired employees. Such cases are unusual, but they do happen from time to time.

If I see the code like this

```
double getPayAmount() {
  double result;
  if (_isDead) result = deadAmount();
  else {
      if (_isSeparated) result = separatedAmount();
      else {
          if (_isRetired) result = retiredAmount();
          else result = normalPayAmount();
      };
  }
  return result;
};
```

Then the checking is masking the normal course of action behind the checking. So instead it is clearer to use guard clauses. I can introduce these one at a time. I like to start at the top:

```
double getPayAmount() {
  double result;
  if (_isDead) return deadAmount();
  if (_isSeparated) result = separatedAmount();
  else {
      if (_isRetired) result = retiredAmount();
      else result = normalPayAmount();
  };
  return result;
};
```

Replace Nested Conditional with Guard Clauses

I continue one at a time:

```
double getPayAmount() {
  double result;
  if (_isDead) return deadAmount();
  if (_isSeparated) return separatedAmount();
  if (_isRetired) result = retiredAmount();
  else result = normalPayAmount();
  return result;
};
```

and then

```
double getPayAmount() {
  double result;
  if (_isDead) return deadAmount();
  if (_isSeparated) return separatedAmount();
  if (_isRetired) return retiredAmount();
  result = normalPayAmount();
  return result;
};
```

By this point the result temp isn't pulling its weight so I nuke it:

```
double getPayAmount() {
  if (_isDead) return deadAmount();
  if (_isSeparated) return separatedAmount();
  if (_isRetired) return retiredAmount();
  return normalPayAmount();
};
```

Nested conditional code often is written by programmers who are taught to have one exit point from a method. I've found that is a too simplistic rule. When I have no further interest in a method, I signal my lack of interest by getting out. Directing the reader to look at an empty else block only gets in the way of comprehension.

Example: Reversing the Conditions

In reviewing the manuscript of this book, Joshua Kerievsky pointed out that you often do *Replace Nested Conditional with Guard Clauses* by reversing the conditional expressions. He kindly came up with an example to save further taxing of my imagination:

```
public double getAdjustedCapital() {
  double result = 0.0;
  if (_capital > 0.0) {
    if (_intRate > 0.0 && _duration > 0.0) {
      result = (_income / _duration) * ADJ_FACTOR;
    }
  }
  return result;
}
```

Replace Nested
Conditional
with Guard
Clauses

Again I make the replacements one at a time, but this time I reverse the conditional as I put in the guard clause:

```
public double getAdjustedCapital() {
  double result = 0.0;
  if (_capital <= 0.0) return result;
  if (_intRate > 0.0 && _duration > 0.0) {
    result = (_income / _duration) * ADJ_FACTOR;
  }
  return result;
}
```

Because the next conditional is a bit more complicated, I can reverse it in two steps. First I add a not:

```
public double getAdjustedCapital() {
  double result = 0.0;
  if (_capital <= 0.0) return result;
  if (!(_intRate > 0.0 && _duration > 0.0)) return result;
  result = (_income / _duration) * ADJ_FACTOR;
  return result;
}
```

Leaving nots in a conditional like that twists my mind around at a painful angle, so I simplify it as follows:

```
public double getAdjustedCapital() {
    double result = 0.0;
    if (_capital <= 0.0) return result;
    if (_intRate <= 0.0 || _duration <= 0.0) return result;
    result = (_income / _duration) * ADJ_FACTOR;
    return result;
}
```

In these situations I prefer to put an explicit value on the returns from the guards. That way you can easily see the result of the guard's failing (I would also consider *Replace Magic Number with Symbolic Constant [204]* here).

Replace Nested Conditional with Guard Clauses

```
public double getAdjustedCapital() {
    double result = 0.0;
    if (_capital <= 0.0) return 0.0;
    if (_intRate <= 0.0 || _duration <= 0.0) return 0.0;
    result = (_income / _duration) * ADJ_FACTOR;
    return result;
}
```

With that done I can also remove the temp:

```
public double getAdjustedCapital() {
    if (_capital <= 0.0) return 0.0;
    if (_intRate <= 0.0 || _duration <= 0.0) return 0.0;
    return (_income / _duration) * ADJ_FACTOR;
}
```

Replace Conditional with Polymorphism

You have a conditional that chooses different behavior depending on the type of an object.

Move each leg of the conditional to an overriding method in a subclass. Make the original method abstract.

```
double getSpeed() {
    switch (_type) {
        case EUROPEAN:
            return getBaseSpeed();
        case AFRICAN:
            return getBaseSpeed() - getLoadFactor() * _numberOfCoconuts;
        case NORWEGIAN_BLUE:
            return (_isNailed) ? 0 : getBaseSpeed(_voltage);
    }
    throw new RuntimeException ("Should be unreachable");
}
```

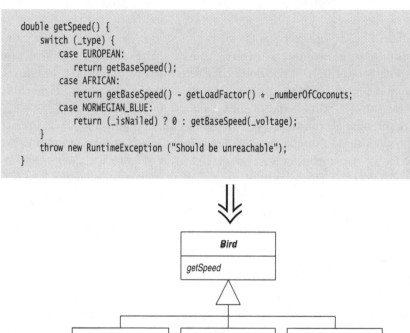

Motivation

One of the grandest sounding words in object jargon is *polymorphism*. The essence of polymorphism is that it allows you to avoid writing an explicit conditional when you have objects whose behavior varies depending on their types.

As a result you find that switch statements that switch on type codes or if-then-else statements that switch on type strings are much less common in an object-oriented program.

Polymorphism gives you many advantages. The biggest gain occurs when this same set of conditions appears in many places in the program. If you want to add a new type, you have to find and update all the conditionals. But with subclasses you just create a new subclass and provide the appropriate methods. Clients of the class don't need to know about the subclasses, which reduces the dependencies in your system and makes it easier to update.

Mechanics

Replace Conditional with Polymorphism

Before you can begin with *Replace Conditional with Polymorphism* you need to have the necessary inheritance structure. You may already have this structure from previous refactorings. If you don't have the structure, you need to create it.

To create the inheritance structure you have two options: *Replace Type Code with Subclasses (223)* and *Replace Type Code with State/Strategy (227)*. Subclasses are the simplest option, so you should use them if you can. If you update the type code after the object is created, however, you cannot use subclassing and have to use the state/strategy pattern. You also need to use the state/strategy pattern if you are already subclassing this class for another reason. Remember that if several case statements are switching on the same type code, you only need to create one inheritance structure for that type code.

You can now attack the conditional. The code you target may be a switch (case) statement or an if statement.

- ❏ If the conditional statement is one part of a larger method, take apart the conditional statement and use *Extract Method (110)*.

- ❏ If necessary use *Move Method (142)* to place the conditional at the top of the inheritance structure.

- ❏ Pick one of the subclasses. Create a subclass method that overrides the conditional statement method. Copy the body of that leg of the conditional statement into the subclass method and adjust it to fit.

  ⇒ *You may need to make some private members of the superclass protected in order to do this.*

- ❏ Compile and test.

- ❏ Remove the copied leg of the conditional statement.

- ❏ Compile and test.

❑ Repeat with each leg of the conditional statement until all legs are turned into subclass methods.

❑ Make the superclass method abstract.

Example

I use the tedious and simplistic example of employee payment. I'm using the classes after using *Replace Type Code with State/Strategy (227)* so the objects look like Figure 9.1 (see the example in Chapter 8 for how we got here).

```
class Employee...
  int payAmount() {
    switch (getType()) {
      case EmployeeType.ENGINEER:
        return _monthlySalary;
      case EmployeeType.SALESMAN:
        return _monthlySalary + _commission;
      case EmployeeType.MANAGER:
        return _monthlySalary + _bonus;
      default:
        throw new RuntimeException("Incorrect Employee");
    }
  }
}
```

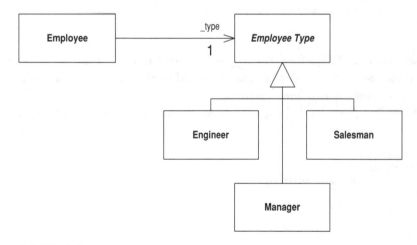

Figure 9.1 *The inheritance structure*

```
    int getType() {
        return _type.getTypeCode();
    }
    private EmployeeType _type;

abstract class EmployeeType...
  abstract int getTypeCode();

class Engineer extends EmployeeType...
  int getTypeCode() {
      return EmployeeType.ENGINEER;
  }
```

... and other subclasses

Replace Conditional with Polymorphism

The case statement is already nicely extracted, so there is nothing to do there. I do need to move it into the employee type, because that is the class that is being subclassed.

```
class EmployeeType...
  int payAmount(Employee emp) {
      switch (getTypeCode()) {
          case ENGINEER:
              return emp.getMonthlySalary();
          case SALESMAN:
              return emp.getMonthlySalary() + emp.getCommission();
          case MANAGER:
              return emp.getMonthlySalary() + emp.getBonus();
          default:
              throw new RuntimeException("Incorrect Employee");
      }
  }
```

Because I need data from the employee, I need to pass in the employee as an argument. Some of this data might be moved to the employee type object, but that is an issue for another refactoring.

When this compiles, I change the payAmount method in Employee to delegate to the new class:

```
class Employee...
  int payAmount() {
      return _type.payAmount(this);
  }
```

Now I can go to work on the case statement. It's rather like the way small boys kill insects—I remove one leg at a time. First I copy the Engineer leg of the case statement onto the Engineer class.

```
class Engineer...
    int payAmount(Employee emp) {
        return emp.getMonthlySalary();
    }
```

This new method overrides the whole case statement for engineers. Because I'm paranoid, I sometimes put a trap in the case statement:

```
class EmployeeType...
    int payAmount(Employee emp) {
        switch (getTypeCode()) {
            case ENGINEER:
                throw new RuntimeException ("Should be being overridden");
            case SALESMAN:
                return emp.getMonthlySalary() + emp.getCommission();
            case MANAGER:
                return emp.getMonthlySalary() + emp.getBonus();
            default:
                throw new RuntimeException("Incorrect Employee");
        }
    }
```

carry on until all the legs are removed:

```
class Salesman...
    int payAmount(Employee emp) {
        return emp.getMonthlySalary() + emp.getCommission();
    }

class Manager...
    int payAmount(Employee emp) {
        return emp.getMonthlySalary() + emp.getBonus();
    }
```

and then declare the superclass method abstract:

```
class EmployeeType...
    abstract int payAmount(Employee emp);
```

Introduce Null Object

You have repeated checks for a null value.

Replace the null value with a null object.

```
if (customer == null) plan = BillingPlan.basic();
else plan = customer.getPlan();
```

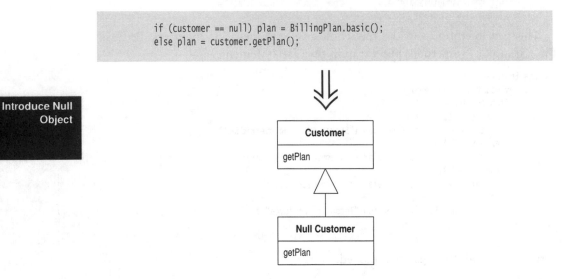

Motivation

The essence of polymorphism is that instead of asking an object what type it is and then invoking some behavior based on the answer, you just invoke the behavior. The object, depending on its type, does the right thing. One of the less intuitive places to do this is where you have a null value in a field. I'll let Ron Jeffries tell the story:

—*Ron Jeffries*

We first started using the null object pattern when Rich Garzaniti found that lots of code in the system would check objects for presence before sending a message to the object. We might ask an object for its person, then ask the result whether it was null. If the object was present, we would ask it for its rate. We were doing this in several places, and the resulting duplicate code was getting annoying.

So we implemented a missing-person object that answered a zero rate (we call our null objects missing objects). Soon missing person knew a lot of methods, such as rate. Now we have more than 80 null-object classes.

Our most common use of null objects is in the display of information. When we display, for example, a person, the object may or may not have any of perhaps 20 instance variables. If these were allowed to be null, the printing of a person would be very complex. Instead we plug in various null objects, all of which know how to display themselves in an orderly way. This got rid of huge amounts of procedural code.

Our most clever use of null object is the missing Gemstone session. We use the Gemstone database for production, but we prefer to develop without it and push the new code to Gemstone every week or so. There are various points in the code where we have to log in to a Gemstone session. When we are running without Gemstone, we simply plug in a missing Gemstone session. It looks the same as the real thing but allows us to develop and test without realizing the database isn't there.

Another helpful use of null object is the missing bin. A bin is a collection of payroll values that often have to be summed or looped over. If a particular bin doesn't exist, we answer a missing bin, which acts just like an empty bin. The missing bin knows it has zero balance and no values. By using this approach, we eliminate the creation of tens of empty bins for each of our thousands of employees.

An interesting characteristic of using null objects is that things almost never blow up. Because the null object responds to all the same messages as a real one, the system generally behaves normally. This can sometimes make it difficult to detect or find a problem, because nothing ever breaks. Of course, as soon as you begin inspecting the objects, you'll find the null object somewhere where it shouldn't be.

Remember, null objects are always constant: nothing about them ever changes. Accordingly, we implement them using the Singleton pattern [Gang of Four]. Whenever you ask, for example, for a missing person, you always get the single instance of that class.

▲————————————————————————————————————▲

You can find more details about the null object pattern in Woolf [Woolf].

Mechanics

❑ Create a subclass of the source class to act as a null version of the class. Create an isNull operation on the source class and the null class. For the source class it should return false, for the null class it should return true.

   ⇒ *You may find it useful to create an explicitly nullable interface for the* isNull *method.*

   ⇒ *As an alternative you can use a testing interface to test for nullness.*

❑ Compile.

❑ Find all places that can give out a null when asked for a source object. Replace them to give out a null object instead.

❏ Find all places that compare a variable of the source type with null and replace them with a call isNull.

⇒ *You may be able to do this by replacing one source and its clients at a time and compiling and testing between working on sources.*
⇒ *A few assertions that check for null in places where you should no longer see it can be useful.*

❏ Compile and test.

❏ Look for cases in which clients invoke an operation if not null and do some alternative behavior if null.

❏ For each of these cases override the operation in the null class with the alternative behavior.

❏ Remove the condition check for those that use the overriden behavior, compile, and test.

Introduce Null Object

Example

A utility company knows about sites: the houses and apartments that use the utility's services. At any time a site has a customer.

```
class Site...
   Customer getCustomer() {
       return _customer;
   }
   Customer _customer;
```

There are various features of a customer. I look at three of them.

```
class Customer...
   public String getName() {...}
   public BillingPlan getPlan() {...}
   public PaymentHistory getHistory() {...}
```

The payment history has its own features:

```
public class PaymentHistory...
   int getWeeksDelinquentInLastYear()
```

The getters I show allow clients to get at this data. However, sometimes I don't have a customer for a site. Someone may have moved out and I don't yet know who has moved in. Because this can happen we have to ensure that any code that uses the customer can handle nulls. Here are a few example fragments:

```
        Customer customer = site.getCustomer();
        BillingPlan plan;
```

```
        if (customer == null) plan = BillingPlan.basic();
        else plan = customer.getPlan();
...

        String customerName;
        if (customer == null) customerName = "occupant";
        else customerName = customer.getName();
...

        int weeksDelinquent;
        if (customer == null) weeksDelinquent = 0;
        else weeksDelinquent = customer.getHistory().getWeeksDelinquentInLastYear();
```

In these situations I may have many clients of site and customer, all of which have to check for nulls and all of which do the same thing when they find one. Sounds like it's time for a null object.

The first step is to create the null customer class and modify the customer class to support a query for a null test:

```
class NullCustomer extends Customer {
  public boolean isNull() {
      return true;
  }
}

class Customer...
  public boolean isNull() {
      return false;
  }

  protected Customer() {} //needed by the NullCustomer
```

If you aren't able to modify the Customer class you can use a testing interface (see page 266).

If you like, you can signal the use of null object by means of an interface:

```
interface Nullable {
  boolean isNull();
}

class Customer implements Nullable
```

I like to add a factory method to create null customers. That way clients don't have to know about the null class:

```
class Customer...
  static Customer newNull() {
      return new NullCustomer();
  }
```

Now comes the difficult bit. Now I have to return this new null object whenever I expect a null and replace the tests of the form foo == null with tests

Introduce Null
Object

of the form foo.isNull(). I find it useful to look for all the places where I ask for a customer and modify them so that they return a null customer rather than null.

```
class Site...
  Customer getCustomer() {
      return (_customer == null) ?
          Customer.newNull():
          _customer;
  }
```

I also have to alter all uses of this value so that they test with isNull() rather than == null.

Introduce Null Object

```
Customer customer = site.getCustomer();
BillingPlan plan;
if (customer.isNull()) plan = BillingPlan.basic();
else plan = customer.getPlan();

...

String customerName;
if (customer.isNull()) customerName = "occupant";
else customerName = customer.getName();

...

int weeksDelinquent;
if (customer.isNull()) weeksDelinquent = 0;
else weeksDelinquent = customer.getHistory().getWeeksDelinquentInLastYear();
```

There's no doubt that this is the trickiest part of this refactoring. For each source of a null I replace, I have to find all the times it is tested for nullness and replace them. If the object is widely passed around, these can be hard to track. I have to find every variable of type customer and find everywhere it is used. It is hard to break this process into small steps. Sometimes I find one source that is used in only a few places, and I can replace that source only. But most of the time, however, I have to make many widespread changes. The changes aren't too difficult to back out of, because I can find calls of isNull without too much difficulty, but this is still a messy step.

Once this step is done, and I've compiled and tested, I can smile. Now the fun begins. As it stands I gain nothing from using isNull rather than == null. The gain comes as I move behavior to the null customer and remove conditionals. I can make these moves one at a time. I begin with the name. Currently I have client code that says

```
String customerName;
if (customer.isNull()) customerName = "occupant";
else customerName = customer.getName();
```

I add a suitable name method to the null customer:

```
class NullCustomer...
  public String getName(){
      return "occupant";
  }
```

Now I can make the conditional code go away:

```
      String customerName = customer.getName();
```

I can do the same for any other method in which there is a sensible general response to a query. I can also do appropriate actions for modifiers. So client code such as

```
      if (! customer.isNull())
          customer.setPlan(BillingPlan.special());
```

can be replaced with

```
customer.setPlan(BillingPlan.special());
```

```
class NullCustomer...
  public void setPlan (BillingPlan arg) {}
```

Remember that this movement of behavior makes sense only when most clients want the same response. Notice that I said *most* not *all*. Any clients who want a different response to the standard one can still test using isNull. You benefit when many clients want to do the same thing; they can simply rely on the default null behavior.

The example contains a slightly different case—client code that uses the result of a call to customer:

```
      if (customer.isNull()) weeksDelinquent = 0;
      else weeksDelinquent = customer.getHistory().getWeeksDelinquentInLastYear();
```

I can handle this by creating a null payment history:

```
class NullPaymentHistory extends PaymentHistory...
  int getWeeksDelinquentInLastYear() {
      return 0;
  }
```

I modify the null customer to return it when asked:

```
class NullCustomer...
  public PaymentHistory getHistory() {
      return PaymentHistory.newNull();
  }
```

Again I can remove the conditional code:

```
int weeksDelinquent = customer.getHistory().getWeeksDelinquentInLastYear();
```

You often find that null objects return other null objects.

Example: Testing Interface

The testing interface is an alternative to defining an isNull method. In this approach I create a null interface with no methods defined:

```
interface Null {}
```

I then implement null in my null objects:

```
class NullCustomer extends Customer implements Null...
```

I then test for nullness with the instanceof operator:

```
aCustomer instanceof Null
```

I normally run away screaming from the instanceof operator, but in this case it is okay to use it. It has the particular advantage that I don't need to change the customer class. This allows me to use the null object even when I don't have access to customer's source code.

Other Special Cases

When carrying out this refactoring, you can have several kinds of null. Often there is a difference between there is no customer (new building and not yet moved in) and there is an unknown customer (we think there is someone there, but we don't know who it is). If that is the case, you can build separate classes for the different null cases. Sometimes null objects actually can carry data, such as usage records for the unknown customer, so that we can bill the customers when we find out who they are.

In essence there is a bigger pattern here, called *special case*. A special case class is a particular instance of a class with special behavior. So UnknownCustomer and NoCustomer would both be special cases of Customer. You often see special cases with numbers. Floating points in Java have special cases for positive and negative infinity and for not a number (NaN). The value of special cases is that they help reduce dealing with errors. Floating point operations don't throw exceptions. Doing any operation with NaN yields another NaN in the same way that accessors on null objects usually result in other null objects.

Introduce Assertion

A section of code assumes something about the state of the program.

Make the assumption explicit with an assertion.

```
double getExpenseLimit() {
    // should have either expense limit or a primary project
    return (_expenseLimit != NULL_EXPENSE) ?
        _expenseLimit:
        _primaryProject.getMemberExpenseLimit();
}
```

⇓

```
double getExpenseLimit() {
    Assert.isTrue (_expenseLimit != NULL_EXPENSE || _primaryProject != null);
    return (_expenseLimit != NULL_EXPENSE) ?
        _expenseLimit:
        _primaryProject.getMemberExpenseLimit();
}
```

Motivation

Often sections of code work only if certain conditions are true. This may be as simple as a square root calculation's working only on a positive input value. With an object it may be assumed that at least one of a group of fields has a value in it.

Such assumptions often are not stated but can only be decoded by looking through an algorithm. Sometimes the assumptions are stated with a comment. A better technique is to make the assumption explicit by writing an assertion.

An assertion is a conditional statement that is assumed to be always true. Failure of an assertion indicates programmer error. As such, assertion failures should always result in unchecked exceptions. Assertions should never be used by other parts of the system. Indeed assertions usually are removed for production code. It is therefore important to signal something is an assertion.

Assertions act as communication and debugging aids. In communication they help the reader understand the assumptions the code is making. In debugging, assertions can help catch bugs closer to their origin. I've noticed the debugging help is less important when I write self-testing code, but I still appreciate the value of assertions in communciation.

Mechanics

Because assertions should not affect the running of a system, adding one is always behavior preserving.

Introduce
Assertion

❑ When you see that a condition is assumed to be true, add an assertion to state it.

⇒ *Have an assert class that you can use for assertion behavior.*

Beware of overusing assertions. Don't use assertions to check everything that you think is true for a section of code. Use assertions only to check things that *need* to be true. Overusing assertions can lead to duplicate logic that is awkward to maintain. Logic that covers an assumption is good because it forces you to rethink the section of the code. If the code works without the assertion, the assertion is confusing rather than helpful and may hinder modification in the future.

Always ask whether the code still works if an assertion fails. If the code does work, remove the assertion.

Beware of duplicate code in assertions. Duplicate code smells just as bad in assertion checks as it does anywhere else. Use *Extract Method (110)* liberally to get rid of the duplication.

Example

Here's a simple tale of expense limits. Employees can be given an individual expense limit. If they are assigned a primary project, they can use the expense limit of that primary project. They don't have to have an expense limit or a primary project, but they must have one or the other. This assumption is taken for granted in the code that uses expense limits:

```
class Employee...
  private static final double NULL_EXPENSE = -1.0;
  private double _expenseLimit = NULL_EXPENSE;
  private Project _primaryProject;
```

```
double getExpenseLimit() {
    return (_expenseLimit != NULL_EXPENSE) ?
        _expenseLimit:
        _primaryProject.getMemberExpenseLimit();
}

boolean withinLimit (double expenseAmount) {
    return (expenseAmount <= getExpenseLimit());
}
```

This code contains an implicit assumption that the employee has either a project or a personal expense limit. Such an assertion should be clearly stated in the code:

```
double getExpenseLimit() {
    Assert.isTrue (_expenseLimit != NULL_EXPENSE || _primaryProject != null);
    return (_expenseLimit != NULL_EXPENSE) ?
        _expenseLimit:
        _primaryProject.getMemberExpenseLimit();
}
```

This assertion does not change any aspect of the behavior of the program. Either way, if the condition is not true, I get a runtime exception: either a null pointer exception in withinLimit or a runtime exception inside Assert.isTrue. In some circumstances the assertion helps find the bug, because it is closer to where things went wrong. Mostly, however, the assertion helps to communicate how the code works and what it assumes.

I often find I use *Extract Method (110)* on the conditional inside the assertion. I either use it in several places and eliminate duplicate code or use it simply to clarify the intention of the condition.

One of the complications of assertions in Java is that there is no simple mechanism to putting them in. Assertions should be easily removable, so they don't affect performance in production code. Having a utility class, such as Assert, certainly helps. Sadly, any expression inside the assertion parameters executes whatever happens. The only way to stop that is to use code like:

```
double getExpenseLimit() {
    Assert.isTrue (Assert.ON &&
        (_expenseLimit != NULL_EXPENSE || _primaryProject != null));
    return (_expenseLimit != NULL_EXPENSE) ?
        _expenseLimit:
        _primaryProject.getMemberExpenseLimit();
}
```

or

```
double getExpenseLimit() {
    if (Assert.ON)
        Assert.isTrue (_expenseLimit != NULL_EXPENSE || _primaryProject != null);
    return (_expenseLimit != NULL_EXPENSE) ?
        _expenseLimit:
        _primaryProject.getMemberExpenseLimit();
}
```

If Assert.ON is a constant, the compiler should detect and eliminate the dead code if it is false. Adding the clause is messy, however, so many programmers prefer the simpler use of Assert and then use a filter to remove any line that uses assert at production time (using perl or the like).

The Assert class should have various methods that are named helpfully. In addition to isTrue, you can have equals, and shouldNeverReachHere.

Introduce Assertion

Chapter 10

Making Method Calls Simpler

Objects are all about interfaces. Coming up with interfaces that are easy to understand and use is a key skill in developing good object-oriented software. This chapter explores refactorings that make interfaces more straightforward.

Often the simplest and most important thing you can do is to change the name of a method. Naming is a key tool in communication. If you understand what a program is doing, you should not be afraid to use *Rename Method (273)* to pass on that knowledge. You can (and should) also rename variables and classes. On the whole these renamings are fairly simple text replacements, so I haven't added extra refactorings for them.

Parameters themselves have quite a role to play with interfaces. *Add Parameter (275)* and *Remove Parameter (277)* are common refactorings. Programmers new to objects often use long parameter lists, which are typical of other development environments. Objects allow you to keep parameter lists short, and several more involved refactorings give you ways to shorten them. If you are passing several values from an object, use *Preserve Whole Object (288)* to reduce all the values to a single object. If this object does not exist, you can create it with *Introduce Parameter Object (295)*. If you can get the data from an object to which the method already has access, you can eliminate parameters with *Replace Parameter with Method (292)*. If you have parameters that are used to determine conditional behavior, you can use *Replace Parameter with Explicit Methods (285)*. You can combine several similar methods by adding a parameter with *Parameterize Method (283)*.

Doug Lea gave me a warning about refactorings that reduce parameter lists. Concurrent programming often uses long parameter lists. Typically this occurs so that you can pass in parameters that are immutable, as built-ins and value

271

objects often are. Usually you can replace long parameter lists with immutable objects, but otherwise you need to be cautious about this group of refactorings.

One of the most valuable conventions I've used over the years is to clearly separate methods that change state (modifiers) from those that query state (queries). I don't know how many times I've got myself into trouble, or seen others get into trouble, by mixing these up. So whenever I see them combined, I use *Separate Query from Modifier (279)* to get rid of them.

Good interfaces show only what they have to and no more. You can improve an interface by hiding things. Of course all data should be hidden (I hope I don't need to tell you to do that), but also any methods that can be should be hidden. When refactoring you often need to make things visible for a while and then cover them up with *Hide Method (303)* and *Remove Setting Method (300)*.

Constructors are a particularly awkward feature of Java and C++, because they force you to know the class of an object you need to create. Often you don't need to know this. The need to know can be removed with *Replace Constructor with Factory Method (304)*.

Casting is another bane of the Java programmer's life. As much as possible try to avoid making the user of a class do downcasting if you can contain it elsewhere by using *Encapsulate Downcast (308)*.

Java, like many modern languages, has an exception-handling mechanism to make error handling easier. Programmers who are not used to this often use error codes to signal trouble. You can use *Replace Error Code with Exception (310)* to use the new exceptional features. But sometimes exceptions aren't the right answer; you should test first with *Replace Exception with Test (315)*.

Rename Method

The name of a method does not reveal its purpose.

Change the name of the method.

Motivation

An important part of the code style I am advocating is small methods to factor complex processes. Done badly, this can lead you on a merry dance to find out what all the little methods do. The key to avoiding this merry dance is naming the methods. Methods should be named in a way that communicates their intention. A good way to do this is to think what the comment for the method would be and turn that comment into the name of the method.

Rename
Method

Life being what it is, you won't get your names right the first time. In this situation you may well be tempted to leave it—after all it's only a name. That is the work of the evil demon *Obfuscatis*; don't listen to him. If you see a badly named method, it is imperative that you change it. Remember your code is for a human first and a computer second. Humans need good names. Take note of when you have spent ages trying to do something that would have been easier if a couple of methods had been better named. Good naming is a skill that requires practice; improving this skill is the key to being a truly skillful programmer. The same applies to other aspects of the signature. If reordering parameters clarifies matters, do it (see *Add Parameter (275)* and *Remove Parameter [277]*).

Mechanics

❏ Check to see whether the method signature is implemented by a superclass or subclass. If it is, perform these steps for each implementation.

❏ Declare a new method with the new name. Copy the old body of code over to the new name and make any alterations to fit.

❏ Compile.

❑ Change the body of the old method so that it calls the new one.

⇒ *If you only have a few references, you can reasonably skip this step.*

❑ Compile and test.

❑ Find all references to the old method name and change them to refer to the new one. Compile and test after each change.

❑ Remove the old method.

⇒ *If the old method is part of the interface and you cannot remove it, leave it in place and mark it as deprecated.*

❑ Compile and test.

Example

I have a method to get a person's telephone number:

```
public String getTelephoneNumber() {
    return ("(" + _officeAreaCode + ") " + _officeNumber);
}
```

I want to rename the method to getOfficeTelephoneNumber. I begin by creating the new method and copying the body over to the new method. The old method now changes to call the new one:

```
class Person...
  public String getTelephoneNumber(){
      return getOfficeTelephoneNumber();
  }
  public String getOfficeTelephoneNumber() {
      return ("(" + _officeAreaCode + ") " + _officeNumber);
  }
```

Now I find the callers of the old method, and switch them to call the new one. When I have switched them all, I can remove the old method.

The procedure is the same if I need to add or remove a parameter.

If there aren't many callers, I change the callers to call the new method without using the old method as a delegating method. If my tests throw a wobbly, I back out and make the changes the slow way.

Add Parameter

A method needs more information from its caller.

Add a parameter for an object that can pass on this information.

Motivation

Add Parameter is a very common refactoring, one that you almost certainly have already done. The motivation is simple. You have to change a method, and the change requires information that wasn't passed in before, so you add a parameter.

Actually most of what I have to say is motivation against doing this refactoring. Often you have other alternatives to adding a parameter. If available, these alternatives are better because they don't lead to increasing the length of parameter lists. Long parameter lists smell bad because they are hard to remember and often involve data clumps.

Look at the existing parameters. Can you ask one of those objects for the information you need? If not, would it make sense to give them a method to provide that information? What are you using the information for? Should that behavior be on another object, the one that has the information? Look at the existing parameters and think about them with the new parameter. Perhaps you should consider *Introduce Parameter Object (295)*.

I'm not saying that you should never add parameters; I do it frequently, but you need to be aware of the alternatives.

Add Parameter

Mechanics

The mechanics of *Add Parameter* are very similar to those of *Rename Method (273)*.

(273)

☐ Check to see whether this method signature is implemented by a superclass or subclass. If it is, carry out these steps for each implementation.

☐ Declare a new method with the added parameter. Copy the old body of code over to the new method.

⇒ *If you need to add more than one parameter, it is easier to add them at the same time.*

☐ Compile.

☐ Change the body of the old method so that it calls the new one.

⇒ *If you only have a few references, you can reasonably skip this step.*
⇒ *You can supply any value for the parameter, but usually you use null for object parameter and a clearly odd value for built-in types. It's often a good idea to use something other than zero for numbers so you can spot this case more easily.*

☐ Compile and test.

☐ Find all references to the old method and change them to refer to the new one. Compile and test after each change.

☐ Remove the old method.

⇒ *If the old method is part of the interface and you cannot remove it, leave it in place and mark it as deprecated.*

☐ Compile and test.

Add Parameter

Remove Parameter

A parameter is no longer used by the method body.

Remove it.

Motivation

Programmers often add parameters but are reluctant to remove them. After all, a spurious parameter doesn't cause any problems, and you might need it again later.

This is the demon *Obfuscatis* speaking; purge him from your soul! A parameter indicates information that is needed; different values make a difference. Your caller has to worry about what values to pass. By not removing the parameter you are making further work for everyone who uses the method. That's not a good trade-off, especially because removing parameters is an easy refactoring.

The case to be wary of here is a polymorphic method. In this case you may well find that other implementations of the method do use the parameter. In this case you shouldn't remove the parameter. You might choose to add a separate method that can be used in those cases, but you need to examine how your callers use the method to see whether it is worth doing that. If some callers already know they are dealing with a certain subclass and doing extra work to find the parameter or are using knowledge of the class hierarchy to know they can get away with a null, add an extra method without the parameter. If they do not need to know about which class has which method, the callers should be left in blissful ignorance.

Remove
Parameter

Mechanics

The mechanics of *Remove Parameter* are very similar to those of *Rename Method (273)* and *Add Parameter (275)*.

- ❏ Check to see whether this method signature is implemented by a superclass or subclass. Check to see whether the class or superclass uses the parameter. If it does, don't do this refactoring.

- ❏ Declare a new method without the parameter. Copy the old body of code to the new method.

    ⇒ *If you need to remove more than one parameter, it is easier to remove them together.*

- ❏ Compile.

- ❏ Change the body of the old method so that it calls the new one.

    ⇒ *If you only have a few references, you can reasonably skip this step.*

- ❏ Compile and test.

- ❏ Find all references to the old method and change them to refer to the new one. Compile and test after each change.

- ❏ Remove the old method.

    ⇒ *If the old method is part of the interface and you cannot remove it, leave it in place and mark it as deprecated.*

- ❏ Compile and test.

Because I'm pretty comfortable with adding and removing parameters, I often do a batch in one go.

Separate Query from Modifier

*You have a method that returns a value but also changes the
state of an object.*

*Create two methods, one for the query and one for
the modification.*

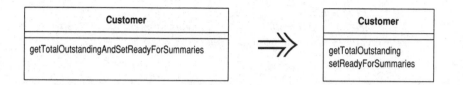

Motivation

When you have a function that gives you a value and has no observable side
effects, you have a very valuable thing. You can call this function as often as
you like. You can move the call to other places in the method. In short, you
have a lot less to worry about.

It is a good idea to clearly signal the difference between methods with side
effects and those without. A good rule to follow is to say that any method that
returns a value should not have observable side effects. Some programmers
treat this as an absolute rule [Meyer]. I'm not 100 percent pure on this (as on
anything), but I try to follow it most of the time, and it has served me well.

If you come across a method that returns a value but also has side effects,
you should try to separate the query from the modifier.

You'll note I use the phrase *observable* side effects. A common optimization
is to cache the value of a query in a field so that repeated calls go quicker.
Although this changes the state of the object with the cache, the change is not
observable. Any sequence of queries will always return the same results for each
query [Meyer].

Mechanics

❏ Create a query that returns the same value as the original method.

    ⇒ *Look in the original method to see what is returned. If the returned value is a temporary, look at the location of the temp assignment.*

❏ Modify the original method so that it returns the result of a call to the query.

    ⇒ *Every return in the original method should say* return newQuery() *instead of returning anything else.*
    ⇒ *If the method used a temp to with a single assignment to capture the return value, you should be able to remove it.*

❏ Compile and test.

❏ For each call, replace the single call to the original method with a call to the query. Add a call to the original method before the line that calls the query. Compile and test after each change to a calling method.

❏ Make the original method have a void return type and remove the return expressions.

Separate Query
from Modifier

Example

Here is a function that tells me the name of a miscreant for a security system and sends an alert. The rule is that only one alert is sent even if there is more than one miscreant:

```
String foundMiscreant(String[] people){
    for (int i = 0; i < people.length; i++) {
        if (people[i].equals ("Don")){
            sendAlert();
            return "Don";
        }
        if (people[i].equals ("John")){
            sendAlert();
            return "John";
        }
    }
    return "";
}
```

It is called by

```
void checkSecurity(String[] people) {
    String found = foundMiscreant(people);
    someLaterCode(found);
}
```

To separate the query from the modifier, I first need to create a suitable query that returns the same value as the modifier does but without doing the side effects.

```
String foundPerson(String[] people){
    for (int i = 0; i < people.length; i++) {
        if (people[i].equals ("Don")){
            return "Don";
        }
        if (people[i].equals ("John")){
            return "John";
        }
    }
    return "";
}
```

Then I replace every return in the original function, one at a time, with calls to the new query. I test after each replacement. When I'm done the original method looks like the following:

```
String foundMiscreant(String[] people){
    for (int i = 0; i < people.length; i++) {
        if (people[i].equals ("Don")){
            sendAlert();
            return foundPerson(people);

        }
        if (people[i].equals ("John")){
            sendAlert();
            return foundPerson(people);

        }
    }
    return foundPerson(people);
}
```

Separate Query
from Modifier

Now I alter all the calling methods to do two calls: first to the modifier and then to the query:

```
void checkSecurity(String[] people) {
    foundMiscreant(people);
    String found = foundPerson(people);
    someLaterCode(found);
}
```

Once I have done this for all calls, I can alter the modifier to give it a void return type:

```
void foundMiscreant (String[] people){
    for (int i = 0; i < people.length; i++) {
```

```
                if (people[i].equals ("Don")){
                    sendAlert();
                    return;
                }
                if (people[i].equals ("John")){
                    sendAlert();
                    return;
                }
            }
        }
    }
```

Now it seems better to change the name of the original:

```
void sendAlert (String[] people){
    for (int i = 0; i < people.length; i++) {
        if (people[i].equals ("Don")){
            sendAlert();
            return;
        }
        if (people[i].equals ("John")){
            sendAlert();
            return;
        }
    }
}
```

Separate Query from Modifier

Of course in this case I have a lot of code duplication because the modifier uses the body of the query to do its work. I can now use *Substitute Algorithm (139)* on the modifier to take advantage of this:

```
void sendAlert(String[] people){
    if (! foundPerson(people).equals(""))
        sendAlert();
}
```

Concurrency Issues

If you are working in a multithreaded system, you'll know that doing test and set operations as a single action is an important idiom. Does this conflict with *Separate Query from Modifier (279)*? I discussed this issue with Doug Lea and concluded that it doesn't, but you need to do some additional things. It is still valuable to have separate query and modifier operations. However, you need to retain a third method that does both. The query-and-modify operation will call the separate query and modify methods and be synchronized. If the query and modify operations are not synchronized, you also might restrict their visibility to package or private level. That way you have a safe, synchronized operation decomposed into two easier-to-understand methods. These lower-level methods then are available for other uses.

Parameterize Method

Several methods do similar things but with different values contained in the method body.

Create one method that uses a parameter for the different values.

Motivation

You may see a couple of methods that do similar things but vary depending on a few values. In this case you can simplify matters by replacing the separate methods with a single method that handles the variations by parameters. Such a change removes duplicate code and increases flexibility, because you can deal with other variations by adding parameters.

Mechanics

❏ Create a parameterized method that can be substituted for each repetitive method.

❏ Compile.

❏ Replace one old method with a call to the new method.

❏ Compile and test.

❏ Repeat for all the methods, testing after each one.

You may find that you cannot do this for the whole method, but you can for a fragment of a method. In this case first extract the fragment into a method, then parameterize that method.

Example

The simplest case is methods along the following lines:

```
class Employee {
  void tenPercentRaise () {
      salary *= 1.1;
  }

  void fivePercentRaise () {
      salary *= 1.05;
  }
```

which can be replaced with

```
void raise (double factor) {
  salary *= (1 + factor);
}
```

Of course that is so simple that anyone would spot it. A less obvious case is as follows:

```
protected Dollars baseCharge() {
    double result = Math.min(lastUsage(),100) * 0.03;
    if (lastUsage() > 100) {
        result += (Math.min (lastUsage(),200) - 100) * 0.05;
    };
    if (lastUsage() > 200) {
        result += (lastUsage() - 200) * 0.07;
    };
    return new Dollars (result);
}
```

this can be replaced with

```
protected Dollars baseCharge() {
    double result = usageInRange(0, 100) * 0.03;
    result += usageInRange (100,200) * 0.05;
    result += usageInRange (200, Integer.MAX_VALUE) * 0.07;
    return new Dollars (result);
}

protected int usageInRange(int start, int end) {
    if (lastUsage() > start) return Math.min(lastUsage(),end) - start;
    else return 0;
}
```

The trick is to spot code that is repetitive on the basis of a few values that can be passed in as parameters.

Parameterize Method

Replace Parameter with Explicit Methods

You have a method that runs different code depending on the values of an enumerated parameter.

Create a separate method for each value of the parameter.

```
void setValue (String name, int value) {
    if (name.equals("height")) {
        _height = value;
        return;
    }
    if (name.equals("width")) {
        _width = value;
        return;
    }
    Assert.shouldNeverReachHere();
}
```

⇓

```
void setHeight(int arg) {
    _height = arg;
}
void setWidth (int arg) {
    _width = arg;
}
```

Motivation

Replace Parameter with Explicit Methods is the reverse of *Parameterize Method (283)*. The usual case for the former is that you have discrete values of a parameter, test for those values in a conditional, and do different things. The caller has to decide what it wants to do by setting the parameter, so you might as well provide different methods and avoid the conditional. You not only avoid the conditional behavior but also gain compile time checking. Furthermore your interface also is clearer. With the parameter, any programmer using the method needs not only to look at the methods on the class but also to determine a valid parameter value. The latter is often poorly documented.

The clarity of the explicit interface can be worthwhile even when the compile time checking isn't an advantage. `Switch.beOn()` is a lot clearer than `Switch.setState(true)`, even when all you are doing is setting an internal boolean field.

You shouldn't use *Replace Parameter with Explicit Methods* when the parameter values are likely to change a lot. If this happens and you are just setting a field to the passed in parameter, use a simple setter. If you need conditional behavior, you need *Replace Conditional with Polymorphism (255)*.

Mechanics

❑ Create an explicit method for each value of the parameter.

❑ For each leg of the conditional, call the appropriate new method.

❑ Compile and test after changing each leg.

❑ Replace each caller of the conditional method with a call to the appropriate new method.

❑ Compile and test.

❑ When all callers are changed, remove the conditional method.

Example

I want to create a subclass of employee on the basis of a passed in parameter, often the result of *Replace Constructor with Factory Method (304)*:

```java
static final int ENGINEER = 0;
static final int SALESMAN = 1;
static final int MANAGER = 2;

static Employee create(int type) {
    switch (type) {
        case ENGINEER:
            return new Engineer();
        case SALESMAN:
            return new Salesman();
        case MANAGER:
            return new Manager();
        default:
            throw new IllegalArgumentException("Incorrect type code value");
    }
}
```

Because this is a factory method, I can't use *Replace Conditional with Polymorphism (255),* because I haven't created the object yet. I don't expect too many new subclasses, so an explicit interface makes sense. First I create the new methods:

```
static Employee createEngineer() {
    return new Engineer();
}
static Employee createSalesman() {
    return new Salesman();
}
static Employee createManager() {
    return new Manager();
}
```

One by one I replace the cases in the switch statements with calls to the explicit methods:

```
static Employee create(int type) {
    switch (type) {
        case ENGINEER:
            return Employee.createEngineer();
        case SALESMAN:
            return new Salesman();
        case MANAGER:
            return new Manager();
        default:
            throw new IllegalArgumentException("Incorrect type code value");
    }
}
```

I compile and test after changing each leg, until I've replaced them all:

```
static Employee create(int type) {
    switch (type) {
        case ENGINEER:
            return Employee.createEngineer();
        case SALESMAN:
            return Employee.createSalesman();
        case MANAGER:
            return Employee.createManager();
        default:
            throw new IllegalArgumentException("Incorrect type code value");
    }
}
```

Now I move on to the callers of the old create method. I change code such as

```
Employee kent = Employee.create(ENGINEER)
```

to

```
Employee kent = Employee.createEngineer()
```

Once I've done that for all the callers of create, I can remove the create method. I may also be able to get rid of the constants.

Preserve Whole Object

You are getting several values from an object and passing these values as parameters in a method call.

Send the whole object instead.

```
int low = daysTempRange().getLow();
int high = daysTempRange().getHigh();
withinPlan = plan.withinRange(low, high);
```

⇓

Preserve Whole Object

```
withinPlan = plan.withinRange(daysTempRange());
```

Motivation

This type of situation arises when an object passes several data values from a single object as parameters in a method call. The problem with this is that if the called object needs new data values later, you have to find and change all the calls to this method. You can avoid this by passing in the whole object from which the data came. The called object then can ask for whatever it wants from the whole object.

In addition to making the parameter list more robust to changes, *Preserve Whole Object* often makes the code more readable. Long parameter lists can be hard to work with because both caller and callee have to remember which values were there. They also encourage duplicate code because the called object can't take advantage of any other methods on the whole object to calculate intermediate values.

There is a down side. When you pass in values, the called object has a dependency on the values, but there isn't any dependency to the object from which the values were extracted. Passing in the required object causes a dependency between the required object and the called object. If this is going to mess up your dependency structure, don't use *Preserve Whole Object*.

Another reason I have heard for not using *Preserve Whole Object* is that when a calling object need only one value from the required object, it is better to pass in the value than to pass in the whole object. I don't subscribe to that view. One value and one object amount to the same thing when you pass them in, at least for clarity's sake (there may be a performance cost with pass by value parameters). The driving force is the dependency issue.

That a called method uses lots of values from another object is a signal that the called method should really be defined on the object from which the values come. When you are considering *Preserve Whole Object*, consider *Move Method (142)* as an alternative.

You may not already have the whole object defined. In this case you need *Introduce Parameter Object (295)*.

A common case is that a calling object passes several of its *own* data values as parameters. In this case you can make the call and pass in this instead of these values, if you have the appropriate getting methods and you don't mind the dependency.

Preserve Whole Object

Mechanics

- ❏ Create a new parameter for the whole object from which the data comes.

- ❏ Compile and test.

- ❏ Determine which parameters should be obtained from the whole object.

- ❏ Take one parameter and replace references to it within the method body by invoking an appropriate method on the whole object parameter.

- ❏ Delete the parameter.

- ❏ Compile and test.

- ❏ Repeat for each parameter that can be got from the whole object.

- ❏ Remove the code in the calling method that obtains the deleted parameters.

    ⇒ *Unless, of course, the code is using these parameters somewhere else.*

- ❏ Compile and test.

Example

Consider a room object that records high and low temperatures during the day. It needs to compare this range with a range in a predefined heating plan:

```
class Room...
    boolean withinPlan(HeatingPlan plan) {
        int low = daysTempRange().getLow();
        int high = daysTempRange().getHigh();
        return plan.withinRange(low, high);
    }
class HeatingPlan...
    boolean withinRange (int low, int high) {
        return (low >= _range.getLow() && high <= _range.getHigh());
    }
    private TempRange _range;
```

Preserve Whole Object

Rather than unpack the range information when I pass it, I can pass the whole range object. In this simple case I can do this in one step. When more parameters are involved, I can do it in smaller steps. First I add the whole object to the parameter list:

```
class HeatingPlan...
    boolean withinRange (TempRange roomRange, int low, int high) {
        return (low >= _range.getLow() && high <= _range.getHigh());
    }

class Room...
    boolean withinPlan(HeatingPlan plan) {
        int low = daysTempRange().getLow();
        int high = daysTempRange().getHigh();
        return plan.withinRange(daysTempRange(), low, high);
    }
```

Then I use a method on the whole object instead of one of the parameters:

```
class HeatingPlan...
    boolean withinRange (TempRange roomRange, int high) {
        return (roomRange.getLow() >= _range.getLow() && high <= _range.getHigh());
    }

class Room...
    boolean withinPlan(HeatingPlan plan) {
        int low = daysTempRange().getLow();
        int high = daysTempRange().getHigh();
        return plan.withinRange(daysTempRange(), high);
    }
```

I continue until I've changed all I need:

```
class HeatingPlan...
  boolean withinRange (TempRange roomRange) {
      return (roomRange.getLow() >= _range.getLow() && roomRange.getHigh() <= _range.getHigh());
  }
class Room...
  boolean withinPlan(HeatingPlan plan) {
      int low = daysTempRange().getLow();
      int high = daysTempRange().getHigh();
      return plan.withinRange(daysTempRange());
  }
```

Now I don't need the temps anymore:

```
class Room...
  boolean withinPlan(HeatingPlan plan) {
      int low = daysTempRange().getLow();
      int high = daysTempRange().getHigh();
      return plan.withinRange(daysTempRange());
  }
```

Preserve Whole Object

Using whole objects this way soon leads you to realize that you can usefully move behavior into the whole object to make it easier to work with.

```
class HeatingPlan...
  boolean withinRange (TempRange roomRange) {
      return (_range.includes(roomRange));
  }
class TempRange...
  boolean includes (TempRange arg) {
      return arg.getLow() >= this.getLow() && arg.getHigh() <= this.getHigh();
  }
```

Replace Parameter with Method

An object invokes a method, then passes the result as a parameter for a method. The receiver can also invoke this method.

Remove the parameter and let the receiver invoke the method.

```
int basePrice = _quantity * _itemPrice;
discountLevel = getDiscountLevel();
double finalPrice = discountedPrice (basePrice, discountLevel);
```

⇓

```
int basePrice = _quantity * _itemPrice;
double finalPrice = discountedPrice (basePrice);
```

**Replace
Parameter with
Method**

Motivation

If a method can get a value that is passed in as parameter by another means, it should. Long parameter lists are difficult to understand, and we should reduce them as much as possible.

One way of reducing parameter lists is to look to see whether the receiving method can make the same calculation. If an object is calling a method on itself, and the calculation for the parameter does not reference any of the parameters of the calling method, you should be able to remove the parameter by turning the calculation into its own method. This is also true if you are calling a method on a different object that has a reference to the calling object.

You can't remove the parameter if the calculation relies on a parameter of the calling method, because that parameter may change with each call (unless, of course, that parameter can be replaced with a method). You also can't remove the parameter if the receiver does not have a reference to the sender, and you don't want to give it one.

In some cases the parameter may be there for a future parameterization of the method. In this case I would still get rid of it. Deal with the parameterization when you need it; you may find out that you don't have the right parameter anyway. I would make an exception to this rule only when the resulting change in the interface would have painful consequences around the whole program, such as a long build or changing of a lot of embedded code. If this worries you, look into how painful such a change would really be. You should also look to see whether you can reduce the dependencies that cause the change to be so painful. Stable interfaces are good, but freezing a poor interface is a problem.

Mechanics

❏ If necessary, extract the calculation of the parameter into a method.

❏ Replace references to the parameter in method bodies with references to the method.

❏ Compile and test after each replacement.

❏ Use *Remove Parameter (277)* on the parameter.

Example

Another unlikely variation on discounting orders is as follows:

```
public double getPrice() {
    int basePrice = _quantity * _itemPrice;
    int discountLevel;
    if (_quantity > 100) discountLevel = 2;
    else discountLevel = 1;
    double finalPrice = discountedPrice (basePrice, discountLevel);
    return finalPrice;
}

private double discountedPrice (int basePrice, int discountLevel) {
    if (discountLevel == 2) return basePrice * 0.1;
    else return basePrice * 0.05;
}
```

I can begin by extracting the calculation of the discount level:

```
public double getPrice() {
    int basePrice = _quantity * _itemPrice;
    int discountLevel = getDiscountLevel();
    double finalPrice = discountedPrice (basePrice, discountLevel);
    return finalPrice;
}

private int getDiscountLevel() {
    if (_quantity > 100) return 2;
    else return 1;
}
```

I then replace references to the parameter in discountedPrice:

```
private double discountedPrice (int basePrice, int discountLevel) {
    if (getDiscountLevel() == 2) return basePrice * 0.1;
    else return basePrice * 0.05;
}
```

Then I can use *Remove Parameter (277)*:

```
public double getPrice() {
    int basePrice = _quantity * _itemPrice;
    int discountLevel = getDiscountLevel();
    double finalPrice = discountedPrice (basePrice);
    return finalPrice;
}

private double discountedPrice (int basePrice) {
    if (getDiscountLevel() == 2) return basePrice * 0.1;
    else return basePrice * 0.05;
}
```

I can now get rid of the temp:

```
public double getPrice() {
    int basePrice = _quantity * _itemPrice;
    double finalPrice = discountedPrice (basePrice);
    return finalPrice;
}
```

Then it's time to get rid of the other parameter and its temp. I am left with

```
public double getPrice() {
    return discountedPrice ();
}

private double discountedPrice () {
    if (getDiscountLevel() == 2) return getBasePrice() * 0.1;
    else return getBasePrice() * 0.05;
}

private double getBasePrice() {
    return _quantity * _itemPrice;
}
```

so I might as well use *Inline Method (117)* on discountedPrice:

```
private double getPrice () {
    if (getDiscountLevel() == 2) return getBasePrice() * 0.1;
    else return getBasePrice() * 0.05;
}
```

Replace
Parameter with
Method

Introduce Parameter Object

You have a group of parameters that naturally go together.

Replace them with an object.

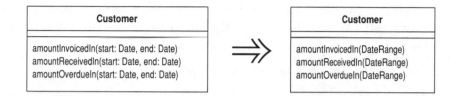

Motivation

Often you see a particular group of parameters that tend to be passed together. Several methods may use this group, either on one class or in several classes. Such a group of classes is a data clump and can be replaced with an object that carries all of this data. It is worthwhile to turn these parameters into objects just to group the data together. This refactoring is useful because it reduces the size of the parameter lists, and long parameter lists are hard to understand. The defined accessors on the new object also make the code more consistent, which again makes it easier to understand and modify.

You get a deeper benefit, however, because once you have clumped together the parameters, you soon see behavior that you can also move into the new class. Often the bodies of the methods have common manipulations of the parameter values. By moving this behavior into the new object, you can remove a lot of duplicated code.

Mechanics

❏ Create a new class to represent the group of parameters you are replacing. Make the class immutable.

❏ Compile.

❑ Use *Add Parameter (275)* for the new data clump. Use a null for this parameter in all the callers.

> ⇒ *If you have many callers, you can retain the old signature and let it call the new method. Apply the refactoring on the old method first. You can then move the callers over one by one and remove the old method when you're done.*

❑ For each parameter in the data clump, remove the parameter from the signature. Modify the callers and method body to use the parameter object for that value.

❑ Compile and test after you remove each parameter.

❑ When you have removed the parameters, look for behavior that you can move into the parameter object with *Move Method (142)*.

> ⇒ *This may be a whole method or part of a method. If it is part of a method, use* Extract Method (110) *first and then move the new method over.*

Introduce
Parameter
Object

Example

I begin with an account and entries. The entries are simple data holders.

```
class Entry...
    Entry (double value, Date chargeDate) {
        _value = value;
        _chargeDate = chargeDate;
    }
    Date getDate(){
        return _chargeDate;
    }
    double getValue(){
        return _value;
    }
    private Date _chargeDate;
    private double _value;
```

My focus is on the account, which holds a collection of entries and has a method for determining the flow of the account between two dates:

```
class Account...
    double getFlowBetween (Date start, Date end) {
        double result = 0;
        Enumeration e = _entries.elements();
        while (e.hasMoreElements()) {
            Entry each = (Entry) e.nextElement();
            if (each.getDate().equals(start) ||
```

```
              each.getDate().equals(end) ||
              (each.getDate().after(start) && each.getDate().before(end)))
        {
              result += each.getValue();
        }
     }
     return result;
  }

  private Vector _entries = new Vector();
```

client code...
```
  double flow = anAccount.getFlowBetween(startDate, endDate);
```

I don't know how many times I come across pairs of values that show a range, such as start and end dates and upper and lower numbers. I can understand why this happens, after all I did it all the time myself. But since I saw the range pattern [Fowler, AP] I always try to use ranges instead. My first step is to declare a simple data holder for the range:

```
class DateRange {
  DateRange (Date start, Date end) {
     _start = start;
     _end = end;
  }
  Date getStart() {
     return _start;
  }
  Date getEnd() {
     return _end;
  }
  private final Date _start;
  private final Date _end;
}
```

I've made the date range class immutable; that is, all the values for the date range are final and set in the constructor, hence there are no methods for modifying the values. This is a wise move to avoid aliasing bugs. Because Java has pass-by-value parameters, making the class immutable mimics the way Java's parameters work, so this is the right assumption for this refactoring.

Next I add the date range into the parameter list for the getFlowBetween method:

```
class Account...
  double getFlowBetween (Date start, Date end, DateRange range) {
     double result = 0;
     Enumeration e = _entries.elements();
     while (e.hasMoreElements()) {
        Entry each = (Entry) e.nextElement();
        if (each.getDate().equals(start) ||
```

```
            each.getDate().equals(end) ||
            (each.getDate().after(start) && each.getDate().before(end)))
        {
            result += each.getValue();
        }
    }
    return result;
}
```

```
client code...
    double flow = anAccount.getFlowBetween(startDate, endDate, null);
```

At this point I only need to compile, because I haven't altered any behavior yet.

The next step is to remove one of the parameters and use the new object instead. To do this I delete the start parameter and modify the method and its callers to use the new object instead:

Introduce
Parameter
Object

```
class Account...
    double getFlowBetween (Date end, DateRange range) {
        double result = 0;
        Enumeration e = _entries.elements();
        while (e.hasMoreElements()) {
            Entry each = (Entry) e.nextElement();
            if (each.getDate().equals(range.getStart()) ||
                each.getDate().equals(end) ||
                (each.getDate().after(range.getStart()) && each.getDate().before(end)))
            {
                result += each.getValue();
            }
        }
        return result;
    }
```

```
client code...
    double flow = anAccount.getFlowBetween(endDate, new DateRange (startDate, null));
```

I then remove the end date:

```
class Account...
    double getFlowBetween (DateRange range) {
        double result = 0;
        Enumeration e = _entries.elements();
        while (e.hasMoreElements()) {
            Entry each = (Entry) e.nextElement();
            if (each.getDate().equals(range.getStart()) ||
                each.getDate().equals(range.getEnd()) ||
                (each.getDate().after(range.getStart()) && each.getDate().before(range.getEnd())))
```

```
            {
                result += each.getValue();
            }
        }
        return result;
    }
```

client code...
```
        double flow = anAccount.getFlowBetween(new DateRange (startDate, endDate));
```

I have introduced the parameter object; however, I can get more value from
this refactoring by moving behavior from other methods to the new object. In
this case I can take the code in the condition and use *Extract Method (110)* and
Move Method (142) to get

```
class Account...
    double getFlowBetween (DateRange range) {
        double result = 0;
        Enumeration e = _entries.elements();
        while (e.hasMoreElements()) {
            Entry each = (Entry) e.nextElement();
            if (range.includes(each.getDate())) {
                result += each.getValue();
            }
        }
        return result;
    }
```

```
class DateRange...
    boolean includes (Date arg) {
        return (arg.equals(_start) ||
                arg.equals(_end) ||
                (arg.after(_start) && arg.before(_end)));
    }
```

Introduce
Parameter
Object

I usually do simple extracts and moves such as this in one step. If I run into a
bug, I can back out and take the two smaller steps.

Remove Setting Method

A field should be set at creation time and never altered.

Remove any setting method for that field.

Motivation

Providing a setting method indicates that a field may be changed. If you don't want that field to change once the object is created, then don't provide a setting method (and make the field final). That way your intention is clear and you often remove the very possibility that the field will change.

This situation often occurs when programmers blindly use indirect variable access [Beck]. Such programmers then use setters even in a constructor. I guess there is an argument for consistency but not compared with the confusion that the setting method will cause later on.

Mechanics

❑ Compile and test.

❑ Check that the setting method is called only in the constructor, or in a method called by the constructor.

❑ Modify the constructor to access the variables directly.

> ⇒ *You cannot do this if you have a subclass setting the private fields of a superclass. In this case you should try to provide a protected superclass method (ideally a constructor) to set these values. Whatever you do, don't give the superclass method a name that will confuse it with a setting method.*

❑ Compile and test.

❑ Remove the setting method and make the field final.

❑ Compile.

Example

A simple example is as follows:

```
class Account {

  private String _id;

  Account (String id) {
      setId(id);
  }

  void setId (String arg) {
      _id = arg;
  }
```

which can be replaced with

```
class Account {

  private final String _id;

  Account (String id) {
      _id = id;
  }
```

The problems come in some variations. First is the case in which you are doing computation on the argument:

```
class Account {

  private String _id;

  Account (String id) {
      setId(id);
  }

  void setId (String arg) {
      _id = "ZZ" + arg;
  }
```

If the change is simple (as here) and there is only one constructor, I can make the change in the constructor. If the change is complex or I need to call it from separate methods, I need to provide a method. In that case I need to name the method to make its intention clear:

```
class Account {

  private final String _id;
```

```
Account (String id) {
    initializeId(id);
}

void initializeId (String arg) {
    _id = "ZZ" + arg;
}
```

An awkward case lies with subclasses that initialize private superclass variables:

```
class InterestAccount extends Account...

    private double _interestRate;

    InterestAccount (String id, double rate) {
        setId(id);
        _interestRate = rate;
    }
```

Remove Setting Method

The problem is that I cannot access id directly to set it. The best solution is to use a superclass constructor:

```
class InterestAccount...

    InterestAccount (String id, double rate) {
        super(id);
        _interestRate = rate;
    }
```

If that is not possible, a well-named method is the best thing to use:

```
class InterestAccount...

    InterestAccount (String id, double rate) {
        initializeId(id);
        _interestRate = rate;
    }
```

Another case to consider is setting the value of a collection:

```
class Person {
  Vector getCourses() {
      return _courses;
  }
  void setCourses(Vector arg) {
      _courses = arg;
  }
  private Vector _courses;
```

Here I want to replace the setter with add and remove operations. I talk about this in *Encapsulate Collection (208)*.

Hide Method

A method is not used by any other class.

Make the method private.

Motivation

Refactoring often causes you to change decisions about the visibility of methods. It is easy to spot cases in which you need to make a method more visible: another class needs it and you thus relax the visibility. It is somewhat more difficult to tell when a method is too visible. Ideally a tool should check all methods to see whether they can be hidden. If it doesn't, you should make this check at regular intervals.

A particularly common case is hiding getting and setting methods as you work up a richer interface that provides more behavior. This case is most common when you are starting with a class that is little more than an encapsulated data holder. As more behavior is built into the class, you may find that many of the getting and setting methods are no longer needed publicly, in which case they can be hidden. If you make a getting or setting method private and you are using direct variable access, you can remove the method.

Mechanics

- ❏ Check regularly for opportunities to make a method more private.

  - ⇒ *Use a lint-style tool, do manual checks every so often, and check when you remove a call to a method in another class.*
  - ⇒ *Particularly look for cases such as this with setting methods.*

- ❏ Make each method as private as you can.

- ❏ Compile after doing a group of hidings.

  - ⇒ *The compiler checks this naturally, so you don't need to compile with each change. If one goes wrong, it is easy to spot.*

Replace Constructor with Factory Method

You want to do more than simple construction when
you create an object.

Replace the constructor with a factory method.

```
Employee (int type) {
    _type = type;
}
```

⟱

```
static Employee create(int type) {
    return new Employee(type);
}
```

Motivation

The most obvious motivation for *Replace Constructor with Factory Method*
comes with replacing a type code with subclassing. You have an object that
often is created with a type code but now needs subclasses. The exact subclass
is based on the type code. However, constructors can only return an instance of
the object that is asked for. So you need to replace the constructor with a factory method [Gang of Four].

You can use factory methods for other situations in which constructors are
too limited. Factory methods are essential for *Change Value to Reference (179)*.
They also can be used to signal different creation behavior that goes beyond the
number and types of parameters.

Mechanics

❑ Create a factory method. Make its body a call to the current constructor.

❑ Replace all calls to the constructor with calls to the factory method.

❑ Compile and test after each replacement.

❑ Declare the constructor private.

❑ Compile.

Example

A quick but wearisome and belabored example is the employee payment system. I have the following employee:

```
class Employee {

    private int _type;
    static final int ENGINEER = 0;
    static final int SALESMAN = 1;
    static final int MANAGER = 2;

    Employee (int type) {
        _type = type;
    }
}
```

Replace
Constructor
with Factory
Method

I want to make subclasses of Employee to correspond to the type codes. So I need to create a factory method:

```
static Employee create(int type) {
    return new Employee(type);
}
```

I then change all callers of the constructor to use this new method and make the constructor private:

```
client code...
  Employee eng = Employee.create(Employee.ENGINEER);

class Employee...
  private Employee (int type) {
      _type = type;
  }
```

Example: Creating Subclasses with a String

So far I do not have a great gain; the advantage comes from the fact that I have separated the receiver of the creation call from the class of object created. If I later apply *Replace Type Code with Subclasses* (Chapter 8) to turn the codes into subclasses of employee, I can hide these subclasses from clients by using the factory method:

```
static Employee create(int type) {
    switch (type) {
        case ENGINEER:
            return new Engineer();
        case SALESMAN:
            return new Salesman();
        case MANAGER:
            return new Manager();
        default:
            throw new IllegalArgumentException("Incorrect type code value");
    }
}
```

The sad thing about this is that I have a switch. Should I add a new subclass, I have to remember to update this switch statement, and I tend toward forgetfulness.

A good way around this is to use Class.forName. The first thing to do is to change the type of the parameter, essentially a variation on *Rename Method (273)*. First I create a new method that takes a string as an argument:

```
static Employee create (String name) {
    try {
        return (Employee) Class.forName(name).newInstance();
    } catch (Exception e) {
        throw new IllegalArgumentException ("Unable to instantiate" + name);
    }
}
```

I then convert the integer create to use this new method:

```
class Employee {
  static Employee create(int type) {
    switch (type) {
        case ENGINEER:
            return create("Engineer");
        case SALESMAN:
            return create("Salesman");
        case MANAGER:
            return create("Manager");
        default:
            throw new IllegalArgumentException("Incorrect type code value");
    }
}
```

I can then work on the callers of create to change statements such as

```
Employee.create(ENGINEER)
```

Replace
Constructor
with Factory
Method

to

```
Employee.create("Engineer")
```

When I'm done I can remove the integer parameter version of the method.

This approach is nice in that it removes the need to update the create method as I add new subclasses of employee. The approach, however, lacks compile time checking: a spelling mistake leads to a runtime error. If this is important, I use an explicit method (see below), but then I have to add a new method every time I add a subclass. It's a trade-off between flexibility and type safety. Fortunately, if I make the wrong choice, I can use either *Parameterize Method (283)* or *Replace Parameter with Explicit Methods (285)* to reverse the decision.

Another reason to be wary of Class.forName is that it exposes subclass names to clients. This is not too bad because you can use other strings and carry out other behavior with the factory method. That's a good reason not to use *Inline Method (117)* to remove the factory.

Example: Creating Subclasses with Explicit Methods

I can use a different approach to hide subclasses with explicit methods. This is useful if you have just a few subclasses that don't change. So I may have an abstract Person class with subclasses for Male and Female. I begin by defining a factory method for each subclass on the superclass:

```
class Person...
  static Person createMale(){
      return new Male();
  }
  static Person createFemale() {
      return new Female();
  }
```

I can then replace calls of the form

```
Person kent = new Male();
```

with

```
Person kent = Person.createMale();
```

This leaves the superclass knowing about the subclasses. If you want to avoid this, you need a more complex scheme, such as a product trader [Bäumer and Riehle]. Most of the time, however, that complexity isn't needed, and this approach works nicely.

Encapsulate Downcast

A method returns an object that needs to be downcasted
by its callers.

Move the downcast to within the method.

```
Object lastReading() {
  return readings.lastElement();
}
```

⇓

```
Reading lastReading() {
  return (Reading) readings.lastElement();
}
```

**Encapsulate
Downcast**

Motivation

Downcasting is one of the most annoying things you have to do with strongly
typed OO languages. It is annoying because it feels unnecessary; you are telling
the compiler something it ought to be able to figure out itself. But because the
figuring out often is rather complicated, you often have to do it yourself. This is
particularly prevalent in Java, in which the lack of templates means that you
have to downcast whenever you take an object out of a collection.

Downcasting may be a necessary evil, but you should do it as little as possible. If you return a value from a method, and you know the type of what is
returned is more specialized than what the method signature says, you are putting unnecessary work on your clients. Rather than forcing them to do the
downcasting, you should always provide them with the most specific type you
can.

Often you find this situation with methods that return an iterator or collection. Look instead to see what people are using the iterator for and provide the
method for that.

Mechanics

❑ Look for cases in which you have to downcast the result from calling a method.

⇒ *These cases often appear with methods that return a collection or iterator.*

❑ Move the downcast into the method.

⇒ *With methods that return collections, use* Encapsulate Collection (208).

Example

I have a method called lastReading, which returns the last reading from a vector of readings:

```
Object lastReading() {
  return readings.lastElement();
}
```

I should replace this with

```
Reading lastReading() {
  return (Reading) readings.lastElement();
}
```

A good lead-in to doing this is where I have collection classes. Say this collection of readings is on a Site class and I see code like this:

```
Reading lastReading = (Reading) theSite.readings().lastElement()
```

I can avoid the downcast and hide which collection is being used with

```
Reading lastReading = theSite.lastReading();

class Site...
  Reading lastReading() {
      return (Reading) readings().lastElement();
  }
```

Altering a method to return a subclass alters the signature of the method but does not break existing code because the compiler knows it can substitute a subclass for the superclass. Of course you should ensure that the subclass does not do anything that breaks the contract of the superclass.

Replace Error Code with Exception

A method returns a special code to indicate an error.

Throw an exception instead.

```java
int withdraw(int amount) {
    if (amount > _balance)
        return -1;
    else {
        _balance -= amount;
        return 0;
    }
}
```

⟱

```java
void withdraw(int amount) throws BalanceException {
    if (amount > _balance) throw new BalanceException();
    _balance -= amount;
}
```

Motivation

In computers, as in life, things go wrong occasionally. When things go wrong, you need to do something about it. In the simplest case, you can stop the program with an error code. This is the software equivalent of committing suicide because you miss a flight. (If I did that I wouldn't be alive even if I were a cat.) Despite my glib attempt at humor, there is merit to the software suicide option. If the cost of a program crash is small and the user is tolerant, stopping the program is fine. However, more important programs need more important measures.

The problem is that the part of a program that spots an error isn't always the part that can figure out what to do about it. When such a routine finds an error, it needs to let its caller know, and the caller may pass the error up the chain. In many languages a special output is used to indicate error. Unix and C-based systems traditionally use a return code to signal success or failure of a routine.

Java has a better way: exceptions. Exceptions are better because they clearly separate normal processing from error processing. This makes programs easier to understand, and as I hope you now believe, understandability is next to godliness.

Mechanics

- ❑ Decide whether the exception should be checked or unchecked.

  ⇒ *If the caller is responsible for testing the condition before calling, make the exception unchecked.*

  ⇒ *If the exception is checked, either create a new exception or use an existing one.*

- ❑ Find all the callers and adjust them to use the exception.

  ⇒ *If the exception is unchecked, adjust the callers to make the appropriate check before calling the method. Compile and test after each such change.*

  ⇒ *If the exception is checked, adjust the callers to call the method in a try block.*

- ❑ Change the signature of the method to reflect the new usage.

If you have many callers, this can be too big a change. You can make it more gradual with the following steps:

- ❑ Decide whether the exception should be checked or unchecked.

- ❑ Create a new method that uses the exception.

- ❑ Modify the body of the old method to call the new method.

- ❑ Compile and test.

- ❑ Adjust each caller of the old method to call the new method. Compile and test after each change.

- ❑ Delete the old method.

Replace Error
Code with
Exception

Example

Isn't it strange that computer textbooks often assume you can't withdraw more than your balance from an account, although in real life you often can?

```
class Account...
    int withdraw(int amount) {
        if (amount > _balance)
            return -1;
        else {
```

```
                _balance -= amount;
                return 0;
            }
        }

    private int _balance;
```

To change this code to use an exception I first need to decide whether to use a checked or unchecked exception. The decision hinges on whether it is the responsibility of the caller to test the balance before withdrawing or whether it is the responsibility of the withdraw routine to make the check. If testing the balance is the caller's responsibility, it is a programming error to call withdraw with an amount greater than the balance. Because it is a programming error—that is, a bug—I should use an unchecked exception. If testing the balance is the withdraw routine's responsibility, I must declare the exception in the interface. That way I signal the caller to expect the exception and to take appropriate measures.

Replace Error
Code with
Exception

Example: Unchecked Exception

Let's take the unchecked case first. Here I expect the caller to do the checking. First I look at the callers. In this case nobody should be using the return code because it is a programmer error to do so. If I see code such as

```
        if (account.withdraw(amount) == -1)
            handleOverdrawn();
        else doTheUsualThing();
```

I need to replace it with code such as

```
        if (!account.canWithdraw(amount))
            handleOverdrawn();
        else {
            account.withdraw(amount);
            doTheUsualThing();
        }
```

I can compile and test after each change.

Now I need to remove the error code and throw an exception for the error case. Because the behavior is (by definition) exceptional, I should use a guard clause for the condition check:

```
    void withdraw(int amount) {
        if (amount > _balance)
            throw new IllegalArgumentException ("Amount too large");
        _balance -= amount;
    }
```

Because it is a programmer error, I should signal even more clearly by using an assertion:

```
class Account...
  void withdraw(int amount) {
      Assert.isTrue ("sufficient funds", amount <= _balance);
      _balance -= amount;
  }

class Assert...
  static void isTrue (String comment, boolean test) {
      if (! test) {
          throw new RuntimeException ("Assertion failed: " + comment);
      }
  }
```

Example: Checked Exception

I handle the checked exception case slightly differently. First I create (or use) an appropriate new exception:

Replace Error
Code with
Exception

```
class BalanceException extends Exception {}
```

Then I adjust the callers to look like

```
try {
    account.withdraw(amount);
    doTheUsualThing();
} catch (BalanceException e) {
    handleOverdrawn();
}
```

Now I change the withdraw method to use the exception:

```
void withdraw(int amount) throws BalanceException {
    if (amount > _balance) throw new BalanceException();
    _balance -= amount;
}
```

The awkward thing about this procedure is that I have to change all the callers and the called routine in one go. Otherwise the compiler spanks us. If there are a lot of callers, this can be too large a change without the compile and test step.

For these cases I can use a temporary intermediate method. I begin with the same case as before:

```
if (account.withdraw(amount) == -1)
    handleOverdrawn();
else doTheUsualThing();

class Account ...
  int withdraw(int amount) {
      if (amount > _balance)
          return -1;
      else {
          _balance -= amount;
          return 0;
      }
  }
```

The first step is to create a new withdraw method that uses the exception:

```
void newWithdraw(int amount) throws BalanceException {
    if (amount > _balance) throw new BalanceException();
    _balance -= amount;
}
```

Next I adjust the current withdraw method to use the new one:

```
int withdraw(int amount) {
    try {
        newWithdraw(amount);
        return 0;
    } catch (BalanceException e) {
        return -1;
    }
}
```

With that done, I can compile and test. Now I can replace each of the calls to the old method with a call to the new one:

```
try {
    account.newWithdraw(amount);
    doTheUsualThing();
} catch (BalanceException e) {
    handleOverdrawn();
}
```

With both old and new methods in place, I can compile and test after each change. When I'm finished, I can delete the old method and use *Rename Method (273)* to give the new method the old name.

Replace Exception with Test

You are throwing an exception on a condition the caller could have checked first.

Change the caller to make the test first.

```
double getValueForPeriod (int periodNumber) {
    try {
        return _values[periodNumber];
    } catch (ArrayIndexOutOfBoundsException e) {
        return 0;
    }
}
```

⇓

```
double getValueForPeriod (int periodNumber) {
    if (periodNumber >= _values.length) return 0;
    return _values[periodNumber];
}
```

Replace
Exception with
Test

Motivation

Exceptions are an important advance in programming languages. They allow us to avoid complex codes by use of *Replace Error Code with Exception (310)*. Like so many pleasures, exceptions can be used to excess, and they cease to be pleasurable. (Even I can tire of Aventinus [Jackson].) Exceptions should be used for exceptional behavior—behavior that is an unexpected error. They should not act as a substitute for conditional tests. If you can reasonably expect the caller to check the condition before calling the operation, you should provide a test, and the caller should use it.

Mechanics

❑ Put a test up front and copy the code from the catch block into the appropriate leg of the if statement.

❑ Add an assertion to the catch block to notify you whether the catch block is executed.

❑ Compile and test.

❑ Remove the catch block and the try block if there are no other catch blocks.

❑ Compile and test.

Example

For this example I use an object that manages resources that are expensive to create but can be reused. Database connections are a good example of this. Such a manager has two pools of resources, one that is available for use and one that is allocated. When a client wants a resource, the manager hands it out and transfers it from the available pool to the allocated pool. When a client releases a resource, the manager passes it back. If a client requests a resource and none is available, the manager creates a new one.

The method for giving out resources might look like this:

```
class ResourcePool
  Resource getResource() {
      Resource result;
      try {
          result = (Resource) _available.pop();
          _allocated.push(result);
          return result;
      } catch (EmptyStackException e) {
          result = new Resource();
          _allocated.push(result);
          return result;
      }
  }
  Stack _available;
  Stack _allocated;
```

In this case running out of resources is not an unexpected occurrence, so I should not use an exception.

To remove the exception I first add an appropriate up-front test and do the empty behavior there:

```
Resource getResource() {
    Resource result;
    if (_available.isEmpty()) {
        result = new Resource();
        _allocated.push(result);
        return result;
    }
    else {
        try {
```

Replace
Exception with
Test

```
            result = (Resource) _available.pop();
            _allocated.push(result);
            return result;
        } catch (EmptyStackException e) {
            result = new Resource();
            _allocated.push(result);
            return result;
        }
    }
}
```

With this the exception should never occur. I can add an assertion to check this:

```
Resource getResource() {
    Resource result;
    if (_available.isEmpty()) {
        result = new Resource();
        _allocated.push(result);
        return result;
    }
    else {
        try {
            result = (Resource) _available.pop();
            _allocated.push(result);
            return result;
        } catch (EmptyStackException e) {
            Assert.shouldNeverReachHere("available was empty on pop");
            result = new Resource();
            _allocated.push(result);
            return result;
        }
    }
}

class Assert...
  static void shouldNeverReachHere(String message) {
      throw new RuntimeException (message);
  }
```

Now I can compile and test. If all goes well, I can remove the try block completely:

```
Resource getResource() {
    Resource result;
    if (_available.isEmpty()) {
        result = new Resource();
        _allocated.push(result);
        return result;
    }
    else {
        result = (Resource) _available.pop();
```

```
        _allocated.push(result);
        return result;
    }
}
```

After this I usually find I can clean up the conditional code. Here I can use *Consolidate Duplicate Conditional Fragments (243):*

```
Resource getResource() {
    Resource result;
    if (_available.isEmpty())
        result = new Resource();
    else
        result = (Resource) _available.pop();
    _allocated.push(result);
    return result;
}
```

Chapter 11

Dealing
with Generalization

Generalization produces its own batch of refactorings, mostly dealing with moving methods around a hierarchy of inheritance. *Pull Up Field (320)* and *Pull Up Method (322)* both promote function up a hierarchy, and *Push Down Method (328)* and *Push Down Field (329)* push function downward. Constructors are a little bit more awkward to pull up, so *Pull Up Constructor Body (325)* deals with those issues. Rather than pushing down a constructor, it is often useful to use *Replace Constructor with Factory Method (304)*.

If you have methods that have a similar outline body but vary in details, you can use *Form Template Method (345)* to separate the differences from the similarities.

In addition to moving function around a hierarchy, you can change the hierarchy by creating new classes. *Extract Subclass (330)*, *Extract Superclass (336)*, and *Extract Interface (341)* all do this by forming new elements out of various points. *Extract Interface (341)* is particularly important when you want to mark a small amount of function for the type system. If you find yourself with unnecessary classes in your hierarchy, you can use *Collapse Hierarchy (344)* to remove them.

Sometimes you find that inheritance is not the best way of handling a situation and that you need delegation instead. *Replace Inheritance with Delegation (352)* helps make this change. Sometimes life is the other way around and you have to use *Replace Delegation with Inheritance (355)*.

Pull Up Field

Two subclasses have the same field.

Move the field to the superclass.

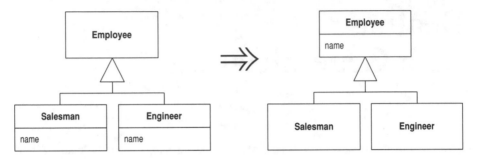

Motivation

If subclasses are developed independently, or combined through refactoring, you often find that they duplicate features. In particular, certain fields can be duplicates. Such fields sometimes have similar names but not always. The only way to determine what is going on is to look at the fields and see how they are used by other methods. If they are being used in a similar way, you can generalize them.

Doing this reduces duplication in two ways. It removes the duplicate data declaration and allows you to move from the subclasses to the superclass behavior that uses the field.

Mechanics

- Inspect all uses of the candidate fields to ensure they are used in the same way.

- If the fields do not have the same name, rename the fields so that they have the name you want to use for the superclass field.

❑ Compile and test.

❑ Create a new field in the superclass.

⇒ *If the fields are private, you will need to protect the superclass field so that the subclasses can refer to it.*

❑ Delete the subclass fields.

❑ Compile and test.

❑ Consider using *Self Encapsulate Field (171)* on the new field.

Pull Up Field

Pull Up Method

You have methods with identical results on subclasses.

Move them to the superclass.

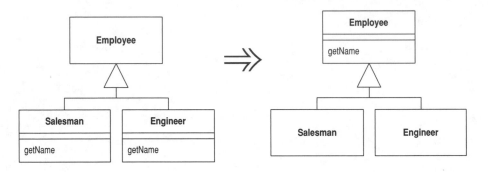

Motivation

Eliminating duplicate behavior is important. Although two duplicate methods work fine as they are, they are nothing more than a breeding ground for bugs in the future. Whenever there is duplication, you face the risk that an alteration to one will not be made to the other. Usually it is difficult to find the duplicates.

The easiest case of using *Pull Up Method* occurs when the methods have the same body, implying there's been a copy and paste. Of course it's not always as obvious as that. You could just do the refactoring and see if the tests croak, but that puts a lot of reliance on your tests. I usually find it valuable to look for the differences; often they show up behavior that I forgot to test for.

Often *Pull Up Method* comes after other steps. You see two methods in different classes that can be parameterized in such a way that they end up as essentially the same method. In that case the smallest step is to parameterize each method separately and then generalize them. Do it in one go if you feel confident enough.

A special case of the need for *Pull Up Method* occurs when you have a subclass method that overrides a superclass method yet does the same thing.

The most awkward element of *Pull Up Method* is that the body of the methods may refer to features that are on the subclass but not on the superclass. If the feature is a method, you can either generalize the other method or create an abstract method in the superclass. You may need to change a method's signature or create a delegating method to get this to work.

If you have two methods that are similar but not the same, you may be able to use *Form Template Method (345)*.

Mechanics

- ❏ Inspect the methods to ensure they are identical.

  ⇒ *If the methods look like they do the same thing but are not identical, use algorithm substitution on one of them to make them identical.*

- ❏ If the methods have different signatures, change the signatures to the one you want to use in the superclass.

- ❏ Create a new method in the superclass, copy the body of one of the methods to it, adjust, and compile.

  ⇒ *If you are in a strongly typed language and the method calls another method that is present on both subclasses but not the superclass, declare an abstract method on the superclass.*
  ⇒ *If the method uses a subclass field, use* Pull Up Field (320) *or* Self Encapsulate Field (171) *and declare and use an abstract getting method.*

- ❏ Delete one subclass method.

- ❏ Compile and test.

- ❏ Keep deleting subclass methods and testing until only the superclass method remains.

- ❏ Take a look at the callers of this method to see whether you can change a required type to the superclass.

Pull Up Method

Example

Consider a customer with two subclasses: regular customer and preferred customer.

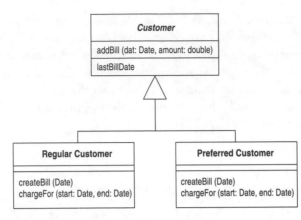

The createBill method is identical for each class:

```
void createBill (Date date) {
  double chargeAmount = chargeFor (lastBillDate, date);
  addBill (date, charge);
}
```

Pull Up Method

I can't move the method up into the superclass, because chargeFor is different on each subclass. First I have to declare it on the superclass as abstract:

```
class Customer...
  abstract double chargeFor(date start, date end)
```

Then I can copy createBill from one of the subclasses. I compile with that in place and then remove the createBill method from one of the subclasses, compile, and test. I then remove it from the other, compile, and test:

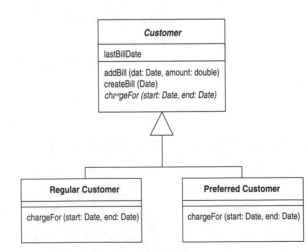

Pull Up Constructor Body

You have constructors on subclasses with mostly identical bodies.

Create a superclass constructor; call this from the subclass methods.

```
class Manager extends Employee...
    public Manager (String name, String id, int grade) {
        _name = name;
        _id = id;
        _grade = grade;
    }
```

⟱

```
    public Manager (String name, String id, int grade) {
        super (name, id);
        _grade = grade;
    }
```

Motivation

Constructors are tricky things. They aren't quite normal methods, so you are more restricted in what you can do with them than you are when you use normal methods.

If you see subclass methods with common behavior, your first thought is to extract the common behavior into a method and pull it up into the superclass. With a constructor, however, the common behavior is often the construction. In this case you need a superclass constructor that is called by subclasses. In many cases this is the whole body of the constructor. You can't use *Pull Up Method (322)* here, because you can't inherit constructors (don't you just hate that?).

If refactoring becomes complex, you might want to consider *Replace Constructor with Factory Method (304)* instead.

Mechanics

❏ Define a superclass constructor.

❏ Move the common code at the beginning from the subclass to the super-class constructor.

⇒ *This may be all the code.*
⇒ *Try to move common code to the beginning of the constructor.*

❏ Call the superclass constructor as the first step in the subclass constructor.

⇒ *If all the code is common, this will be the only line of the subclass constructor.*

❏ Compile and test.

⇒ *If there is any common code later, use* Extract Method (110) *to factor out common code and use* Pull Up Method *to pull it up.*

Example

Pull Up
Constructor
Body

Here are a manager and an employee:

```
class Employee...
  protected String _name;
  protected String _id;

class Manager extends Employee...
  public Manager (String name, String id, int grade) {
      _name = name;
      _id = id;
      _grade = grade;
  }

  private int _grade;
```

The fields from Employee should be set in a constructor for Employee. I define one and make it protected to signal that subclasses should call it:

```
class Employee
  protected Employee (String name, String id) {
      _name = name;
      _id = id;
  }
```

Then I call it from the subclass:

```
public Manager (String name, String id, int grade) {
    super (name, id);
    _grade = grade;
}
```

A variation occurs when there is common code later. Say I have the following code:

```
class Employee...
  boolean isPriviliged() {..}
  void assignCar() {..}
class Manager...
  public Manager (String name, String id, int grade) {
      super (name, id);
      _grade = grade;
      if (isPriviliged()) assignCar(); //every subclass does this
  }
  boolean isPriviliged() {
      return _grade > 4;
  }
```

I can't move the assignCar behavior into the superclass constructor because it must be executed after grade has been assigned to the field. So I need *Extract Method (110)* and *Pull Up Method (322)*.

```
class Employee...
  void initialize() {
      if (isPriviliged()) assignCar();
  }
class Manager...
  public Manager (String name, String id, int grade) {
      super (name, id);
      _grade = grade;
      initialize();
  }
```

Pull Up Constructor Body

Push Down Method

Behavior on a superclass is relevant only for some of its subclasses.

Move it to those subclasses.

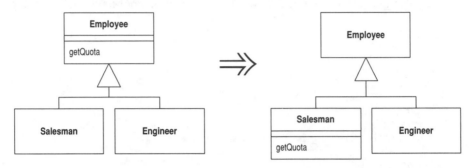

Motivation

Push Down Method is the opposite of *Pull Up Method (322)*. I use it when I need to move behavior from a superclass to a specific subclass, usually because it makes sense only there. You often do this when you use *Extract Subclass (330)*.

Mechanics

❑ Declare a method in all subclasses and copy the body into each subclass.

   ⇒ *You may need to declare fields as protected for the method to access them. Usually you do this if you intend to push down the field later. Otherwise use an accessor on the superclass. If this accessor is not public, you need to declare it as protected.*

❑ Remove method from superclass.

   ⇒ *You may have to change callers to use the subclass in variable and parameter declarations.*

   ⇒ *If it makes sense to access the method through a superclass variable, you don't intend to remove the method from any subclasses, and the superclass is abstract, you can declare the method as abstract, in the superclass.*

❑ Compile and test.

❑ Remove the method from each subclass that does not need it.

❑ Compile and test.

Push Down Field

A field is used only by some subclasses.

Move the field to those subclasses.

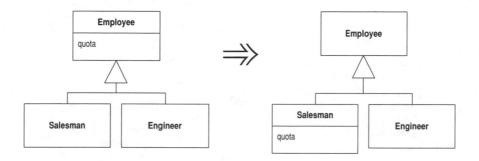

Motivation

Push Down Field (329) is the opposite of *Pull Up Field (320)*. Use it when you don't need a field in the superclass but only in a subclass.

Mechanics

❏ Declare the field in all subclasses.

❏ Remove the field from the superclass.

❏ Compile and test.

❏ Remove the field from all subclasses that don't need it.

❏ Compile and test.

Extract Subclass

A class has features that are used only in some instances.

Create a subclass for that subset of features.

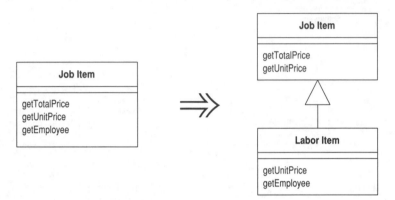

Motivation

The main trigger for use of *Extract Subclass* is the realization that a class has behavior used for some instances of the class and not for others. Sometimes this is signaled by a type code, in which case you can use *Replace Type Code with Subclasses (223)* or *Replace Type Code with State/Strategy (227)*. But you don't have to have a type code to suggest the use for a subclass.

The main alternative to *Extract Subclass* is *Extract Class (149)*. This is a choice between delegation and inheritance. *Extract Subclass (330)* is usually simpler to do, but it has limitations. You can't change the class-based behavior of an object once the object is created. You can change the class-based behavior with *Extract Class (149)* simply by plugging in different components. You can also use only subclasses to represent one set of variations. If you want the class to vary in several different ways, you have to use delegation for all but one of them.

Mechanics

❑ Define a new subclass of the source class.

❑ Provide constructors for the new subclass.

⇒ *In the simple cases, copy the arguments of the superclass and call the superclass constructor with* super.

⇒ *If you want to hide the use of the subclass from clients, you can use* Replace Constructor with Factory Method (304).

❑ Find all calls to constructors of the superclass. If they need the subclass, replace with a call to the new constructor.

⇒ *If the subclass constructor needs different arguments, use* Rename Method (273) *to change it. If some of the constructor parameters of the superclass are no longer needed, use* Rename Method (273) *on that too.*

⇒ *If the superclass can no longer be directly instantiated, declare it abstract.*

❑ One by one use *Push Down Method (328)* and *Push Down Field (329)* to move features onto the subclass.

⇒ *Unlike* Extract Class (149) *it usually is easier to work with the methods first and the data last.*

⇒ *When a public method is pushed, you may need to redefine a caller's variable or parameter type to call the new method. The compiler will catch these cases.*

❑ Look for any field that designates information now indicated by the hierarchy (usually a boolean or type code). Eliminate it by using *Self Encapsulate Field (171)* and replacing the getter with polymorphic constant methods. All users of this field should be refactored with *Replace Conditional with Polymorphism (255).*

⇒ *For any methods outside the class that use an accessor, consider using* Move Method (142) *to move the method into this class; then use* Replace Conditional with Polymorphism (255).

❑ Compile and test after each push down.

**Extract
Subclass**

Example

I'll start with a job item class that determines prices for items of work at a local garage:

```
class JobItem ...
    public JobItem (int unitPrice, int quantity, boolean isLabor, Employee employee) {
        _unitPrice = unitPrice;
        _quantity = quantity;
        _isLabor = isLabor;
        _employee = employee;
    }
    public int getTotalPrice() {
        return getUnitPrice() * _quantity;
    }
    public int getUnitPrice(){
        return (_isLabor) ?
            _employee.getRate():
            _unitPrice;
    }
    public int getQuantity(){
        return _quantity;
    }
    public Employee getEmployee() {
        return _employee;
    }
    private int _unitPrice;
    private int _quantity;
    private Employee _employee;
    private boolean _isLabor;

class Employee...
    public Employee (int rate) {
        _rate = rate;
    }
    public int getRate() {
        return _rate;
    }
    private int _rate;
```

I extract a LaborItem subclass from this class because some of the behavior and data are needed only in that case. I begin by creating the new class:

```
class LaborItem extends JobItem {}
```

The first thing I need is a constructor for the labor item because job item does not have a no-arg constructor. For this I copy the signature of the parent constructor:

```
public LaborItem (int unitPrice, int quantity, boolean isLabor, Employee employee) {
    super (unitPrice, quantity, isLabor, employee);
}
```

This is enough to get the new subclass to compile. However, the constructor is messy; some arguments are needed by the labor item, and some are not. I deal with that later.

The next step is to look for calls to the constructor of the job item, and to look for cases where the constructor of the labor item should be called instead. So statements like

```
JobItem j1 = new JobItem (0, 5, true, kent);
```

become

```
JobItem j1 = new LaborItem (0, 5, true, kent);
```

At this stage I have not changed the type of the variable; I have changed only the type of the constructor. This is because I want to use the new type only where I have to. At this point I have no specific interface for the subclass, so I don't want to declare any variations yet.

Now is a good time to clean up the constructor parameter lists. I use *Rename Method (273)* on each of them. I work with the superclass first. I create the new constructor and make the old one protected (the subclass still needs it):

```
class JobItem...
    protected JobItem (int unitPrice, int quantity, boolean isLabor, Employee employee) {
        _unitPrice = unitPrice;
        _quantity = quantity;
        _isLabor = isLabor;
        _employee = employee;
    }
    public JobItem (int unitPrice, int quantity) {
        this (unitPrice, quantity, false, null)
    }
```

Calls from outside now use the new constructor:

```
JobItem j2 = new JobItem (10, 15);
```

Once I've compiled and tested, I use *Rename Method (273)* on the subclass constructor:

```
class LaborItem
    public LaborItem (int quantity, Employee employee) {
        super (0, quantity, true, employee);
    }
```

For the moment, I still use the protected superclass constructor.

Extract
Subclass

Now I can start pushing down the features of the job item. I begin with the methods. I start with using *Push Down Method (328)* on getEmployee:

```
class LaborItem...
  public Employee getEmployee() {
      return _employee;
  }
class JobItem...
  protected Employee _employee;
```

Because the employee field will be pushed down later, I declare it as protected for the moment.

Once the employee field is protected, I can clean up the constructors so that employee is set only in the subclass into which it is being pushed down:

```
class JobItem...
  protected JobItem (int unitPrice, int quantity, boolean isLabor) {
      _unitPrice = unitPrice;
      _quantity = quantity;
      _isLabor = isLabor;
  }
class LaborItem ...
  public LaborItem (int quantity, Employee employee) {
      super (0, quantity, true);
       _employee = employee;
  }
```

Extract Subclass

The field _isLabor is used to indicate information that is now inherent in the hierarchy. So I can remove the field. The best way to do this is to first use *Self Encapsulate Field (171)* and then change the accessor to use a polymorphic constant method. A polymorphic constant method is one whereby each implementation returns a (different) fixed value:

```
class JobItem...
  protected boolean isLabor() {
      return false;
  }
```

```
class LaborItem...
  protected boolean isLabor() {
      return true;
  }
```

Then I can get rid of the isLabor field.

Now I can look at users of the isLabor methods. These should be refactored with *Replace Conditional with Polymorphism (255)*. I take the method

```
class JobItem...
  public int getUnitPrice(){
      return (isLabor()) ?
          _employee.getRate():
          _unitPrice;
  }
```

and replace it with

```
class JobItem...
  public int getUnitPrice(){
      return _unitPrice;
  }
class LaborItem...
  public int getUnitPrice(){
      return _employee.getRate();
  }
```

Once a group of methods that use some data have been pushed down, I can use *Push Down Field (329)* on the data. That I can't use it because a method uses the data is a signal for more work on the methods, either with *Push Down Method (328)* or *Replace Conditional with Polymorphism (255)*.

Because the unit price is used only by items that are nonlabor (parts job items), I can use *Extract Subclass (330)* on job item again to create a parts item class. When I've done that, the job item class will be abstract.

Extract Superclass

You have two classes with
similar features.

Create a superclass and move the common
features to the superclass.

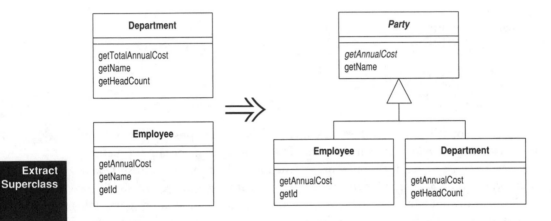

**Extract
Superclass**

Motivation

Duplicate code is one of the principal bad things in systems. If you say things in multiple places, then when it comes time to change what you say, you have more things to change than you should.

One form of duplicate code is two classes that do similar things in the same way or similar things in different ways. Objects provide a built-in mechanism to simplify this situation with inheritance. However, you often don't notice the commonalities until you have created some classes, in which case you need to create the inheritance structure later.

An alternative is *Extract Class (149)*. The choice is essentially between inheritance and delegation. Inheritance is the simpler choice if the two classes share interface as well as behavior. If you make the wrong choice, you can always use *Replace Inheritance with Delegation (352)* later.

Mechanics

- ❑ Create a blank abstract superclass; make the original classes subclasses of this superclass.

- ❑ One by one, use *Pull Up Field (320)*, *Pull Up Method (322)*, and *Pull Up Constructor Body (325)* to move common elements to the superclass.

  ⇒ *It's usually easier to move the fields first.*
  ⇒ *If you have subclass methods that have different signatures but the same purpose, use* Rename Method (273) *to get them to the same name and then use* Pull Up Method (322).
  ⇒ *If you have methods with the same signature but different bodies, declare the common signature as an abstract method on the superclass.*
  ⇒ *If you have methods with different bodies that do the same thing, you may try using* Substitute Algorithm (139) *to copy one body into the other. If this works, you can then use* Pull Up Method (322).

- ❑ Compile and test after each pull.

- ❑ Examine the methods left on the subclasses. See if there are common parts, if there are you can use *Extract Method (110)* followed by *Pull Up Method (322)* on the common parts. If the overall flow is similar, you may be able to use *Form Template Method (345)*.

- ❑ After pulling up all the common elements, check each client of the subclasses. If they use only the common interface you can change the required type to the superclass.

Extract Superclass

Example

For this case I have an employee and a department:

```
class Employee...
    public Employee (String name, String id, int annualCost) {
        _name = name;
        _id = id;
        _annualCost = annualCost;
    }
    public int getAnnualCost() {
        return _annualCost;
    }
```

```
    public String getId(){
        return _id;
    }
    public String getName() {
        return _name;
    }
    private String _name;
    private int _annualCost;
    private String _id;

public class Department...
    public Department (String name) {
        _name = name;
    }
    public int getTotalAnnualCost(){
        Enumeration e = getStaff();
        int result = 0;
        while (e.hasMoreElements()) {
            Employee each = (Employee) e.nextElement();
            result += each.getAnnualCost();
        }
        return result;
    }
    public int getHeadCount() {
        return _staff.size();
    }
    public Enumeration getStaff() {
        return _staff.elements();
    }
    public void addStaff(Employee arg) {
        _staff.addElement(arg);
    }
    public String getName() {
        return _name;
    }
    private String _name;
    private Vector _staff = new Vector();
```

Extract Superclass

There are a couple of areas of commonality here. First, both employees and departments have names. Second, they both have annual costs, although the methods for calculating them are slightly different. I extract a superclass for both of these features. The first step is to create the new superclass and define the existing superclasses to be subclasses of this superclass:

```
abstract class Party {}
class Employee extends Party...
class Department extends Party...
```

Now I begin to pull up features to the superclass. It is usually easier to use *Pull Up Field (320)* first:

```
class Party...
  protected String _name;
```

Then I can use *Pull Up Method (322)* on the getters:

```
class Party {

  public String getName() {
      return _name;
  }
```

I like to make the field private. To do this I need to use *Pull Up Constructor Body (325)* to assign the name:

```
class Party...
  protected Party (String name) {
      _name = name;
  }
  private String _name;

class Employee...
  public Employee (String name, String id, int annualCost) {
      super (name);
      _id = id;
      _annualCost = annualCost;
  }

class Department...
  public Department (String name) {
      super (name);
  }
```

Extract
Superclass

The methods Department.getTotalAnnualCost and Employee.getAnnualCost, do carry out the same intention, so they should have the same name. I first use *Rename Method (273)* to get them to the same name:

```
class Department extends Party {
  public int getAnnualCost(){
      Enumeration e = getStaff();
      int result = 0;
      while (e.hasMoreElements()) {
          Employee each = (Employee) e.nextElement();
          result += each.getAnnualCost();
      }
      return result;
  }
```

Their bodies are still different, so I cannot use *Pull Up Method (322);* however, I can declare an abstract method on the superclass:

```
abstract public int getAnnualCost()
```

Once I've made the obvious changes, I look at the clients of the two classes to see whether I can change any of them to use the new superclass. One client of these classes is the department class itself, which holds a collection of employees. The getAnnualCost method uses only the annual cost method, which is now declared on the party:

```
class Department...
  public int getAnnualCost(){
      Enumeration e = getStaff();
      int result = 0;
      while (e.hasMoreElements()) {
          Party each = (Party) e.nextElement();
          result += each.getAnnualCost();
      }
      return result;
  }
```

This behavior suggests a new possibility. I could treat department and employee as a *composite* [Gang of Four]. This would allow me to let a department include another department. This would be new functionality, so it is not strictly a refactoring. If a composite were wanted, I would obtain it by changing the name of the staff field to better represent the picture. This change would involve making a corresponding change in the name addStaff and altering the parameter to be a party. The final change would be to make the headCount method recursive. I could do this by creating a headcount method for employee that just returns 1 and using *Substitute Algorithm (139)* on the department's headcount to sum the headcounts of the components.

Extract Interface

Several clients use the same subset of a class's interface, or two classes have part of their interfaces in common.

Extract the subset into an interface.

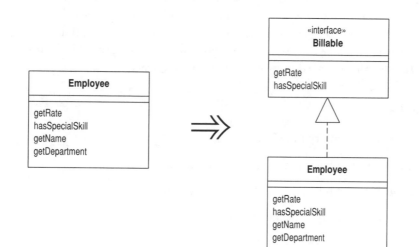

Motivation

Classes use each other in several ways. Use of a class often means ranging over the whole area of responsibilities of a class. Another case is use of only a particular subset of a class's responsibilities by a group of clients. Another is that a class needs to work with any class that can handle certain requests.

For the second two cases it is often useful to make the subset of responsibilities a thing in its own right, so that it can be made clear in the use of the system. That way it is easier to see how the responsibilities divide. If new classes are needed to support the subset, it is easier to see exactly what fits in the subset.

In many object-oriented languages, this capability is supported by multiple inheritance. You create a class for each segment of behavior and combine them in an implementation. Java has single inheritance but allows you to state and implement this kind of requirement using interfaces. Interfaces have had a big influence on the way programmers design Java programs. Even Smalltalk programmers think interfaces are a step forward!

There is some similarity between *Extract Superclass (336)* and *Extract Interface (341)*. *Extract Interface (341)* can only bring out common interfaces, not common code. Using *Extract Interface (341)* can lead to smelly duplicate code. You can reduce this problem by using *Extract Class (149)* to put the behavior into a component and delegating to it. If there is substantial common behavior *Extract Superclass (336)* is simpler, but you do only get to have one superclass.

Interfaces are good to use whenever a class has distinct roles in different situations. Use *Extract Interface (341)* for each role. Another useful case is that in which you want to describe the outbound interface of a class, that is, the operations the class makes on its server. If you want to allow other kinds of servers in the future, all they need do is implement the interface.

Mechanics

- Create an empty interface.
- Declare the common operations in the interface.
- Declare the relevant class(es) as implementing the interface.
- Adjust client type declarations to use the interface.

Example

A timesheet class generates charges for employees. In order to do this the timesheet needs to know the employee's rate and whether the employee has a special skill:

```
double charge(Employee emp, int days) {
    int base = emp.getRate() * days;
    if (emp.hasSpecialSkill())
        return base * 1.05;
    else return base;
}
```

Employee has many other aspects to it than the charge rate and the special skill information, but those are the only pieces that this application needs. I can highlight the fact that I need only this subset by defining an interface for it:

```
interface Billable {
  public int getRate();
  public boolean hasSpecialSkill();
}
```

I then declare the employee as implementing the interface:

```
class Employee implements Billable ...
```

With that done I can change the declaration of charge to show only this part of the employee's behavior is used:

```
double charge(Billable emp, int days) {
    int base = emp.getRate() * days;
    if (emp.hasSpecialSkill())
        return base * 1.05;
    else return base;
}
```

At the moment the gain is a modest gain in documentability. Such a gain would not be worthwhile for one method, but if several classes were to use the billable interface on person, that would be useful. The big gain appears when I want to bill computers too. To make them billable I know that all I have to do is implement the billable interface and I can put computers on timesheets.

Extract
Interface

Collapse Hierarchy

A superclass and subclass are not very different.

Merge them together.

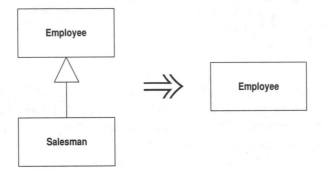

Motivation

If you have been working for a while with a class hierarchy, it can easily become too tangled for its own good. Refactoring the hierarchy often involves pushing methods and fields up and down the hierarchy. After you've done this you can well find you have a subclass that isn't adding any value, so you need to merge the classes together.

Mechanics

❑ Choose which class is going to be removed: the superclass or the subclasses.

❑ Use *Pull Up Field (320)* and *Pull Up Method (322)* or *Push Down Method (328)* and *Push Down Field (329)* to move all the behavior and data of the removed class to the class with which it is being merged.

❑ Compile and test with each move.

❑ Adjust references to the class that will be removed to use the merged class. This will affect variable declarations, parameter types, and constructors.

❑ Remove the empty class.

❑ Compile and test.

Form Template Method

You have two methods in subclasses that perform similar steps
in the same order, yet the steps are different.

*Get the steps into methods with the same signature, so
that the original methods become the same. Then you
can pull them up.*

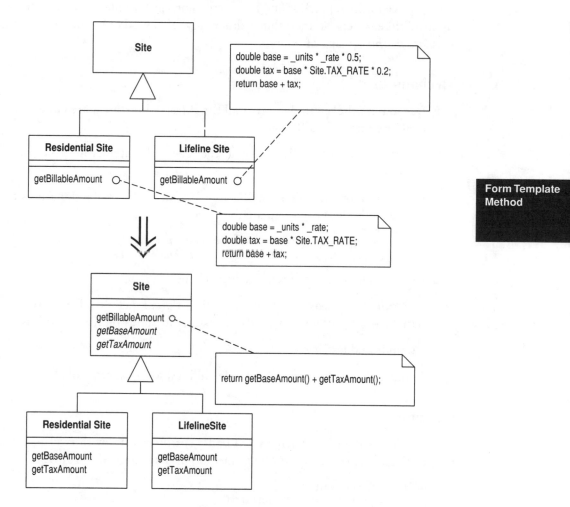

Motivation

Inheritance is a powerful tool for eliminating duplicate behavior. Whenever we see two similar methods in a subclass, we want to bring them together in a superclass. But what if they are not exactly the same? What do we do then? We still need to eliminate all the duplication we can but keep the essential differences.

A common case is two methods that seem to carry out broadly similar steps in the same sequence, but the steps are not the same. In this case we can move the sequence to the superclass and allow polymorphism to play its role in ensuring the different steps do their things differently. This kind of method is called a *template method* [Gang of Four].

Mechanics

□ Decompose the methods so that all the extracted methods are either identical or completely different.

□ Use *Pull Up Method (322)* to pull the identical methods into the superclass.

□ For the different methods use *Rename Method (273)* so the signatures for all the methods at each step are the same.

⇒ *This makes the original methods the same in that they all issue the same set of method calls, but the subclasses handle the calls differently.*

□ Compile and test after each signature change.

□ Use *Pull Up Method (322)* on one of the original methods. Define the signatures of the different methods as abstract methods on the superclass.

□ Compile and test.

□ Remove the other methods, compile, and test after each removal.

Example

I finish where I left off in Chapter 1. I had a customer class with two methods for printing statements. The `statement` method prints statements in ASCII:

```
public String statement() {
    Enumeration rentals = _rentals.elements();
    String result = "Rental Record for " + getName() + "\n";
    while (rentals.hasMoreElements()) {
        Rental each = (Rental) rentals.nextElement();
```

Form Template Method

```
                    //show figures for this rental
                    result += "\t" + each.getMovie().getTitle()+ "\t" +
                        String.valueOf(each.getCharge()) + "\n";
            }

            //add footer lines
            result +=  "Amount owed is " + String.valueOf(getTotalCharge()) + "\n";
            result += "You earned " + String.valueOf(getTotalFrequentRenterPoints()) +
                    " frequent renter points";
            return result;
    }
```

while the `htmlStatement` does them in HTML:

```
    public String htmlStatement() {
        Enumeration rentals = _rentals.elements();
        String result = "<H1>Rentals for <EM>" + getName() + "</EM></H1><P>\n";
        while (rentals.hasMoreElements()) {
            Rental each = (Rental) rentals.nextElement();
            //show figures for each rental
            result += each.getMovie().getTitle()+ ": " +
                String.valueOf(each.getCharge()) + "<BR>\n";
        }
        //add footer lines
        result +=  "<P>You owe <EM>" + String.valueOf(getTotalCharge()) + "</EM><P>\n";
        result += "On this rental you earned <EM>" +
            String.valueOf(getTotalFrequentRenterPoints()) +
            "</EM> frequent renter points<P>";
        return result;
    }
```

Before I can use *Form Template Method (345)* I need to arrange things so that the two methods are subclasses of some common superclass. I do this by using a method object [Beck] to create a separate strategy hierarchy for printing the statements (Figure 11.1).

```
class Statement {}
class TextStatement extends Statement {}
class HtmlStatement extends Statement {}
```

Now I use *Move Method (142)* to move the two statement methods over to the subclasses:

```
class Customer...
public String statement() {
    return new TextStatement().value(this);
}
public String htmlStatement() {
    return new HtmlStatement().value(this);
}
```

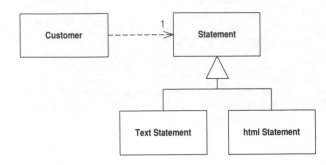

Figure 11.1 *Using a strategy for statements*

Form Template Method

```
class TextStatement {
  public String value(Customer aCustomer) {
      Enumeration rentals = aCustomer.getRentals();
      String result = "Rental Record for " + aCustomer.getName() + "\n";
      while (rentals.hasMoreElements()) {
          Rental each = (Rental) rentals.nextElement();

          //show figures for this rental
          result += "\t" + each.getMovie().getTitle()+ "\t" +
              String.valueOf(each.getCharge()) + "\n";
      }

      //add footer lines
      result +=  "Amount owed is " + String.valueOf(aCustomer.getTotalCharge()) + "\n";
      result += "You earned " + String.valueOf(aCustomer.getTotalFrequentRenterPoints()) +
        " frequent renter points";
      return result;
  }
}
class HtmlStatement {
  public String value(Customer aCustomer) {
      Enumeration rentals = aCustomer.getRentals();
      String result = "<H1>Rentals for <EM>" + aCustomer.getName() + "</EM></H1><P>\n";
      while (rentals.hasMoreElements()) {
          Rental each = (Rental) rentals.nextElement();
          //show figures for each rental
          result += each.getMovie().getTitle()+ ": " +
                    String.valueOf(each.getCharge()) + "<BR>\n";
      }
      //add footer lines
      result +=  "<P>You owe <EM>" + String.valueOf(aCustomer.getTotalCharge()) +
          "</EM><P>\n";
      result += "On this rental you earned <EM>"
             String.valueOf(aCustomer.getTotalFrequentRenterPoints()) +
             "</EM> frequent renter points<P>";
      return result;
  }
}
```

As I moved them I renamed the statement methods to better fit the strategy. I gave them the same name because the difference between the two now lies in the class rather than the method. (For those trying this from the example, I also had to add a `getRentals` method to customer and relax the visibility of `getTotalCharge` and `getTotalFrequentRenterPoints`.)

With two similar methods on subclasses, I can start to use *Form Template Method (345)*. The key to this refactoring is to separate the varying code from the similar code by using *Extract Method (110)* to extract the pieces that are different between the two methods. Each time I extract I create methods with different bodies but the same signature.

The first example is the printing of the header. Both methods use the customer to obtain information, but the resulting string is formatted differently. I can extract the formatting of this string into separate methods with the same signature:

```
class TextStatement...
  String headerString(Customer aCustomer) {
    return "Rental Record for " + aCustomer.getName() + "\n";
  }
  public String value(Customer aCustomer) {
      Enumeration rentals = aCustomer.getRentals();
      String result = headerString(aCustomer);
      while (rentals.hasMoreElements()) {
          Rental each = (Rental) rentals.nextElement();

          //show figures for this rental
          result += "\t" + each.getMovie().getTitle()+ "\t" +
              String.valueOf(each.getCharge()) + "\n";
      }

      //add footer lines
      result +=  "Amount owed is " + String.valueOf(aCustomer.getTotalCharge()) + "\n";
      result += "You earned " + String.valueOf(aCustomer.getTotalFrequentRenterPoints()) +
            " frequent renter points";
      return result;
  }
```

Form Template
Method

```
class HtmlStatement...
  String headerString(Customer aCustomer) {
      return "<H1>Rentals for <EM>" + aCustomer.getName() + "</EM></H1><P>\n";
  }
  public String value(Customer aCustomer) {
      Enumeration rentals = aCustomer.getRentals();
      String result = headerString(aCustomer);
      while (rentals.hasMoreElements()) {
          Rental each = (Rental) rentals.nextElement();
          //show figures for each rental
          result += each.getMovie().getTitle()+ ": " +
                  String.valueOf(each.getCharge()) + "<BR>\n";
      }
      //add footer lines
      result +=  "<P>You owe <EM>" + String.valueOf(aCustomer.getTotalCharge()) + "</EM><P>\n";
```

```
            result += "On this rental you earned <EM>" +
                String.valueOf(aCustomer.getTotalFrequentRenterPoints()) +
                "</EM> frequent renter points<P>";
            return result;
    }
```

I compile and test and then continue with the other elements. I did the steps one at a time. Here is the result:

```
class TextStatement …
    public String value(Customer aCustomer) {
        Enumeration rentals = aCustomer.getRentals();
        String result = headerString(aCustomer);
        while (rentals.hasMoreElements()) {
            Rental each = (Rental) rentals.nextElement();
            result += eachRentalString(each);
        }
        result += footerString(aCustomer);
        return result;
    }

String eachRentalString (Rental aRental) {
        return "\t" + aRental.getMovie().getTitle()+ "\t" +
                String.valueOf(aRental.getCharge()) + "\n";
    }
```

Form Template Method

```
String footerString (Customer aCustomer) {
        return "Amount owed is " + String.valueOf(aCustomer.getTotalCharge()) + "\n" +
            "You earned " + String.valueOf(aCustomer.getTotalFrequentRenterPoints()) +
            " frequent renter points";
    }

class HtmlStatement…
    public String value(Customer aCustomer) {
        Enumeration rentals = aCustomer.getRentals();
        String result = headerString(aCustomer);
        while (rentals.hasMoreElements()) {
            Rental each = (Rental) rentals.nextElement();
            result += eachRentalString(each);
        }
        result += footerString(aCustomer);
        return result;
    }

    String eachRentalString (Rental aRental) {
        return aRental.getMovie().getTitle()+ ": " +
                String.valueOf(aRental.getCharge()) + "<BR>\n";
    }

    String footerString (Customer aCustomer) {
        return "<P>You owe <EM>" + String.valueOf(aCustomer.getTotalCharge()) +
        "</EM><P>\n" + "On this rental you earned <EM>" +
        String.valueOf(aCustomer.getTotalFrequentRenterPoints()) +
            "</EM> frequent renter points<P>";
    }
```

Once these changes have been made, the two value methods look remarkably similar. So I use *Pull Up Method (322)* on one of them, picking the text version at random. When I pull up, I need to declare the subclass methods as abstract:

```
class Statement...
  public String value(Customer aCustomer) {
        Enumeration rentals = aCustomer.getRentals();
        String result = headerString(aCustomer);
        while (rentals.hasMoreElements()) {
            Rental each = (Rental) rentals.nextElement();
            result += eachRentalString(each);
        }
        result += footerString(aCustomer);
        return result;
   }

  abstract String headerString(Customer aCustomer);
  abstract String eachRentalString (Rental aRental);
  abstract String footerString (Customer aCustomer);
```

I remove the value method from text statement, compile, and test. When that works I remove the value method from the HTML statement, compile, and test again. The result is shown in Figure 11.2.

After this refactoring, it is easy to add new kinds of statements. All you have to do is create a subclass of statement that overrides the three abstract methods.

Form Template Method

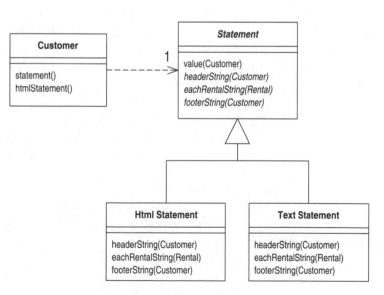

Figure 11.2 *Classes after forming the template method*

Replace Inheritance with Delegation

A subclass uses only part of a superclasses interface or does not want to inherit data.

Create a field for the superclass, adjust methods to delegate to the superclass, and remove the subclassing.

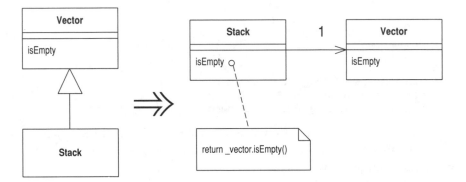

Motivation

Inheritance is a wonderful thing, but sometimes it isn't what you want. Often you start inheriting from a class but then find that many of the superclass operations aren't really true of the subclass. In this case you have an interface that's not a true reflection of what the class does. Or you may find that you are inheriting a whole load of data that is not appropriate for the subclass. Or you may find that there are protected superclass methods that don't make much sense with the subclass.

You can live with the situation and use convention to say that although it is a subclass, it's using only part of the superclass function. But that results in code that says one thing when your intention is something else—a confusion you should remove.

By using delegation instead, you make it clear that you are making only partial use of the delegated class. You control which aspects of the interface to take and which to ignore. The cost is extra delegating methods that are boring to write but are too simple to go wrong.

Mechanics

❑ Create a field in the subclass that refers to an instance of the superclass. Initialize it to this.

❑ Change each method defined in the subclass to use the delegate field. Compile and test after changing each method.

⇒ *You won't be able to replace any methods that invoke a method on* super *that is defined on the subclass, or they may get into an infinite recurse. These methods can be replaced only after you have broken the inheritance.*

❑ Remove the subclass declaration and replace the delegate assignment with an assignment to a new object.

❑ For each superclass method used by a client, add a simple delegating method.

❑ Compile and test.

Example

One of the classic examples of inappropriate inheritance is making a stack a subclass of vector. Java 1.1 does this in its utilities (naughty boys!), but in this case I use a simplified form of stack:

```java
class MyStack extends Vector {

    public void push(Object element) {
        insertElementAt(element,0);
    }

    public Object pop() {
        Object result = firstElement();
        removeElementAt(0);
        return result;
    }
}
```

Looking at the users of the class, I realize that clients do only four things with stack: push, pop, size, and isEmpty. The latter two are inherited from Vector.

I begin the delegation by creating a field for the delegated vector. I link this field to this so that I can mix delegation and inheritance while I carry out the refactoring:

```
private Vector _vector = this;
```

Now I start replacing methods to get them to use the delegation. I begin with push:

```
public void push(Object element) {
   _vector.insertElementAt(element,0);
}
```

I can compile and test here, and everything will still work. Now pop:

```
public Object pop() {
   Object result = _vector.firstElement();
   _vector.removeElementAt(0);
   return result;
}
```

Once I've completed these subclass methods, I need to break the link to the superclass:

```
class MyStack extends Vector

private Vector _vector = new Vector();
```

I then add simple delegating methods for superclass methods used by clients:

```
public int size() {
   return _vector.size();
}

public boolean isEmpty() {
   return _vector.isEmpty();
}
```

Now I can compile and test. If I forgot to add a delegating method, the compilation will tell me.

Replace
Inheritance
with Delegation

Replace Delegation with Inheritance

You're using delegation and are often writing many simple delegations for the entire interface.

Make the delegating class a subclass of the delegate.

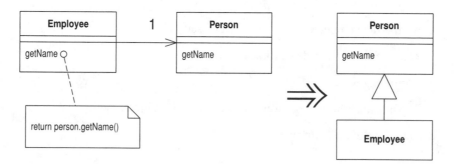

Motivation

This is the flip side of *Replace Inheritance with Delegation (352)*. If you find yourself using all the methods of the delegate and are sick of writing all those simple delegating methods, you can switch back to inheritance pretty easily.

There are a couple of caveats to bear in mind. If you aren't using all the methods of the class to which you are delegating, you shouldn't use *Replace Delegation with Inheritance,* because a subclass should always follow the interface of the superclass. If the delegating methods are tiresome, you have other options. You can let the clients call the delegate themselves with *Remove Middle Man (160)*. You can use *Extract Superclass (336)* to separate the common interface and then inherit from the new class. You can use *Extract Interface (341)* in a similar way.

Another situation to beware of is that in which the delegate is shared by more than one object and is mutable. In this case you can't replace the delegate with inheritance because you'll no longer share the data. Data sharing is a responsibility that cannot be transferred back to inheritance. When the object is immutable, data sharing is not a problem, because you can just copy and nobody can tell.

Mechanics

- ❑ Make the delegating object a subclass of the delegate.

- ❑ Compile.

  ⇒ *You may get some method clashes at this point; methods may have the same name but vary in return type, exceptions, or visibility. Use Rename Method (273) to fix these.*

- ❑ Set the delegate field to be the object itself.

- ❑ Remove the simple delegation methods.

- ❑ Compile and test.

- ❑ Replace all other delegations with calls to the object itself.

- ❑ Remove the delegate field.

Example

A simple employee delegates to a simple person:

```
class Employee {
  Person _person = new Person();

  public String getName() {
      return _person.getName();
  }
  public void setName(String arg) {
      _person.setName(arg);
  }
  public String toString () {
      return "Emp: " + _person.getLastName();
  }
}


class Person {
  String _name;

  public String getName() {
      return _name;
  }
  public void setName(String arg) {
      _name = arg;
  }
  public String getLastName() {
      return _name.substring(_name.lastIndexOf(' ')+1);
  }
}
```

Replace Delegation with Inheritance

The first step is just to declare the subclass:

```
class Employee extends Person
```

Compiling at this point alerts me to any method clashes. These occur if methods with the name have different return types or throw different exceptions. Any such problems need to be fixed with *Rename Method (273)*. This simple example is free of such encumbrances.

The next step is to make the delegate field refer to the object itself. I must remove all simple delegation methods such as getName and setName. If I leave any in, I will get a stack overflow error caused by infinite recursion. In this case this means removing getName and setName from Employee.

Once I've got the class working, I can change the methods that use the delegate methods. I switch them to use calls directly:

```
public String toString () {
    return "Emp: " + getLastName();
}
```

Once I've got rid of all methods that use delegate methods, I can get rid of the _person field.

Replace
Delegation with
Inheritance

Chapter 12

Big Refactorings

by Kent Beck and Martin Fowler

The preceding chapters present the individual "moves" of refactoring. What is missing is a sense of the whole "game." You are refactoring to some purpose, not just to avoid making progress (at least usually you are refactoring to some purpose). What does the whole game look like?

The Nature of the Game

One thing you'll surely notice in what follows is that the steps aren't nearly as carefully spelled out as in the previous refactorings. That's because the situations change so much in the big refactorings. We can't tell you exactly what to do, because we don't know exactly what you'll be seeing when you do it. When you are adding a parameter to a method, the mechanics are clear because the scope is clear. When you are untangling an inheritance mess, every mess is different.

Another thing to realize about these refactorings is that they take time. All the refactorings in Chapters 6 through 11 can be accomplished in a few minutes or an hour at most. We have worked at some of the big refactorings for months or years on running systems. When you have a system and it's in production and you need to add functionality, you'll have a hard time persuading managers that they should stop progress for a couple of months while you tidy up. Instead, you have to make like Hansel and Gretel and nibble around the edges, a little today, a little more tomorrow.

As you do this, you should be guided by your need to do something else. Do the refactorings as you need to add function and fix bugs. You don't have to complete the refactoring when you begin. Do as much as you need to achieve your real task. You can always come back tomorrow.

This philosophy is reflected in the examples. To show you each of the refactorings in this book would easily take a hundred pages each. We know this, because Martin tried it. So we've compressed the examples into a few sketchy diagrams.

Because they can take such a long time, the big refactorings also don't have the instant gratification of the refactorings in the other chapters. You will have to have a little faith that you are making the world a little safer for your program each day.

The big refactorings require a degree of agreement among the entire programming team that isn't needed with the smaller refactorings. The big refactorings set the direction for many, many changes. The whole team has to recognize that one of the big refactorings is "in play" and make their moves accordingly. You don't want to get in the situation of the two guys whose car stops near the top of a hill. They get out to push, one on each end of the car. After a fruitless half-hour the guy in front says, "I never thought pushing a car downhill would be so hard." To which the other guy replies, "What do you mean 'downhill'?"

Why Big Refactorings Are Important

If the big refactorings lack so many of the qualities that make the little refactorings valuable (predictability, visible progress, instant satisfaction), why are they important enough that we wanted to put them in this book? Because without them you run the risk of investing time and effort into learning to refactor and then actually refactoring and not getting the benefit. That would reflect badly on us. We can't stand that.

Seriously, you refactor not because it is fun but because there are things you expect to be able to do with your programs if you refactor that you just can't do if you don't refactor.

Accumulation of half-understood design decisions eventually chokes a program as a water weed chokes a canal. By refactoring you can ensure that your full understanding of how the program should be designed is always reflected in the program. As a water weed quickly spreads its tendrils, partially understood design decisions quickly spread their effects throughout your program. No one or two or even ten individual actions will be enough to eradicate the problem.

Big Refactorings

Four Big Refactorings

In this chapter we describe four examples of big refactorings. These are examples of the kind of thing, rather than any attempt to cover the whole ground. Most of the research and practice on refactoring so far has concentrated on the smaller refactorings. Talking about big refactorings in this way is very new and has come primarily out of Kent's experience, which is greater than anyone's with doing this on a large scale.

Tease Apart Inheritance (362) deals with a tangled inheritance hierarchy that seems to combine several variations in a confusing way. *Convert Procedural Design to Objects (368)* helps solve the classic problem of what to do with procedural code. A lot of programmers use object-oriented languages without really knowing about objects, so this is a refactoring you often have to do. If you see code written with the classic two-tier approach to user interfaces and databases, you'll find you need *Separate Domain from Presentation (370)* when you want to isolate business logic from user interface code. Experienced object-oriented developers have learned that this separation is vital to a long-lived and prosperous system. *Extract Hierarchy (375)* simplifies an overly-complex class by turning it into a group of subclasses.

Tease Apart Inheritance

You have an inheritance hierarchy that is doing two jobs at once.

Create two hierarchies and use delegation to invoke one from the other.

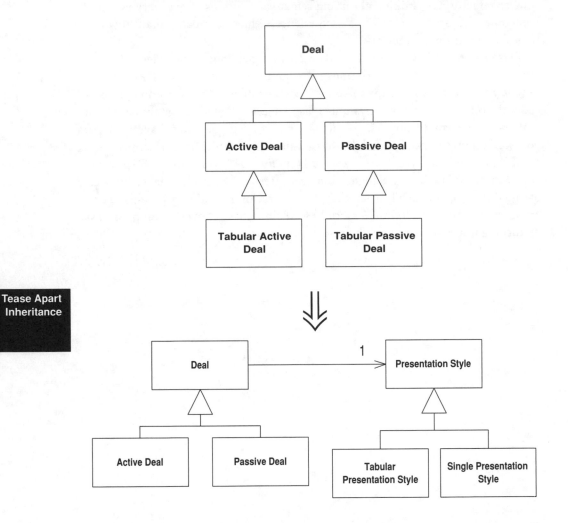

Tease Apart
Inheritance

Motivation

Inheritance is great. It helps you write dramatically "compressed" code in sub-classes. A single method can take on importance out of proportion with its size because of where it sits in the hierarchy.

Not surprisingly for such a powerful mechanism, it is easy to misuse inheritance. And the misuse can easily creep up on you. One day you are adding one little subclass to do a little job. The next day you are adding other subclasses to do the same job in other parts of the hierarchy. A week (or month or year) later you are swimming in spaghetti. Without a paddle.

Tangled inheritance is a problem because it leads to code duplication, the bane of the programmer's existence. It makes changes more difficult, because the strategies for solving a certain kind of problem are spread around. Finally, the resulting code is hard to understand. You can't just say, "This hierarchy here, it computes results." You have to say, "Well, it computes results, and there are subclasses for the tabular versions, and each of those has subclasses for each of the countries."

You can easily spot a single inheritance hierarchy that is doing two jobs. If every class at a certain level in the hierarchy has subclasses that begin with the same adjective, you probably are doing two jobs with one hierarchy.

Mechanics

- ❑ Identify the different jobs being done by the hierarchy. Create a two-dimensional grid (or three- or four-dimensional, if your hierarchy is a real mess and you have some really cool graph paper) and label the axes with the different jobs. We assume two or more dimensions require repeated applications of this refactoring (one at a time, of course).

- ❑ Decide which job is more important and is to be retained in the current hierarchy and which is to be moved to another hierarchy.

- ❑ Use *Extract Class (149)* at the common superclass to create an object for the subsidiary job and add an instance variable to hold this object.

- ❑ Create subclasses of the extracted object for each of the subclasses in the original hierarchy. Initialize the instance variable created in the previous step to an instance of this subclass.

- ❑ Use *Move Method (142)* in each of the subclasses to move the behavior in the subclass to the extracted object.

- ❑ When the subclass has no more code, eliminate it.

- ❑ Continue until all the subclasses are gone. Look at the new hierarchy for possible further refactorings such as *Pull Up Method (322)* or *Pull Up Field (320)*.

Tease Apart
Inheritance

Examples

Let's take the example of a tangled hierarchy (Figure 12.1).

This hierarchy got the way it did because Deal was originally being used only to display a single deal. Then someone got the bright idea of displaying a table of deals. A little experiment with the quick subclass Active Deal shows you can indeed display a table with little work. Oh, you want tables of passive deals, too? No problem, another little subclass and away we go.

Two months later the table code has become complicated but there is no simple place to put it, time is pressing, the usual story. Now adding a new kind of deal is hard, because the deal logic is tangled with the presentation logic.

Following the recipe, the first step is to identify the jobs being done by the hierarchy. One job is capturing variation according to type of deal. Another job is capturing variation according to presentation style. So here's our grid:

Deal	Active Deal	Passive Deal
Tabular Deal		

The next step tells us to decide which job is more important. The dealness of the object is far more important than the presentation style, so we leave Deal alone and extract the presentation style to its own hierarchy. Practically speaking, we should probably leave alone the job that has the most code associated with it, so there is less code to move.

**Tease Apart
Inheritance**

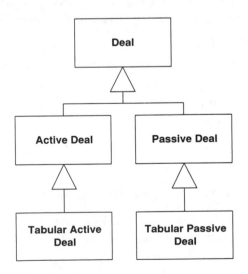

Figure 12.1 *A tangled hierarchy*

The next step tells us to use *Extract Class (149)* to create a presentation style (Figure 12.2).

The next step tells us to create subclasses of the extracted class or for each of the subclasses in the original hierarchy (Figure 12.3) and to initialize the instance variable to the appropriate subclass:

```
ActiveDeal constructor
    ...presentation= new SingleActivePresentationStyle();...
```

You may well be saying, "Don't we have more classes now than we did before? How is this supposed to make my life better?" It is true that sometimes you have to take a step backward before you can take two steps forward. In cases such as this tangled hierarchy, the hierarchy of the extracted object can almost always be dramatically simplified once the object has been extracted. However, it is safer to take the refactoring one step at a time than to jump ten steps ahead to the already simplified design.

Now we use *Move Method (142)* and *Move Field (146)* to move the presentation-related methods and variables of the deal subclasses to the presentation style subclasses. We don't have a good way of simulating this with the example as drawn, so we ask you to imagine it happening. When we're done, though, there should be no code left in the classes Tabular Active Deal and Tabular Passive Deal, so we remove them (Figure 12.4).

Now that we've separated the two jobs, we can work to simplify each separately. When we've done this refactoring, we've always been able to dramatically

Tease Apart
Inheritance

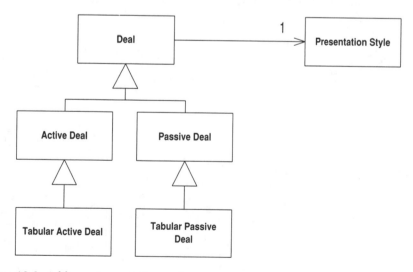

Figure 12.2 *Adding a presentation style*

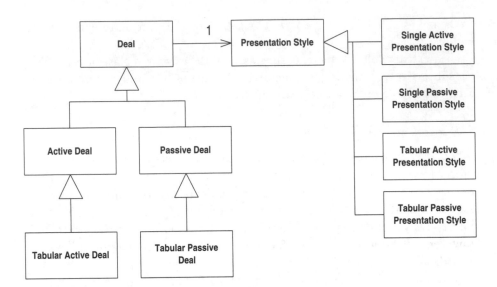

Figure 12.3 *Adding subclasses of presentation style*

simplify the extracted class and often further simplify the original object. The next move will get rid of the active-passive distinction in the presentation style in Figure 12.5.

Even the distinction between single and tabular can be captured by the values of a few variables. You don't need subclasses at all (Figure 12.6).

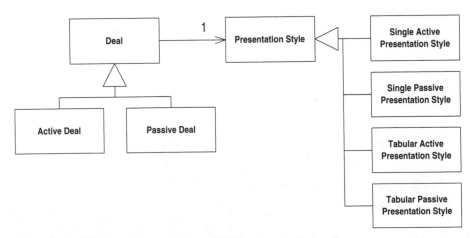

Figure 12.4 *The tabular subclasses of Deal have been removed*

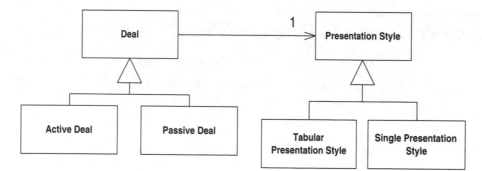

Figure 12.5 *The hierarchies are now separated*

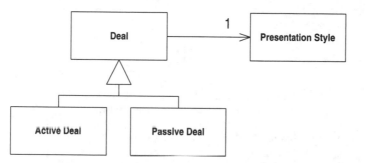

Figure 12.6 *Presentation differences can be handled with a couple of variables*

Convert Procedural Design to Objects

You have code written in a procedural style.

Turn the data records into objects, break up the behavior, and move the behavior to the objects.

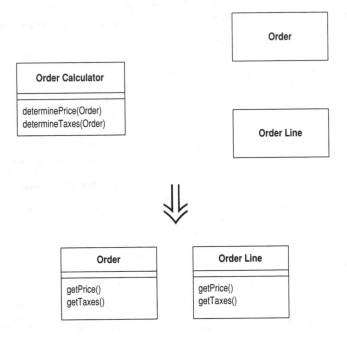

Motivation

A client of ours once started a project with two absolute principles the developers had to follow: (1) you must use Java, (2) you must not use objects.

We may laugh, but although Java is an object-oriented language, there is more to using objects than calling a constructor. Using objects well takes time to learn. Often you're faced with the problem of procedure-like code that has to be more object oriented. The typical situation is long procedural methods on a class with little data and dumb data objects with nothing more than accessors. If you are converting from a purely procedural program, you may not even have this, but it's a good place to start.

We are not saying that you should never have objects with behavior and little or no data. We often use small strategy objects when we need to vary behavior.

However, such procedural objects usually are small and are used when we have a particular need for flexibility.

Mechanics

- ❑ Take each record type and turn it into a dumb data object with accessors.

  ⇒ *If you have a relational database, take each table and turn it into a dumb data object.*

- ❑ Take all the procedural code and put it into a single class.

  ⇒ *You can either make the class a singleton (for ease of reinitialization) or make the methods static.*

- ❑ Take each long procedure and apply *Extract Method (110)* and the related refactorings to break it down. As you break down the procedures, use *Move Method (142)* to move each one to the appropriate dumb data class.

- ❑ Continue until you've removed all the behavior away from the original class. If the original class was a purely procedural class, it's very gratifying to delete it.

Example

The example in Chapter 1 is a good example of the need for *Convert Procedural Design to Objects,* particularly the first stage, in which the statement method is broken up and distributed. When you're finished, you can work on now-intelligent data objects with other refactorings.

Convert
Procedural
Design to
Objects

Separate Domain from Presentation

You have GUI classes that contain domain logic.

Separate the domain logic into separate domain classes

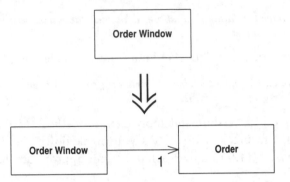

Motivation

Whenever you hear people talking about objects, you hear about modei-view-controller (MVC). This idea underpinned the relationship between the graphical user interface (GUI) and domain objects in Smalltalk-80.

The gold at the heart of MVC is the separation between the user interface code (the *view,* these days often called the *presentation*) and the domain logic (the *model*). The presentation classes contain only the logic needed to deal with the user interface. Domain objects contain no visual code but all the business logic. This separates two complicated parts of the program into pieces that are easier to modify. It also allows multiple presentations of the same business logic. Those experienced in working with objects use this separation instinctively, and it has proved its worth.

But this is not how most people who work with GUIs do their design. Most environments with client-server GUIs use a logical two-tier design: the data sits in the database and the logic sits in the presentation classes. The environment often forces you toward this style of design, making it hard for you to put the logic anywhere else.

Java is a proper object-oriented environment, so you can create nonvisual domain objects that contain business logic. However, you'll often come across code written in the two-tier style.

Mechanics

❑ Create a domain class for each window.

❑ If you have a grid, create a class to represent the rows on the grid. Use a collection on the domain class for the window to hold the row domain objects.

❑ Examine the data on the window. If it is used only for user interface purposes, leave it on the window. If it is used within the domain logic but is not actually displayed on the window, use *Move Method (142)* to move it to the domain object. If it is used by both the user interface and the domain logic, use *Duplicate Observed Data (189)* so that it is in both places and kept in sync.

❑ Examine the logic in the presentation class. Use *Extract Method (110)* to separate logic about the presentation from domain logic. As you isolate the domain logic, use *Move Method (142)* to move it to the domain object.

❑ When you are finished, you will have presentation classes that handle the GUI and domain objects that contain all the business logic. The domain objects will not be well factored, but further refactorings will deal with that.

Example

A program that allows users to enter and price orders. The GUI looks like Figure 12.7. The presentation class interacts with a relational database laid out like Figure 12.8.

All the behavior, both for the GUI and for pricing the orders, is in a single Order Window class.

We begin by creating a suitable order class. We link this to the order window as in Figure 12.9. Because the window contains a grid to display the order lines, we also create an order line class for the rows of the grid.

We work from the window rather than the database. Basing an initial domain model on the database is a reasonable strategy, but our biggest risk is mixing presentation and domain logic. So we separate these on the basis of the windows and refactor the rest later.

With this kind of program it's useful to look at the structured query language (SQL) statements embedded in the window. Data pulled back from SQL statements is domain data.

Figure 12.7 *The user interface for a starting program*

The easiest domain data to deal with is that which isn't directly displayed in the GUI. In the example the database has a codes field in the customers table. The code isn't directly displayed on the GUI; it is converted to a more human-readable phrase. As such the field is a simple class, such as string, rather than an AWT component. We can safely use *Move Field (146)* to move that field to the domain class.

We aren't so lucky with the other fields. They contain AWT components that are displayed on the window and used in the domain objects. For these we need to use *Duplicate Observed Data (189)*. This puts a domain field on the order class with a corresponding AWT field on the order window.

This is a slow process, but by the end we can get all the domain logic fields into the domain class. A good way to drive this process is to try to move all the SQL calls to the domain class. You can do this to move the database logic and the domain data to the domain class together. You can get a nice sense of com-

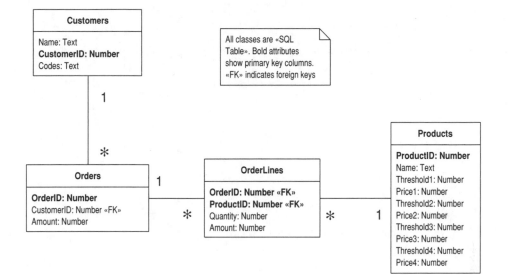

Figure 12.8 *The database for the order program*

pletion by removing the import of java.sql from the order window. This means you do a lot of *Extract Method (110)* and *Move Method (142)*.

The resulting classes, as in Figure 12.10, are a long way from being well factored. But this model is enough to separate the domain logic. As you do this refactoring you have to pay attention to where your risk is. If the intermingling of presentation and domain logic is the biggest risk, get them completely separated before you do much else. If other things are more important, such as

Separate
Domain from
Presentation

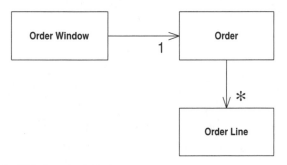

Figure 12.9 *Order Window and Order*

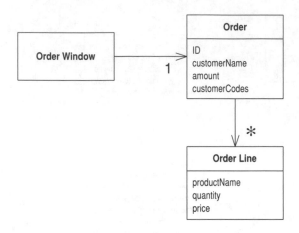

Figure 12.10 *Distributing the data to the domain classes*

pricing strategies for the products, get the logic for the important part out of the window and refactor around that logic to create a suitable structure for the area of high risk. Chances are that most of the domain logic will have to be moved out of the order window. If you can refactor and leave some logic in the window, do so to address your biggest risk first.

Separate Domain from Presentation

Extract Hierarchy

You have a class that is doing too much work, at least in part through many conditional statements.

Create a hierarchy of classes in which each subclass represents a special case.

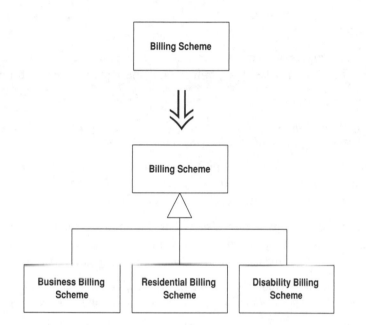

Motivation

In evolutionary design, it is common to think of a class as implementing one idea and come to realize later that it is really implementing two or three or ten. You create the class simply at first. A few days or weeks later you see that if only you add a flag and a couple of tests, you can use it in a new case. A month later you have another such opportunity. A year later you have a real mess: flags and conditional expressions all over the place.

When you encounter a Swiss-Army-knife class that has grown to open cans, cut down small trees, shine a laser point at reluctant presentation bullet items, and, oh yes, I suppose cut things, you need a strategy for teasing apart the various strands. The strategy here works only if your conditional logic remains static during the life of the object. If not, you may have to use *Extract Class (149)* before you can begin separating the cases from each other.

Don't be discouraged if *Extract Hierarchy* is a refactoring that you can't finish in a day. It can take weeks or months to untangle a design that has become snarled. Do the steps that are easy and obvious, then take a break. Do some visibly productive work for a few days. When you've learned something, come back and do a few more easy and obvious steps.

Mechanics

We've put in two sets of mechanics. In the first case you aren't sure what the variations should be. In this case you want to take one step at a time, as follows:

- ❑ Identify a variation.

    ⇒ *If the variations can change during the life of the object, use* Extract Class (149) *to pull that aspect into a separate class.*

- ❑ Create a subclass for that special case and use *Replace Constructor with Factory Method (304)* on the original. Alter the factory method to return an instance of the subclass where appropriate.

- ❑ One at a time, copy methods that contain conditional logic to the subclass, then simplify the methods given what you can say for certain about instances of the subclass that you can't say about instances of the superclass.

    ⇒ *Use* Extract Method (110) *in the superclass if necessary to isolate the conditional parts of methods from the unconditional parts.*

- ❑ Continue isolating special cases until you can declare the superclass abstract.

- ❑ Delete the bodies of methods in the superclass that are overridden in all subclasses and make the superclass declarations abstract.

When the variations are very clear from the outset, you can use a different strategy, as follows:

- ❑ Create a subclass for each variation.

- ❑ Use *Replace Constructor with Factory Method (304)* to return the appropriate subclass for each variation.

    ⇒ *If the variations are marked with a type code, use* Replace Type Code with Subclasses (223). *If the variations can change within the life of the class, use* Replace Type Code with State/Strategy (227).

❑ Take methods that have conditional logic and apply *Replace Conditional with Polymorphism (255)*. If the whole method does not vary, isolate the varying part with *Extract Method (110)*.

Example

The example is a nonobvious case. You can follow the refactorings for *Replace Type Code with Subclasses (223)*, *Replace Type Code with State/Strategy (227)*, and *Replace Conditional with Polymorphism (255)* to see how the obvious case works.

We start with a program that calculates an electricity bill. The initial objects look like Figure 12.11.

The billing scheme contains a lot of conditional logic for billing in different circumstances. Different charges are used for summer and winter, and different billing plans are used for residential, small business, customers receiving Social Security (lifeline), and those with a disability. The resulting complex logic makes the Billing Scheme class rather complex.

Our first step is to pick a variant aspect that keeps cropping up in the conditional logic. This might be various conditions that depend on whether the customer is on a disability plan. This can be a flag in Customer, Billing Scheme, or somewhere else.

We create a subclass for the variation. To use the subclass we need to make sure it is created and used. So we look at the constructor for Billing Scheme. First we use *Replace Constructor with Factory Method (304)*. Then we look at the factory method and see how the logic depends on disability. We then create a clause that returns a disability billing scheme when appropriate.

We look at the various methods on Billing Scheme and look for those that contain conditional logic that varies on the basis of disability. CreateBill is one of those methods, so we copy it to the subclass (Figure 12.12).

Extract Hierarchy

Figure 12.11 *Customer and billing scheme*

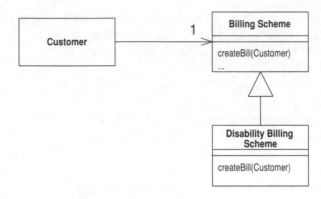

Figure 12.12 *Adding a subclass for disability*

Now we examine the subclass copy of createBill and simplify it on the basis that we know it is now within the context of a disability scheme. So code that says

```
if (disabilityScheme()) doSomething
```

can be replaced with

```
doSomething
```

Extract
Hierarchy

If disabilities are exclusive of the business scheme we can eliminate any code that is conditional on the business scheme.

As we do this, we like to ensure that varying code is separated from code that stays the same. We use *Extract Method (110)* and *Decompose Conditional (238)* to do that. We continue doing this for various methods of Billing Scheme until we feel we've dealt with most of the disability conditionals. Then we pick another variation, say lifeline, and do the same for that.

As we do the second variation, however, we look at how the variations for lifeline compare with those for disability. We want to identify cases in which we can have methods that have the same intention but carry it out differently in the two separate cases. We might have variation in the calculation of taxes for the two cases. We want to ensure that we have two methods on the subclasses that have the same signature. This may mean altering disability so we can line up the subclasses. Usually we find that as we do more variations, the pattern of similar and varying methods tends to stabilize, making additional variations easier.

Chapter 13

Refactoring, Reuse, and Reality

by William Opdyke

Martin Fowler and I first met in Vancouver during OOPSLA 92. A few months earlier, I had completed my doctoral dissertation on refactoring object-oriented frameworks[1] at the University of Illinois. While I was considering continuing my research into refactoring, I was also exploring other options, such as medical informatics. Martin was working on a medical informatics application at the time, which is what brought us together to chat over breakfast in Vancouver. As Martin relates earlier in this book, we spent a few minutes discussing my refactoring research. He had limited interest in the topic at the time, but as you are now aware, his interest in the topic has grown.

At first glance, it might appear that refactoring began in academic research labs. In reality, it began in the software development trenches, where object-oriented programmers, then using Smalltalk, encountered situations in which techniques were needed to better support the process of framework development or, more generally, to support the process of change. This spawned research that has matured to the point at which we feel it is "ready for prime time"—the point at which a broader set of software professionals can experience the benefits of refactoring.

When Martin offered me the opportunity to write a chapter in this book, several ideas came to mind. I could describe the early refactoring research, the era in which Ralph Johnson and I came together from very different technical backgrounds to focus on support for change in object-oriented software. I could discuss how to provide automated support for refactoring, an area of my research quite different from the focus of this book. I could share some of the lessons I have learned about how refactoring relates to the day-to-day concerns of software professionals, especially those who work on large projects in industry.

Many of the insights I gained during my refactoring research have been useful in a wide range of areas—in assessing software technologies and formulating product evolution strategies, in developing prototypes and products in the telecommunication industry, and in training and consulting with product development groups.

I decided to focus briefly on many of these issues. As the title of this chapter implies, many of the insights regarding refactoring apply more generally to issues such as software reuse, product evolution, and platform selection. Although parts of this chapter briefly touch on some of the more interesting theoretical aspects of refactoring, the primary focus is on practical, real-world concerns and how they can be addressed.

If you want to explore refactoring further, see Resources and References for Refactoring later in this chapter.

A Reality Check

I worked at Bell Labs for several years before I decided to pursue my doctoral studies. Most of that time was spent working in a part of the company that developed electronic switching systems. Such products have very tight constraints with respect to both reliability and the speed with which they handle phone calls. Thousands of staff-years have been invested in developing and evolving such systems. Product lifetimes have spanned decades. Most of the cost of developing these systems comes not in developing the initial release but in changing and adapting the systems over time. Ways to make such changes easier and less costly would result in a big win for the company.

Because Bell Labs was funding my doctoral studies, I wanted a field of research that was not only technically interesting but also related to a practical business need. In the late 1980s, object-oriented technology was just beginning to emerge from the research labs. When Ralph Johnson proposed a research topic that focused both on object-oriented technology and on supporting the process of change and software evolution, I grabbed it.

I've been told that when people finish their doctoral studies, they rarely are neutral about their topic. Some are sick of the topic and quickly move on to something else. Others remain enthusiastic about the topic. I was in the latter camp.

When I returned to Bell Labs after receiving my degree, a strange thing happened. The people around me were not nearly as excited about refactoring as I was.

I can vividly recall presenting a talk in early 1993 at a technology exchange forum for staff at AT&T Bell Labs and NCR (we were all part of the same company at the time). I was given 45 minutes to speak on refactoring. At first the talk seemed to go well. My enthusiasm for the topic came across. But at the end of the talk, there were very few questions. One of the attendees came up afterward to learn more; he was beginning his graduate work and was fishing around for a research topic. I had hoped to see some members of development projects show eagerness in applying refactoring to their jobs. If they were eager, they didn't express it at the time.

People just didn't seem to get it.

Ralph Johnson taught me an important lesson about research: if someone (a reviewer of a paper, an attendee at a talk) comments, "I don't understand" or just doesn't get it, it's *our* fault. It is *our* responsibility to work hard to develop and communicate our ideas.

Over the next couple years, I had numerous opportunities to talk about refactoring at AT&T Bell Labs internal forums and at outside conferences and workshops. As I talked more with developers in the trenches, I started to understand why my earlier messages didn't come across clearly. The disconnect was caused partly by the newness of object-oriented technology. Those who had worked with it had rarely progressed beyond the initial release and hence had not yet faced the tough evolution problems refactoring can help solve. This was the typical researcher's dilemma—the state of the art was beyond the state of common practice. However, there was another, troubling cause for the disconnect. There were several commonsense reasons developers, even if they bought into the benefits of refactoring, were reluctant to refactor *their* programs. These concerns had to be addressed before refactoring could be embraced by the development community.

Why Are Developers Reluctant to Refactor *Their* Programs?

Suppose you are a software developer. If your project is a fresh start (with no backward compatibility concerns) *and* if you understand the problem your system is intended to solve *and* if your funder is willing to pay until *you* are satisfied with the results, consider yourself very fortunate. Although such a scenario may be ideal for applying object-oriented techniques, for most of us such a scenario is only a dream.

More often you are asked to extend an existing piece of software. You have a less-than-complete understanding of what you are doing. You are under schedule pressure to produce. What can you do?

You can rewrite the program. You can leverage your design experience and correct the ills of the past and be creative and have fun. Who will foot the bill? How can you be sure that the new system does everything the old system used to do?

You can copy and modify parts of the existing system to extend its capabilities. This may seem expedient and may even be viewed as a way to demonstrate reuse; you don't even have to understand what you are reusing. However, over time, errors propagate themselves, programs become bloated, program design becomes corrupted, and the incremental cost of change escalates.

Refactoring is a middle ground between the two extremes. It is a way to restructure software to make design insights more explicit, to develop frameworks and extract reusable components, to clarify the software architecture, and to prepare to make additions easier. Refactoring can help you leverage your past investment, reduce duplication, and streamline a program.

Suppose you as a developer buy into these advantages. You agree with Fred Brooks that dealing with change is one of the "essential complexities" of developing software.[2] You agree that in the abstract refactoring can provide the stated advantages.

Why might you still not refactor *your* programs? Here are four possible reasons:

1. You might not understand how to refactor.

2. If the benefits are long-term, why exert the effort now? In the long term, you might not be with the project to reap the benefits.

3. Refactoring code is an overhead activity; you're paid to write *new* features.

4. Refactoring might break the existing program.

These are all valid concerns. I have heard them expressed by staff at telecommunication and at high technology companies. Some of these are technical concerns; others are management concerns. All must be addressed before developers will consider refactoring their software. Let's deal with each of these issues in turn.

Understanding How and Where to Refactor

How can you learn how to refactor? What are the tools and techniques? How can they be combined to accomplish something useful? When should we apply them? This book defines several dozen refactorings that Martin found useful in his work. It presents examples of how the refactorings can be applied to support significant changes to programs.

In the Software Refactory project at the University of Illinois, we chose a minimalist approach. We defined a smaller set of refactorings[1,3] and showed how they could be applied. We based our collection of refactorings on our own programming experiences. We evaluated the structural evolution of several object-oriented frameworks, mostly in C++, and talked with and read the retrospectives of several experienced Smalltalk developers. Most of our refactorings are low level, such as creating or deleting a class, variable, or function; changing attributes of variables and functions, such as their access permissions (e.g., public or protected) and function arguments; or moving variables and functions between classes. A smaller set of high-level refactorings are used for operations such as creating an abstract superclass, simplifying a class by means of subclassing and simplifying conditionals, or splitting off part of an existing class to create a new, reusable component class (often converting between inheritance and delegation or aggregation). The more complex refactorings are defined in terms of the low-level refactorings. Our approach was motivated by concern for automated support and safety, which I discuss later.

Given an existing program, what refactorings should you apply? That depends, of course, on your goals. One common reason, which is the focus of this book, is to restructure a program to make it easier to add (near term) a new feature. I discuss this in the next section. There are, however, other reasons why you might apply refactorings.

Experienced object-oriented programmers and those who have been trained in design patterns and good design techniques have learned that several desirable structural qualities and characteristics of programs have been shown to support extensibility and reuse.[4-6] Object-oriented design techniques such as CRC[7] focus on defining classes and their protocols. Although the focus is on upfront design, there are ways to evaluate existing programs against such guidelines.

An automated tool can be used to identify structural weaknesses in a program, such as functions that have an excessively large number of arguments or are excessively long. These are candidates for refactoring. An automated tool also can identify structural similarities that may indicate redundancies. For example, if two functions are nearly identical (as often happens when a copy-and-modify process is applied to a first function to produce a second), such similarities can be detected and refactorings suggested that can move common code to one place. If two variables in different parts of a program have the same name, they sometimes can be replaced with a single variable that is inherited in both places. These are a few very simple examples. Many other, more complex cases can be detected and corrected with an automated tool. These structural abnormalities or structural similarities don't always mean that you'd want to apply a refactoring, but often they do.

Much of the work on design patterns has focused on good programming style and on useful patterns of interactions among parts of a program that can be mapped into structural characteristics and into refactoring. For example, the applicability section of the template method pattern[8] refers to our abstract superclass refactoring.[9]

I have listed[1] some of the heuristics that can help identify candidates for refactoring in a C++ program. John Brant and Don Roberts[10,11] have created a tool that applies an extensive set of heuristics to automatically analyze Smalltalk programs. They suggest refactorings that might improve the program design and where to apply them.

Applying such a tool to analyze your program is somewhat analogous to applying lint to a C or C++ program. The tool isn't smart enough to understand the meaning of the program. Only some of the suggestions it makes on the basis of structural program analysis may be changes you really want to make. As a programmer, you make the call. You decide which recommendations to apply to your program. Those changes should improve the structure of your program and better support changes down the road.

Before programmers can convince themselves that they ought to refactor their code, they need to understand how and where to refactor. There is no substitute for experience. We leveraged the insights of experienced object-oriented developers in our research to obtain a set of useful refactorings and insights about where they ought to be applied. Automated tools can analyze the structure of a program and suggest refactorings that might improve that structure. As with most disciplines, tools and techniques can help *but only if you use them*. As programmers refactor their code, their understanding grows.

Refactoring C++ Programs

—Bill Opdyke

When Ralph Johnson and I began our refactoring research in 1989, the C++ programming language was evolving and was becoming very popular within the object-oriented community. The importance of refactoring had first been recognized within the Smalltalk community. We felt that demonstrating its applicability to C++ programs would interest a broader community of object-oriented developers.

C++ has language features, most notably its static type checking, that simplify some program analysis and refactoring tasks. On the other hand, the C++ language is complex, largely because of its history and evolution from the C programming language. Some programming styles allowable in C++ make it difficult to refactor and evolve a program.

Language Features and Programming Styles That Support Refactoring

The static typing features of C++ make it relatively easy to narrow possible references to the part of the program that you might want to refactor. To pick a simple but frequent case, suppose you want to rename a member function of a C++ class. To correctly apply the renaming, you must change the function declaration and all references to that function. Finding and changing the references can be difficult if the program is large.

Compared with Smalltalk, C++ has class inheritance and protection-access control mode (public, protected, private) features that make it easier to determine where references to the function being renamed might be. If the function to be renamed is declared private to the class, then references to that function can occur only within the class itself or in classes that are declared as friends of that class. If the function is declared protected, references can be found only in the class, its subclasses (and their descendents), and in friends of the class. If the function is declared public (the least restrictive protection mode), the analysis is still limited to the classes listed for "protected" functions and operations on instances of the class that contains the function, its subclasses, and its descendents.

In some very large programs, functions with the same name might be declared in different places in the program. In some cases, two or more functions with the same name might be better replaced with a single function; there are refactorings that can often be applied to make this change. On the other hand, it is sometimes the case that one of the functions ought to be renamed while the other function is kept the same. In a multiperson project, two or more programmers might have given the same name to functions that are independent of each other. In C++, when changing the name of one of these functions it is almost always easy to determine which references refer to the function being renamed and which refer to the other function. In Smalltalk, that analysis is more difficult.

Because C++ uses subclassing to implement subtyping, the scope to a variable or function usually can be generalized or specialized by moving it up or down an inheritance hierarchy. The efforts to analyze a program and perform the refactoring are fairly straightforward.

Several good design principles applied during initial development and throughout the software development process ease the process of refactoring and make it easier to evolve software. Defining member variables and most member functions as private or protected is an abstraction technique that often makes it easier to refactor the internals of a class while minimizing changes made elsewhere in a program. Using inheritance to model generalization and specialization hierarchies (as is natural in C++) makes it fairly straightforward to later generalize or specialize the scope of member variables or functions using refactorings to move these members within inheritance hierarchies.

Features in C++ environments support refactoring. If while refactoring a program a programmer introduces a bug, often the C++ compiler flags the error. Many C++ software development environments provide powerful capabilities for cross referencing and code browsing.

Language Features and Programming Styles That Complicate Refactoring

The compatibility C++ with C is, as most of you well know, a double-edged sword. Many programs have been written in C and many programmers have been training in C, which (on the surface, at least) makes it easier to migrate to C++ than to other object-oriented languages. However, C++ supports many programming styles, some of which violate the principles of sound design.

Programs that use C++ language features such as pointers, cast operations, and sizeof(object) are difficult to refactor. Pointers and cast operations introduce aliasing, which makes it difficult to determine all references to an object that you might want to refactor. Each of these features exposes the internal representation of an object, which violates principles of abstraction.

For example, C++ uses a V-table mechanism for representing member variables in the executable program. The set of inherited member variables appears first followed by the locally defined member variables. One generally safe refactoring is to move a variable to a superclass. Because the variable now is inherited rather than locally defined in the subclass, the physical location of the variable in the executable is likely to have changed as a result of refactoring. If all variable references in the program are through the class interface, such a reordering of physical locations of the variable will not change the program's behavior.

On the other hand, if the variable was referenced through pointer arithmetic (for example, a programmer had a pointer to an object, used to know that the variable was in the fifth byte, and assigned a value to the fifth byte of the object using pointer arithmetic), then moving the variable to the superclass will likely change the program's behavior. Similarly, if a programmer wrote a conditional of the form if (sizeof(object)==15)), and refactored the program to remove an unreferenced variable from a class, the size of instances of that class would change, and a conditional that once tested true would test false.

It might seem absurd for someone to write programs that do conditional tests based on the size of objects or to use pointer arithmetic when C++ provides a much cleaner interface to class variables. My point is that these features (and others that depend on the physical layout of an object) are provided in C++, and there are programmers experienced in using them. Migrating from C to C++ does not an object-oriented programmer or designer make.

Because C++ is such a complicated language (compared with Smalltalk and, to a lesser extent, Java), it is much more difficult to create the kinds of representations of program structure that are useful for automating support for checking whether a refactoring is safe and, if it is, for performing the refactoring.

Because C++ resolves most references at compile time, refactoring a program usually requires recompiling at least part of a program and linking the executable before testing of the effects of a change. By contrast, Smalltalk and CLOS (Common Lisp Object System) provide environments for interpretation and incremental compilation. Whereas applying (and possibly backing out) a series of incremental refactorings is fairly natural for Smalltalk and CLOS, the cost per iteration (in terms of recompilation and retesting) is higher for C++ programs; thus programmers tend to be less willing to make these small changes.

Many applications use a database. Changes to the structure of objects in a C++ program may require that corresponding schematic changes be made to the database. (Many of the ideas I applied in my refactoring work came from research into object-oriented database schema evolution.)

Another limitation, which may interest software researchers more than many software practitioners, is that C++ does not provide support for metalevel program analysis and change. There is nothing analogous to the metaobject protocol available for CLOS. The metaobject protocol of CLOS, for example, supports a sometimes useful refactoring for changing selected instances of a class into instances of a different class while having all references to the old objects automatically point to the new objects. Fortunately, the cases in which I wanted or needed these features were few and far between.

Closing Comments

Refactoring techniques can and have been applied to C++ programs in a variety of contexts. C++ programs often are expected to be evolved over several years. It is during that process of evolving software that the benefits of refactoring can most easily be seen. The language provides some features that simplify refactoring, whereas other language features if applied make refactoring more difficult. Fortunately, it is widely recognized that using language features such as pointer arithmetic is a bad idea, so most good object-oriented programmers avoid using them.

Many thanks to Ralph Johnson, Mick Murphy, James Roskind, and others for introducing me to some of the power and complexity of C++ with respect to refactoring.

Refactoring to Achieve Near-term Benefits

It is relatively easy to describe the mid-to-long range benefits of refactoring. Many organizations, however, are increasingly judged by the investment community and by others on near-term performance. Can refactoring make a difference in the near term?

Refactoring has been applied successfully for more than ten years by experienced object-oriented developers. Many of these programmers cut their teeth in a Smalltalk culture that valued clarity and simplicity of code and embraced reuse. In such a culture, programmers would invest time to refactor because it was the right thing to do. The Smalltalk language and its implementations made refactoring possible in ways that hadn't been true for most prior languages and software development environments. Much of the early Smalltalk programming was done in research groups such as Xerox, PARC, or small programming teams at leading-edge companies and consulting firms. The values of these groups were somewhat different from the values of many industrial software groups. Martin and I are both aware that for refactoring to be embraced by the mainstream software development community, at least some of its benefits must be near term.

Our research team[3,9,12–15] has described several examples of how refactorings can be interleaved with extensions to a program in a way that achieves both near-term and long-term benefits. One of our examples is the Choices file system framework. Initially the framework implemented the BSD (Berkeley Software Distribution) Unix file system format. Later it was extended to support UNIX System V, MS-DOS, persistent, and distributed file systems. System V file systems bear many similarities to BSD UNIX file systems. The approach taken by the framework developer was first to clone parts of BSD Unix implementation then modify the clone to support System V. The resultant implementation worked, but there was lots of duplicate code. After adding the new code, the framework developer refactored the code, creating abstract superclasses to contain the behavior common to the two Unix file system implementations. Common variables and functions were moved to superclasses. In cases in which corresponding functions were nearly but not entirely identical for the two file system implementations, new functions were defined in each subclass to contain the differences. In the original functions those code segments were replaced with calls to the new functions. Code was incrementally made more similar in the two subclasses. When the functions were identical, they were moved to a common superclass.

These refactorings provide several near-term and mid-term benefits. In the near term, errors found in the common code base during testing needed to be modified only *in one place*. The overall code size was smaller. The behavior specific to a particular file system format was cleanly separated from the code common to the two file system formats. This made it easier to track down and fix behaviors specific to that file system format. In the mid term, the abstractions that resulted from refactoring often were useful in defining subsequent file systems. Granted, the behavior common to the two existing file system formats might not be entirely common for a third format, but the existing base of common code was a valuable starting point. Subsequent refactorings could be applied to clarify what was really common. The framework development team found that over time it took less effort to incrementally add support for a new file system format. Even though the newer formats were more complex, development was done by less experienced staff.

I could cite other examples of near-term and long-term benefit from refactoring, but Martin has already done this. Rather than add to his list, let me draw an analogy to something that is near and dear to many of us, our physical health.

In many ways, refactoring is like exercise and eating a proper diet. Many of us know that we ought to exercise more and eat a more balanced diet. Some of us live in cultures that highly encourage these habits. Some of us can get by for a while without practicing these good habits, even without visible effects. We can always make excuses, but we are only fooling ourselves if we continue to ignore good behavior.

Some of us are motivated by the near-term benefits of exercise and eating a proper diet, such as high energy levels, greater flexibility, higher self-esteem, and other benefits. Nearly all of us know that these near-term benefits are *very* real. Many but not all of us make at least sporadic efforts in these areas. Others, however, aren't sufficiently motivated to do something until they reach a crisis point.

Yes, there are cautions that need to be applied; people should consult with an expert before embarking on a program. In the case of exercise and dieting, they should consult with their physician. In the case of refactoring, they should seek resources such as this book and the papers cited elsewhere in this chapter. Staff experienced in refactoring can provide more focused assistance.

Several people I've met are role models with respect to fitness and refactoring. I admire their energy and their productivity. Negative models show the visible signs of neglect. Their future and the future of the software systems they produce may not be rosy.

Refactoring can achieve near-term benefits and make the software easier to modify and maintain. Refactoring is a means rather than an end. It is part of a broader context of how programmers or programming teams develop and maintain their software.[3]

Reducing the Overhead of Refactoring

"Refactoring is an overhead activity. I'm paid to write new, revenue-generating features." My response, in summary, is this:

- Tools and technologies are available to allow refactoring to be done quickly and relatively painlessly.

- Experiences reported by some object-oriented programmers suggest that the overhead of refactoring is more than compensated by reduced efforts and intervals in other phases of program development.

- Although refactoring may seem a bit awkward and an overhead item at first, as it becomes part of a software development regimen, it stops feeling like overhead and starts feeling like an essential.

Perhaps the most mature tool for automated refactoring has been developed for Smalltalk by the Software Refactory team at the University of Illinois (see Chapter 14). It is freely available at their Web site (http://st-www.cs.uiuc.edu). Although refactoring tools for other languages are not so readily available, many of the techniques described in our papers and in this book can be applied in a relatively straightforward manner with a text editor or, better yet, a browser. Software development environments and browsers have progressed substantially in recent years. We hope to see a growing set of refactoring tools available in the future.

Kent Beck and Ward Cunningham, both experienced Smalltalk programmers, have reported at OOPSLA conferences and other forums that refactoring has enabled them to develop software rapidly in domains such as bond trading. I have heard similar testimonials from C++ and CLOS developers. In this book, Martin describes the benefits of refactoring with respect to Java programs. We expect to hear more testimonials from those who read this book and apply these principles.

My experience suggests that as refactoring becomes part of a routine, it stops feeling like overhead. This statement is easy to make but difficult to substantiate. To the skeptics among you, my advice is just do it, then decide for yourself. Give it time, though.

Refactoring Safely

Safety is a concern, especially for organizations developing and evolving large systems. In many applications, there are compelling financial, legal, and ethical considerations for providing continuous, reliable, and error-free service. Many organizations provide extensive training and attempt to apply disciplined development processes to help ensure the safety of their products.

For many programmers, though, safety often seems to be less of a concern. It's more than a little ironic that many of us preach safety first to our children, nieces, and nephews but in our roles as programmers scream for freedom, a hybrid of the Wild West gunslinger and teenage driver. Give us freedom, give us the resources, and watch us fly. After all, do we really want our organization to miss out on the fruits of our creativity merely for the sake of repeatability and conformity?

In this section, I discuss approaches to safe refactoring. I focus on an approach that compared with what Martin describes earlier in this book is somewhat more structured and rigorous but that can eliminate many errors that might be introduced in refactoring.

Safety is a difficult concept to define. An intuitive definition is that a safe refactoring is one that doesn't break a program. Because a refactoring is intended to restructure a program without changing its behavior, a program should perform the same way after a refactoring as it does before.

How does one safely refactor? There are several options:

- Trust your coding abilities.

- Trust that your compiler will catch errors that you miss.

- Trust that your test suite will catch errors that you and your compiler miss.

- Trust that code review will catch errors that you, your compiler, and your test suite miss.

Martin focuses on the first three options in his refactoring. Mid-to-large-size organizations often supplement these steps with code reviews.

Whereas compilers, test suites, code reviews, and disciplined coding styles all are valuable, there are limits to all of these approaches, as follows:

- Programmers are fallible, even you (I know I am).

- There are subtle and not-so-subtle errors that compilers can't catch, especially scoping errors related to inheritance.[1]

- Perry and Kaiser[16] and others have shown that although it is or at least used to be common wisdom that the testing task is simplified when inheritance is used as an implementation technique, in reality an extensive set of tests often is needed to cover all the cases in which operations that used to be requested on an instance of class are now requested on instances of its subclasses. Unless your test designer is omniscient or pays great attention to detail, there are likely to be cases your test suite won't cover. Testing all possible execution paths in a program is a computationally undecidable problem. In other words, you can't be guaranteed to have caught all of the cases with your test suite.

- Code reviewers, like programmers, are fallible. Furthermore, reviewers may be too busy with their main job to thoroughly review someone else's code.

Another approach, which I took in my research, is to define and prototype a refactoring tool to check whether a refactoring can be safely applied to a program and, if it is, refactor the program. This avoids many of the bugs that may be introduced through human error.

Herein I provide a high-level description of my approach to safe refactoring. This may be the most valuable part of this chapter. For more details, see my dissertation[1] and other references at the end of this chapter; also see Chapter 14. If you find this section to be overly technical, skim ahead to the last several paragraphs of this section.

Part of my refactoring tool is a program analyzer, which is a program that analyzes the structure of another program (in this case, a C++ program to which a refactoring might be applied). The tool can answer a series of questions regarding scoping, typing, and program semantics (the meaning or intended operations of a program). Scoping issues related to inheritance make this analysis more complex than with many non-object-oriented programs, but for C++, language features such as static typing make the analysis easier than for, say, Smalltalk.

Consider, for example, the refactoring to delete a variable from a program. A tool can determine what other parts of a program (if any) reference the variable. If there are any references, removing the variable would leave dangling references; thus this refactoring would not be safe. A user who asks the tool to refactor the program would receive an error flag. The user might then decide that the refactoring is a bad idea after all or to change the parts of the program that refer to that variable and apply the refactoring to remove the variable. There are many other checks, most as simple as this, some more complex.

In my research, I defined safety in terms of program properties (related to activities such as scoping and typing) that need to continue to hold after refactoring. Many of these program properties are similar to integrity constraints that must be maintained when database schemas change.[17] Each refactoring has associated with it a set of necessary preconditions that if true would ensure that the program properties are preserved. Only if the tool were to determine that everything is safe would the tool perform the refactoring.

Fortunately, determining whether a refactoring is safe often is trivial, especially for the low-level refactorings that constitute most of our refactoring. To ensure that the higher-level, more complicated refactorings are safe, we defined them in terms of the low-level refactorings. For example, the refactoring to create an abstract superclass is defined in terms of steps, which are simpler refactorings such as creating and moving variables and methods. By showing that each step of a more complicated refactoring is safe, we can know by construction that the refactoring is safe.

There are some (relatively rare) cases in which a refactoring might actually be safe to apply to a program but a tool can't be sure. In these cases the tool takes the safe route and disallows the refactoring. For instance, consider again the case in which you want to remove a variable from a program, but there is a reference to it somewhere else in the program. Perhaps the reference is contained in a code segment that will never be executed. For example, the reference may appear inside a conditional, such as an if-then loop, that will never test true. If you can be sure that the conditional would never test true, you could remove the conditional test, including the code referring to the variable or function that you want to delete. You then could safely remove the variable or function. In general it isn't possible to know for certain whether the condition will always be false. (Suppose you inherited code that was developed by someone else. How confident would you be in deleting this code?)

A refactoring tool can flag the reference and alert the user. The user might decide to leave the code alone. If or when the user became sure that the referencing code would never be executed, he or she could remove the code and apply the refactoring. The tool makes the user aware of the implications of the reference rather than blindly applying the change.

This may sound like complicated stuff. It is fine for a doctoral dissertation (the primary audience, the thesis committee, wants to see some attention to theoretical issues), but is it practical for real refactoring?

All of the safety checking can be implemented under the hood of a refactoring tool. A programmer who wants to refactor a program merely needs to ask the tool to check the code and, if it is safe, perform the refactoring. My tool was a research prototype. Don Roberts, John Brant, Ralph Johnson, and I[10] have implemented a far more robust and featured tool (see Chapter 14) as part of our research into refactoring Smalltalk programs.

Many levels of safety can be applied to refactoring. Some are easy to apply but don't guarantee a high level of safety. Using a refactoring tool can provide many benefits. It can make many simple but tedious checks and flag in advance problems that if left unchecked would cause the program to break as a result of refactoring.

Although applying a refactoring tool avoids introducing many of the errors that you otherwise hope will be flagged during compilation, testing, and code review, the latter techniques are still of value, particularly in the development or evolution of real-time systems. Programs often don't execute in isolation; they are parts of a larger network of communicating systems. Some refactorings not only clean up code but also make a program run more quickly. Speeding up one program might result in performance bottlenecks elsewhere. This is similar to the effects of upgrading microprocessors that speed up parts of a system and require similar approaches to tune and test overall system performance. Conversely, some refactorings may slow overall performance a bit, but in general such effects on performance are minimal.

Safety approaches are intended to guarantee that refactoring does not introduce *new* errors into a program. These approaches don't detect or fix bugs that were in the program before it was refactored. However, refactoring may make it easier to spot such bugs and correct them.

A Reality Check (Revisited)

Making refactoring real requires addressing the real-world concerns of software professionals. Four commonly expressed concerns are as follows:

- The programmers might not understand how to refactor.

- If the benefits are long-term, why exert the effort now? In the long term, you might not be with the project to reap the benefits.

- Refactoring code is an overhead activity; programmers are paid to write *new* features.

- Refactoring might break the existing program.

In this chapter, I briefly address each of these concerns and provide pointers for those who want to delve further into these topics.

The following issues are of concern to some projects:

- What if the code to be refactored is collectively owned by several programmers? In some cases, many of the traditional change management mechanisms are relevant. In other cases, if the software has been well designed and refactored, subsystems will be sufficiently decoupled that many refactorings will affect only a small subset of the code base.

- What if there are multiple versions or lines of code from a code base? In some cases, refactoring may be relevant for all of the versions, in which case all need to be checked for safety before the refactoring is applied. In other cases, the refactorings may be relevant for only some versions, which simplifies the process of checking and refactoring the code. Managing changes to multiple versions often requires applying many of the traditional version-management techniques. Refactoring can be useful in merging variants or versions into an updated code base, which may simplify version management downstream.

In summary, persuading software professionals of the practical value of refactoring is quite different from persuading a doctoral committee that refactoring research is worthy of a Ph.D. It took me some time after completing my graduate studies to fully appreciate these differences.

Resources and References for Refactoring

By this point in the book, I hope you are planning to apply refactoring techniques in your work and are encouraging others in your organization to do so. If you are still undecided, you may want to refer to the references I have provided or contact Martin (Fowler@acm.org), me, or others who are experienced in refactoring.

If you want to explore refactoring further, here are a few references that you may want to check out. As Martin has noted, this book isn't the first written work on refactoring, but (I hope) it will expose a broadening audience to the concepts and benefits of refactoring. Although my doctoral dissertation was the first major written work on the topic, most readers interested in exploring the early foundational work on refactoring probably should look first at several papers.[3,9,12,13] Refactoring was a tutorial topic at OOPSLA 95 and OOPSLA 96.[14,15] For those with an interest in both design patterns and refactoring, the paper "Lifecycle and Refactoring Patterns That Support Evolution and Reuse,"[3] which Brian Foote and I presented at PLoP '94 and which appears in the first volume of the Addison-Wesley Pattern Languages of Program Design series, is a good place to start. My refactoring research was largely built on work by Ralph Johnson and Brian regarding object-oriented application frameworks and the design of reusable classes.[4] Subsequent refactoring research by John Brant, Don Roberts, and Ralph Johnson at the University of Illinois has focused on refactoring Smalltalk programs.[10,11] Their Web site (http://st-www.cs.uiuc.edu) includes some of their most recent work. Interest in refactoring has grown within the object-oriented research community. Several related papers were presented at OOPSLA 96 in a session titled Refactoring and Reuse.[18]

Implications Regarding Software Reuse and Technology Transfer

The real-world concerns addressed earlier don't apply to refactoring alone. They apply more broadly to software evolution and reuse.

For much of the past several years, I have focused on issues related to software reuse, platforms, frameworks, patterns, and the evolution of legacy systems, often involving software that was not object oriented. In addition to working with projects within Lucent and Bell Labs, I have participated in forums with staff at other organizations who have been grappling with similar issues.[19–22]

The real-world concerns regarding a reuse program are similar to those related to refactoring.

- Technical staff may not understand what to reuse or how to reuse it.

- Technical staff may not be motivated to apply a reuse approach unless short-term benefits can be achieved.

- Overhead, learning curve, and discovery cost issues must be addressed for a reuse approach to be successfully adopted.

- Adopting a reuse approach should not be disruptive to a project; there may be strong pressures to leverage existing assets or implementation albeit with legacy constraints. New implementations should interwork or be backward compatible with existing systems.

Geoffrey Moore[23] described the technology adoption process in terms of a bell-shaped curve in which the front tail includes innovators and early adopters, the large middle hump includes early majority and late majority, and the trailing tail includes laggards. For an idea and product to succeed, they must ultimately be adopted by the early and late majorities. Put another way, many ideas that appeal to the innovators and early adopters ultimately fail because they never make it across the chasm to the early and late majorities. The disconnect lies mainly in the differing motivators of these customer groups. Innovators and early adopters are attracted by new technologies, visions of paradigm shifts and breakthroughs. The early and late majorities are concerned primarily with maturity, cost, support, and seeing whether the new idea or product has been successfully applied by others with needs similar to theirs.

Software development professionals are impressed and convinced in very different ways than are software researchers. Software researchers are most often what Moore refers to as innovators. Software developers and especially software managers often are part of the early and late majorities. Recognizing these differences is important in reaching each of these groups. With software reuse, as with refactoring, it is important to reach software development professionals on their terms.

Within Lucent/Bell Labs I found that encouraging application of reuse and platforms required reaching a variety of stakeholders. It required formulating strategy with executives, organizing leadership team meetings among middle managers, consulting with development projects, and publicizing the benefits of these technologies to broad research and development audiences through seminars and publications. Throughout it was important to train staff in the principles, address near-term benefits, provide ways to reduce overhead, and address how these techniques could be introduced safely. I had gained these insights from my refactoring research.

As Ralph Johnson, who was my thesis advisor, pointed out when reviewing a draft of this chapter, these principles don't apply only to refactoring and to software reuse; they are generic issues of technology transfer. If you find yourself trying to persuade other people to refactor (or to adopt another technology or practice), make sure that you focus on these issues and reach people where they are. Technology transfer is difficult, but it can be done.

A Final Note

Thanks for taking the time to read this chapter. I've tried to address many of the concerns that you might have about refactoring and tried to show that many of the real-world concerns regarding refactoring apply more broadly to software evolution and reuse. I hope that you came away enthusiastic about applying these ideas in your work. Best wishes as you move forward in your software development tasks.

References

1. Opdyke, William F. "Refactoring Object-Oriented Frameworks." Ph.D. diss., University of Illinois at Urbana-Champaign. Also available as Technical Report UIUCDCS-R-92-1759, Department of Computer Science, University of Illinois at Urbana-Champaign.

2. Brooks, Fred. "No Silver Bullet: Essence and Accidents of Software Engineering." In *Information Processing 1986: Proceedings of the IFIP Tenth World Computing Conference*, edited by H.-L. Kugler. Amsterdam: Elsevier, 1986.

3. Foote, Brian, and William F. Opdyke. "Lifecycle and Refactoring Patterns That Support Evolution and Reuse." In *Pattern Languages of Program Design*, edited by J. Coplien and D. Schmidt. Reading, Mass.: Addison-Wesley, 1995.

4. Johnson, Ralph E., and Brian Foote. "Designing Reusable Classes." *Journal of Object-Oriented Programming* 1(1988): 22–35.

5. Rochat, Roxanna. "In Search of Good Smalltalk Programming Style." Technical report CR-86-19, Tektronix, 1986.

6. Lieberherr, Karl J., and Ian M. Holland. "Assuring Good Style For Object-Oriented Programs." *IEEE Software* (September 1989) 38–48.

7. Wirfs-Brock, Rebecca, Brian Wilkerson, and Luaren Wiener. *Design Object-Oriented Software*. Upper Saddle River, N.J.: Prentice Hall, 1990.

8. Gamma, Erich, Richard Helm, Ralph Johnson, and John Vlissides. *Design Patterns: Elements of Reusable Object-Oriented Software*. Reading, Mass.: Addison-Wesley, 1985.

9. Opdyke, William F., and Ralph E. Johnson. "Creating Abstract Superclasses by Refactoring." In *Proceedings of CSC '93: The ACM 1993 Computer Science Conference*. 1993.

10. Roberts, Don, John Brant, Ralph Johnson, and William Opdyke. "An Automated Refactoring Tool." In *Proceedings of ICAST 96: 12th International Conference on Advanced Science and Technology.* 1996.

11. Roberts, Don, John Brant, and Ralph E. Johnson. "A Refactoring Tool for Smalltalk." *TAPOS* 3(1997) 39–42.

12. Opdyke, William F., and Ralph E. Johnson. "Refactoring: An Aid in Designing Application Frameworks and Evolving Object-Oriented Systems." In *Proceedings of SOOPPA '90: Symposium on Object-Oriented Programming Emphasizing Practical Applications.* 1990.

13. Johnson, Ralph E., and William F. Opdyke. "Refactoring and Aggregation." In *Proceedings of ISOTAS '93: International Symposium on Object Technologies for Advanced Software.* 1993.

14. Opdyke, William, and Don Roberts. "Refactoring." Tutorial presented at OOPSLA 95: 10th Annual Conference on Object-Oriented Program Systems, Languages and Applications, Austin, Texas, October 1995.

15. Opdyke, William, and Don Roberts. "Refactoring Object-Oriented Software to Support Evolution and Reuse." Tutorial presented at OOPSLA 96: 11th Annual Conference on Object-Oriented Program Systems, Languages and Applications, San Jose, California, October 1996.

16. Perry, Dewayne E., and Gail E. Kaiser. "Adequate Testing and Object-Oriented Programming." *Journal of Object-Oriented Programming* (1990).

17. Banerjee, Jay, and Won Kim. "Semantics and Implementation of Schema Evolution in Object-Oriented Databases." In *Proceedings of the ACM SIG-MOD Conference,* 1987.

18. Proceedings of OOPSLA 96: Conference on Object-Oriented Programming Systems, Languages and Applications, San Jose, California, October 1996.

19. Report on WISR '97: Eighth Annual Workshop on Software Reuse, Columbus, Ohio, March 1997. *ACM Software Engineering Notes.* (1997).

20. Beck, Kent, Grady Booch, Jim Coplien, Ralph Johnson, and Bill Opdyke. "Beyond the Hype: Do Patterns and Frameworks Reduce Discovery Costs?" Panel session at OOPSLA 97: 12th Annual Conference on Object-Oriented Program Systems, Languages and Applications, Atlanta, Georgia, October 1997.

21. Kane, David, William Opdyke, and David Dikel. "Managing Change to Reusable Software." Paper presented at PLoP 97: 4th Annual Conference on the Pattern Languages of Programs, Monticello, Illinois, September 1997.

22. Davis, Maggie, Martin L. Griss, Luke Hohmann, Ian Hopper, Rebecca Joos, and William F. Opdyke. "Software Reuse: Nemesis or Nirvana?" Panel session at OOPSLA 98: 13th Annual Conference on Object-Oriented Program Systems, Languages and Applications, Vancouver, British Columbia, Canada, October 1998.

23. Moore, Geoffrey A. *Cross the Chasm: Marketing and Selling Technology Products to Mainstream Customers*. New York: HarperBusiness, 1991.

Chapter 14

Refactoring Tools

by Don Roberts and John Brant

One of the largest barriers to refactoring code has been the woeful lack of tool support for it. Languages in which refactoring is part of the culture, such as Smalltalk, usually have powerful environments that support many of the features necessary to refactor code. Even there, the process has been only partially supported until recently, and most of the work is still being done by hand.

Refactoring with a Tool

Refactoring with automated tool support feels different from manual refactoring. Even with the safety net of a test suite in place, refactoring by hand is time consuming. This simple fact prevents programmers from making refactorings they know they should, simply because refactoring costs too much. By making refactoring as inexpensive as adjusting the format of code, cleanup work can be done in a similar manner to cleaning up the look of code. However, this type of cleanup can have a profound, positive effect on the maintainability, reusability, and understandability of code. Kent Beck says:

▼ ——— ▼

—Kent Beck

[The Refactoring Browser] completely changes the way you think about programming. All those niggling little "well, I should change this name but . . ." thoughts go away, because you just change the name because there is always a single menu item to just change the name.

    When I started using this tool, I spent about two hours refactoring at my old pace. I would do a refactoring, then just kind of stare off into space for the five minutes it would have taken me to do the refactoring by hand, then do another

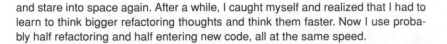

and stare into space again. After a while, I caught myself and realized that I had to learn to think bigger refactoring thoughts and think them faster. Now I use probably half refactoring and half entering new code, all at the same speed.

With this level of tool support for refactoring, it becomes less and less a separate activity from programming. Very rarely do we say, "Now I'm programming" and "Now I'm refactoring." We're more likely to say, "Extract this portion of the method, push it up to the superclass, then add a call to the new method in the new subclass that I'm working on." Because I don't have to test after the automated refactorings, the activities flow into each other, and the process of switching hats becomes much less evident, although it is still occurring.

Consider *Extract Method (110),* an important refactoring. You have many things to check for when you do it by hand. With the Refactoring Browser, you simply select the text to extract and find the menu item named Extract Method. The tool determines whether the selected text is legal to extract. There are several reasons the selection might be illegal. It could contain only a portion of an identifier, or it might contain assignments to a variable without containing all of the references. You don't have to worry about all of the cases, because the tool deals with them. The tool then computes how many parameters must be passed into the new method. It then prompts you for a name for the new method and allows you to specify the order of the parameters in the call to the new function. Once this is done, the tool extracts the code from the original method and replaces it with a call. It then creates the new method in the same class as the original method and with the name that the user specified. The entire process takes about 15 seconds. Compare this with the time necessary to perform the steps in *Extract Method (110).*

As refactoring becomes less expensive, design mistakes become less costly. Because it is less expensive to fix design mistakes, less design needs to be done up front. Upfront design is a predictive activity because the requirements will be incomplete. Because the code is not available, the correct way to design to simplify the code is not obvious. In the past, we had to live with whatever design we initially created because the cost to change the design was too great. With automatic refactoring tools, we can allow the design to be more fluid because changing it is much less costly. Given this new set of costs, we can design to the level of the current problem knowing that we can inexpensively extend the design to add additional flexibility in the future. No longer do we need to attempt to predict every possible way the system might change in the future. If we find that the current design makes the code awkward with the smells described in Chapter 3, we can quickly change the design to make the code clean and maintainable.

Tool-assisted refactoring affects testing. Much less testing has to occur because many of the refactorings are performed automatically. There will always be refactorings that cannot be automated, so the testing step will never be eliminated. The empirical observation has been that the tests are run the same number of times per day as in environments without automatic testing tools but that more refactoring is done.

As Martin has pointed out, Java needs tools to support this kind of behavior by programmers. We want to point out some of the criteria that such a tool must have to be successful. Although we have included the technical criteria, we believe that the practical criteria are much more important.

Technical Criteria for a Refactoring Tool

The main purpose of a refactoring tool is to allow the programmer to refactor code without having to retest the program. Testing is time consuming even when automated, and eliminating it can accelerate the refactoring process by a significant factor. This section briefly discusses the technical requirements for a refactoring tool that are necessary to allow it to transform a program while preserving the behavior of the program.

Program Database

One of the first requirements recognized was the ability to search for various program entities across the entire program, such as with a particular method, finding all calls that can potentially refer to the method in question, or with a particular instance variable, finding all of the methods that read or write it. In tightly integrated environments such as Smalltalk, this information is maintained constantly in a searchable form. This is not a database as traditionally understood, but it *is* a searchable repository. The programmer can perform a search to find cross references to any program element, mainly because of the dynamic compilation of the code. As soon as a change is made to any class, the change is immediately compiled into bytecodes, and the "database" is updated. In more static environments such as Java, programmers enter the code in text files. Updates to the database must be performed by running a program to process these files and extract the relevant information. These updates are similar to compilation of the Java code itself. Some of the more modern environments, such as IBM VisualAge for Java, mimic Smalltalk's dynamic update of the program database.

A naïve approach is to use textual tools such as grep to do the search. This approach breaks down quickly because it cannot differentiate between a variable named *foo* and a function named *foo*. Creating a database requires using semantic analysis (parsing) to determine the "part of speech" of every token in the program. This must done at both the class definition level, to determine instance variable and method definitions, and at the method level, to determine instance variable and method references.

Parse Trees

Most refactorings have to manipulate portions of the system below the method level. These are usually references to program elements that are being changed. For example, if an instance variable is renamed (simply a definition change), all references within the methods of that class and its subclasses must be updated. Other refactorings are entirely below the method level, such as extracting a portion of a method into its own, stand-alone method. Any update to a method has to be able to manipulate the structure of the method. To do this requires parse trees. A parse tree is a data structure that represents the internal structure of the method itself. As a simple example, consider the following method:

```
public void hello( ){
   System.out.println("Hello World");
}
```

The parse tree corresponding to this would look like Figure 14.1.

Accuracy

The refactorings implemented by a tool must reasonably preserve the behavior of programs. Total preservation of behavior is impossible to achieve. For example, what if a refactoring makes a program a few milliseconds faster or slower? This usually would not affect a program, but if the program requirements include hard real-time constraints, this could cause a program to be incorrect.

Even more traditional programs can be broken. For example, if your program constructs a string and uses the Java Reflection API to execute the method that the String names, renaming the method will cause the program to throw an exception that the original did not.

However, refactorings can be made reasonably accurate for most programs. As long as the cases that will break a refactoring are identified, programmers

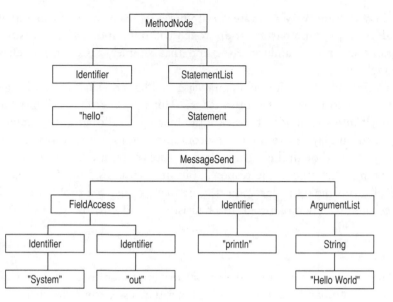

Figure 14.1 *Parse tree for hello world*

who use those techniques can either avoid the refactoring or manually fix the parts of the program that the refactoring tool cannot fix.

Practical Criteria for a Refactoring Tool

Tools are created to support a human in a particular task. If a tool does not fit the way a person works, the person will not use it. The most important criteria are the ones that integrate the refactoring process with other tools.

Speed

The analysis and transformations needed to perform refactorings can be time consuming if they are very sophisticated. The relative costs of time and accuracy always must be considered. If a refactoring takes too long, a programmer will never use the automatic refactoring but will just perform it by hand and live with the consequences. Speed should always be considered. In the process of developing the Refactoring Browser, we had a few refactorings that we did not implement simply because we could not implement them safely in a reasonable amount of time. However, we did a decent job, and most of the refactorings are extremely fast and very accurate. Computer scientists tend to focus on all of the boundary cases that a particular approach will not handle. The fact is that most programs are not boundary cases and that simpler, faster approaches work amazingly well.

An approach to consider if an analysis would be too slow is simply to ask the programmer to provide the information. This puts the responsibility for accuracy back into the hands of the programmer while allowing the analysis to be performed quickly. Quite often the programmer knows the information that is required. Even though this approach is not provably safe because the programmer can make mistakes, the responsibility for error rests on the programmers. Ironically, this makes programmers more likely to use the tool because they are not required to rely on a program's heuristic to find information.

Undo

Automatic refactoring allows an exploratory approach to design. You can push the code around and see how it looks under the new design. Because a refactoring is supposed to be behavior preserving, the inverse refactoring, which undoes the original, also is a refactoring and is behavior preserving. Earlier versions of the Refactoring Browser did not incorporate the undo feature. This made refactoring a little more tentative because undoing some refactorings, although behavior preserving, was difficult. Quite often we would have to find an old version of the program and start again. This was annoying. With the addition of undo, yet another fetter was thrown off. Now we can explore with impunity, knowing that we can roll back to any prior version. We can create classes, move methods into them to see how the code will look, and change our minds and go a completely different direction, all very quickly.

Integrated with Tools

In the past decade the integrated development environment (IDE) has been at the core of most development projects. The IDE integrates the editor, compiler, linker, debugger, and any other tool necessary for developing programs. An early implementation of the Refactoring Browser for Smalltalk was a separate tool from the standard Smalltalk development tools. What we found was that no one used it. We did not even use it ourselves. Once we integrated the refactorings directly into the Smalltalk Browser, we used them extensively. Simply having them at our fingertips made all the difference.

Wrap Up

We have spent several years developing and using the Refactoring Browser. It is quite common for us to use it to refactor its own code. One of the reasons for its success is that we are programmers and we have tried constantly to make it fit the way we work. If we ran across a refactoring that we had to perform by hand and we felt it was general, we would implement it and add it. If something took too long, we would make it faster. If something wasn't accurate enough, we would improve it.

We believe that automatic refactoring tools are the best way to manage the complexity that arises as a software project evolves. Without tools to deal with this complexity, software becomes bloated, buggy, and brittle. Because Java is much simpler than the language with which it shares syntax, it is much easier to develop tools to refactor it. We hope this will occur and that we can avoid the sins of C++.

Chapter 15

Putting It All Together

by Kent Beck

Now you have all the pieces of the puzzle. You've learned the refactorings. You've studied the catalog. You've practiced all of the checklists. You've gotten good at testing, so you aren't afraid. Now you may think you know how to refactor. Not yet.

The list of techniques is only the beginning. It is the gate you must pass through. Without the techniques, you can't manipulate the design of running programs. With them, you still can't, but at least you can start.

Why are all these wonderful techniques really only the beginning? Because you don't yet know when to use them and when not to, when to start and when to stop, when to go and when to wait. It is the rhythm that makes for refactoring, not the individual notes.

How will you know when you are really getting it? You'll know when you start to calm down. When you feel absolute confidence that no matter how screwed up someone left it, you can make the code better, enough better to keep making progress.

Mostly, though, you'll know you're getting it when you can stop with confidence. Stopping is the strongest move in the refactorer's repertoire. You see a big goal—a host of subclasses can be eliminated. You begin to move toward that goal, each step small and sure, each step backed up by keeping all the tests running. You're getting close. You only have two methods to unify in each of the subclasses, and then they can go away.

That's when it happens. You run out of gas. Maybe it's getting late and you are becoming fatigued. Maybe you were wrong in the first place and you can't really get rid of all of those subclasses. Maybe you don't have the tests to back you up. Whatever the cause, your confidence is gone. You can't make the next step with certainty. You don't think you will screw anything up, but you're not sure.

That's when you stop. If the code is already better, integrate and release what you've done. If it isn't better, walk away. Flush it. Glad to have learned a lesson, pity it didn't work out. What's on for tomorrow?

Tomorrow or the next day or the next month or maybe even next year (my personal record is nine years waiting for the second half of a refactoring), the insight comes. Either you understand why you were wrong, or you understand why you were right. In any case, the next step is clear. You take the step with the confidence you had when you started. Maybe you're even a little abashed at how stupid you could have been not to have seen it all along. Don't be. It happens to everyone.

It's a little like walking along a narrow trail above a one-thousand-foot drop. As long as the light holds, you can step forward cautiously but with confidence. As soon as the sun sets, though, you'd better stop. You bed down for the night, sure the sun will rise again in the morning.

This may sound mystical and vague. In a sense it is, because it is a new kind of relationship with your program. When you really understand refactoring, the design of the system is as fluid and plastic and moldable to you as the individual characters in a source code file. You can feel the whole design at once. You can see how it might flex and change—a little this way and this is possible, a little that way and that is possible.

In another sense, though, it is not at all mystical or vague. Refactoring is a learnable skill, the components of which you have read about in this book and begun to learn about. You get those little skills together and polished. Then you begin to see development in a new light.

I said this was a learnable skill. How do you learn it?

■ **Get used to picking a goal.** Somewhere your code smells bad. Resolve to get rid of the problem. Then march toward that goal. You aren't refactoring to pursue truth and beauty (at least that's not all there is to it). You are trying to make your world easier to understand, to regain control of a program that is flapping loose.

■ **Stop when you are unsure.** As you move toward your goal, a time may come when you can't exactly prove to yourself and others that what you are doing will preserve the semantics of your program. Stop. If the code is already better, go ahead and release your progress. If it isn't, throw away your changes.

■ **Backtrack.** The discipline of refactoring is hard to learn and easy to lose sight of, even if only for a moment. I still lose sight more often than I care to admit. I'll do two or three or four refactorings in a row without rerunning the test cases. Of course I can get away with it. I'm confident. I've practiced. Boom! A test fails, and I can't see which of my changes caused the problem.

At this moment you will be mightily tempted to just debug your way out of trouble. After all, you got those tests to run in the first place. How hard could it be to get them running again? Stop. You are out of control, and you have no idea what it will take to get back in control by going forward. Go back to your last known good configuration. Replay your changes one by one. Run the tests after each one.

This may sound obvious here in the comfort of your recliner. When you are hacking and you can smell a big simplification centimeters away, it is the hardest thing to do to stop and back up. But think about it now, while your head is clear. If you have refactored for an hour, it will take only about ten minutes to replay what you did. So you can be guaranteed to be back on track in ten minutes. If, however, you try to move forward, you might be debugging for five seconds or for two hours.

It is easy for me to tell you what to do now. It is brutally hard to actually do it. I think my personal record for failing to follow my own advice is four hours and three separate tries. I got out of control, backtracked, moved forward slowly at first, got out of control again, and again, for four painful hours. It is no fun. That's why you need help.

- **Duets**. For goodness' sake, refactor with someone. There are many advantages to working in pairs for all kinds of development. The advantages work in spades for refactoring. In refactoring there is a premium on working carefully and methodically. Your partner is there to keep you moving step by step, and you are there for him or her. In refactoring there is a premium on seeing possibly far-ranging consequences. Your partner is there to see things you don't see and know things you don't know. In refactoring, there is a premium on knowing when to quit. When your partner doesn't understand what you are doing, it is a sure sign that you don't either. Above all, in refactoring there is an absolute premium on quiet confidence. Your partner is there to gently encourage you when you might otherwise stop.

Another aspect of working with a partner is talking. You want to talk about what you think is about to happen, so the two of you are pointed in the same direction. You want to talk about what you think is happening, so you can spot trouble as soon as possible. You want to talk about what just happened, so you'll know better next time. All that talking cements in your mind exactly where the individual refactorings fit into the rhythm of refactoring.

You are likely to see new possibilities in your code, even if you have worked with it for years, once you know about the smells and the refactorings that can sterilize them. You may even want to jump in and clean up every problem in sight. Don't. No manager wants to hear the team say it has to stop for three months to clean up the mess it has created. And, well, they shouldn't. A big refactoring is a recipe for disaster.

As ugly as the mess looks now, discipline yourself to nibble away at the problem. When you are going to add some new functionality to an area, take a few minutes to clean it up first. If you have to add some tests before you can clean up with confidence, add them. You'll be glad you did. Refactoring first is less dangerous than adding new code. Touching the code will remind you how it works. You'll get done faster, and you'll have the satisfaction of knowing that the next time you pass this way, the code will look better than it did this time.

Never forget the two hats. When you refactor, you will inevitably discover cases in which the code doesn't work right. You'll be absolutely certain of it. Resist temptation. When you are refactoring, your goal is to leave the code computing exactly the same answers it was when you found it. Nothing more, nothing less. Keep a list (I always have an index card beside my computer) of things to change later—test cases to add or change, unrelated refactorings, documents to write, diagrams to draw. That way you won't lose those thoughts, but you won't let them mess up what you are doing now.

References

[Auer]

Auer, Ken. "Reusability through Self-Encapsulation." In *Pattern Languages of Program Design 1*, edited by J.O. Coplien and D.C. Schmidt. Reading, Mass.: Addison-Wesley, 1995.

Patterns paper on the concept of self-encapsulation.

[Bäumer and Riehle]

Bäumer, Dirk, and Dirk Riehle. "Product Trader." In *Pattern Languages of Program Design 3*, edited by R. Martin, F. Buschmann, and D. Riehle. Reading, Mass.: Addison-Wesley, 1998.

A pattern for flexibly creating objects without knowing in what class they should be.

[Beck]

Beck, Kent. *Smalltalk Best Practice Patterns*. Upper Saddle River, N.J.: Prentice Hall, 1997a.

An essential book for any Smalltalker, and a damn useful book for any object-oriented developer. Rumors of a Java version abound.

[Beck, hanoi]

Beck, Kent. "Make it Run, Make it Right: Design Through Refactoring." *The Smalltalk Report*, 6: (1997b): 19–24.

The first published writing that really gets the sense of how the process of refactoring works. The source of many ideas for Chapter 1.

[Beck, XP]

Beck, Kent. *eXtreme Programming eXplained: Embrace Change*. Reading, Mass.: Addison-Wesley, 2000.

[Fowler, UML]

Fowler, M., with K. Scott. *UML Distilled, Second Edition: A Brief Guide to the Standard Object Modeling Language*. Reading, Mass.: Addison-Wesley, 2000.

> A concise guide to the Unified Modeling Language used for various diagrams in this book.

[Fowler, AP]

Fowler, M. *Analysis Patterns: Reusable Object Models*. Reading, Mass.: Addison-Wesley, 1997.

> A book of domain model patterns. Includes a discussion of the range pattern.

[Gang of Four]

Gamma, E., R. Helm, R. Johnson, and J. Vlissides. *Design Patterns: Elements of Reusable Object Oriented Software*. Reading, Mass.: Addison-Wesley, 1995.

> Probably the single most valuable book on object-oriented design. It's now impossible to look as if you know anything about objects if you can't talk intelligently about strategy, singleton, and chain of responsibility.

[Jackson, 1993]

Jackson, Michael. *Michael Jackson's Beer Guide*, Mitchell Beazley, 1993.

> A useful guide to a subject that rewards considerable practical study.

[Java Spec]

Gosling, James, Bill Joy, and Guy Steele. *The Java Language Specification, Second Edition*. Boston, Mass.: Addison-Wesley, 2000.

> The authoritative answer to Java questions.

[JUnit]

Beck, Kent, and Erich Gamma. JUnit Open-Source Testing Framework. Available on the Web (http://www.junit.org).

> Essential tool for working in Java. A simple framework that helps you write, organize, and run unit tests. Similar frameworks are available for Smalltalk and C++.

[Lea]

Lea, Doug. *Concurrent Programming in Java: Design Principles and Patterns*, Reading, Mass.: Addison-Wesley, 1997.

> The compiler should stop anyone implementing Runnable who hasn't read this book.

[McConnell]

McConnell, Steve. *Code Complete: A Practical Handbook of Software Construction*. Redmond, Wash.: Microsoft Press, 1993.

> An excellent guide to programming style and software construction. Written before Java, but almost all of its advice applies.

[Meyer]

Meyer, Bertrand. *Object Oriented Software Construction*. 2 ed. Upper Saddle River, N.J.: Prentice Hall, 1997.

> A very good, if very large, book on object-oriented design. Includes a thorough discussion of design by contract.

[Opdyke]

Opdyke, William F. "Refactoring Object-Oriented Frameworks." Ph.D. diss., University of Illinois at Urbana-Champaign, 1992.

> See ftp://st.cs.uiuc.edu/pub/papers/refactoring/opdyke-thesis.ps.Z. The first decent-length writing on refactoring. Tackles it from a somewhat academic and tools-oriented angle (after all it is a dissertation) but is well worth reading for those who want more on the theory of refactoring.

[Refactoring Browser]

Brant, John, and Don Roberts. Refactoring Browser Tool,

> http://st-www.cs.uiuc.edu/~brant/RefactoringBrowser. The future of software development tools.

[Woolf]

Woolf, Bobby. "Null Object." In *Pattern Languages of Program Design 3*, edited by R. Martin, F. Buschmann, and D. Riehle. Reading, Mass.: Addison-Wesley, 1998.

> A discussion on the null object pattern.

List of Soundbites

Page 90   *A suite of tests is a powerful bug detector that decapitates the time it takes to find bugs.*

Page 94   *Run your tests frequently. Localize tests whenever you compile—every test at least every day.*

Page 97   *When you get a bug report, start by writing a unit test that exposes the bug.*

Page 98   *It is better to write and run incomplete tests than not to run complete tests.*

Page 99   *Think of the boundary conditions under which things might go wrong and concentrate your tests there.*

Page 100   *Don't forget to test that exceptions are raised when things are expected to go wrong.*

Page 101   *Don't let the fear that testing can't catch all bugs stop you from writing the tests that will catch most bugs.*

Index

Object Solutions
Managing the Object-Oriented Project
Grady Booch
Addison-Wesley Object Technology Series

Object Solutions is a direct outgrowth of Grady Booch's experience with object-oriented projects in development around the world. This book focuses on the development process, and is the perfect resource for developers and managers—whether they want to implement object technologies for the first time or refine their existing object-oriented development practice. Drawing upon his knowledge of strategies used in both successful and unsuccessful projects, the author offers pragmatic advice for applying object technologies and controlling projects effectively.

0-8053-0594-7 • Paperback • 336 pages • ©1996

The Unified Modeling Language User Guide
Grady Booch, James Rumbaugh, and Ivar Jacobson
Addison-Wesley Object Technology Series

The Unified Modeling Language User Guide is a two-color introduction to the core eighty percent of the Unified Modeling Language, approaching it in a layered fashion and showing the application of the UML to modeling problems across a wide variety of application domains. This landmark book is suitable for developers unfamiliar with the UML or modeling in general, and will also be useful to experienced developers who wish to learn how to apply the UML to advanced problems.

0-201-57168-4 • Hardcover • 512 pages • ©1999

Surviving Object-Oriented Projects
A Manager's Guide
Alistair Cockburn
Addison-Wesley Object Technology Series

This book allows you to survive and ultimately succeed with an object-oriented project. Alistair Cockburn draws on his personal experience and extensive knowledge to provide the information that managers need to combat the unforeseen challenges that await them during project implementation. *Surviving Object-Oriented Projects* supports its key points through short case studies taken from real object-oriented projects. In addition, an appendix collects these guidelines and solutions into brief "crib sheets" that are ideal for handy reference.

0-201-49834-0 • Paperback • 272 pages • ©1998

Objects, Components, and Frameworks with UML

The Catalysis℠ Approach

Desmond Francis D'Souza and Alan Cameron Wills

Addison-Wesley Object Technology Series

Catalysis is a rapidly emerging UML-based method for component- and framework-based development with objects. The authors describe a unique UML-based approach to precise specification of component interfaces using a type model, enabling precise external description of behavior without constraining implementations. This approach provides application developers and system architects with well-defined and reusable techniques that help them build open distributed object systems from components and frameworks.

0-201-31012-0 • Paperback • 816 pages • ©1999

Analysis Patterns

Reusable Object Models

Martin Fowler

Addison-Wesley Object Technology Series

Martin Fowler shares with you his wealth of object modeling experience and his keen eye for solving repeating problems and transforming the solutions into reusable models. *Analysis Patterns* provides a catalog of patterns that have emerged in a wide range of domains, including trading, measurement, accounting, and organizational relationships.

0-201-89542-0 • Hardcover • 384 pages • ©1997

UML Distilled

Applying the Standard Object Modeling Language

Martin Fowler with Kendall Scott

Addison-Wesley Object Technology Series

Recipient of *Software Development* magazine's 1997 Productivity Award, this concise overview introduces you to the Unified Modeling Language, highlighting the key elements of its notation, semantics, and processes. Included is a brief explanation of UML's history, development, and rationale, as well as discussions on how UML can be integrated into the object-oriented development process. The book also profiles various modeling techniques associated with UML: use cases, CRC cards, design by contract, dynamic classification, interfaces, and abstract classes.

0-201-32563-2 • Paperback • 208 pages • ©1997

Software Reuse
Architecture, Process, and Organization for Business Success
Ivar Jacobson, Martin Griss, and Patrik Jonsson
Addison-Wesley Object Technology Series

This book brings software engineers, designers, programmers, and their managers a giant step closer to a future in which object-oriented component-based software engineering is the norm. Jacobson, Griss, and Jonsson develop a coherent model and set of guidelines for ensuring success with large-scale, systematic, object-oriented reuse. Their framework, referred to as "Reuse-Driven Software Engineering Business" (Reuse Business), deals systematically with the key business process, architecture, and organization issues that hinder success with reuse.

0-201-92476-5 • Hardcover • 560 pages • ©1997

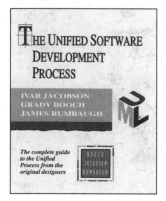

The Unified Software Development Process
Ivar Jacobson, Grady Booch, and James Rumbaugh
Addison-Wesley Object Technology Series

The Unified Software Development Process goes beyond other object-oriented analysis and design methods by detailing a family of processes that incorporate the complete lifecycle of software development. This new book, representing the collaboration of Ivar Jacobson, Grady Booch, and James Rumbaugh, clearly describes the different higher-level constructs—notation as well as semantics—used in the models. Thus stereotypes such as use cases and actors, packages, classes, interfaces, active classes, processes and threads, nodes, and most relations are described intuitively in the context of a model.

0-201-57169-2 • Hardcover • 512 pages • ©1999

The Rational Unified Process
An Introduction
Philippe Kruchten
Addison-Wesley Object Technology Series

This concise book offers a quick introduction to the concepts, structure, content, and motivation of the Rational Unified Process. This revolutionary software development process provides a disciplined approach to assigning, managing, and completing tasks within a software development organization and is the first development process to exploit the full capabilities of the industry-standard Unified Modeling Language. *The Rational Unified Process* is unique in that it captures many of the proven best practices in modern software development and presents them in a form that can be tailored to a wide range of projects and organizations.

0-201-60459-0 • Paperback • 272 pages • ©1999

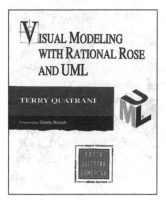

Visual Modeling with Rational Rose and UML

Terry Quatrani
Addison-Wesley Object Technology Series

Terry Quatrani, the Rose Evangelist for Rational Software Corporation, teaches you visual modeling and the UML, enabling you to apply an iterative and incremental process to analysis and design. With the practical direction offered in this book, you will be able to specify, visualize, document, and create software solutions. Highlights of this book include an examination of system behavior from a use case approach; a discussion of the concepts and notations used for finding objects and classes; an introduction to the notation needed to create and document a system's architecture; and a review of the iteration planning process.

0-201-31016-3 • Paperback • 240 pages • ©1998

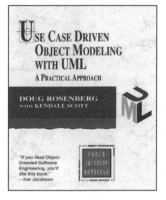

Use Case Driven Object Modeling with UML

A Practical Approach
Doug Rosenberg and Kendall Scott
Addison-Wesley Object Technology Series

This book presents a streamlined approach to UML modeling that includes a minimal—but sufficient—set of diagrams and techniques you can use to get from use cases to code quickly and efficiently. *Use Case Driven Object Modeling with UML* provides practical guidance that will allow software developers to produce UML models quickly and efficiently, while maintaining traceability from user requirements through detailed design and coding. The authors draw upon their extensive industry experience to present proven methods for driving the object modeling process forward from use cases in a simple and straightforward manner.

0-201-43289-7 • Paperback • 192 pages • ©1999

Software Project Management

A Unified Framework
Walker Royce
Addison-Wesley Object Technology Series

This book presents a new management framework uniquely suited to the complexities of modern software development. Walker Royce's pragmatic perspective exposes the shortcomings of many well-accepted management priorities and equips software professionals with state-of-the-art knowledge derived from his twenty years of successful from-the-trenches management experience. In short, the book provides the software industry with field-proven benchmarks for making tactical decisions and strategic choices that will enhance an organization's probability of success.

0-201-30958-0 • Hardcover • 448 pages • ©1998

The Unified Modeling Language Reference Manual

James Rumbaugh, Ivar Jacobson, and Grady Booch
Addison-Wesley Object Technology Series

James Rumbaugh, Ivar Jacobson, and Grady Booch have created the definitive reference to the UML. This two-color book covers every aspect and detail of the UML and presents the modeling language in a useful reference format that serious software architects or programmers should have on their bookshelf. The book is organized by topic and designed for quick access. The authors also provide the necessary information to enable existing OMT, Booch, and OOSE notation users to make the transition to UML. The text also includes an overview of the semantic foundation of the UML in a concise appendix.

0-201-30998-X • Hardcover with CD-ROM • 576 pages • ©1999

Applying Use Cases

A Practical Guide
Geri Schneider and Jason P. Winters
Addison-Wesley Object Technology Series

Applying Use Cases provides a practical and clear introduction to developing use cases, demonstrating their use via a continuing case study. Using the Unified Software Development Process as a framework and the Unified Modeling Language as a notation, the authors lead the reader through applying use cases in the different phases of the process, focusing on where and how use cases are best applied. The book also offers insight into the common mistakes and pitfalls that can plague an object-oriented project.

0-201-30981-5 • Paperback • 208 pages • ©1998

Enterprise Computing with Objects

From Client/Server Environments to the Internet
Yen-Ping Shan and Ralph H. Earle
Addison-Wesley Object Technology Series

This book helps you place rapidly evolving technologies—such as the Internet, the World Wide Web, distributed computing, object technology, and client/server systems—in their appropriate contexts when preparing for the development, deployment, and maintenance of information systems. The authors distinguish what is essential from what is incidental, while imparting a clear understanding of how the underlying technologies fit together. Among the essential topics examined in the book are data persistence, security, performance, scalability, and development tools.

0-201-32566-7 • Paperback • 448 pages • ©1998

The Object Constraint Language
Precise Modeling with UML
Jos Warmer and Anneke Kleppe
Addison-Wesley Object Technology Series

The Object Constraint Language is a new notational language, a subset of the Unified Modeling Language, that allows software developers to express a set of rules that govern very specific aspects of an object in object-oriented applications. With the OCL, developers are able to more easily express unique limitations and write the fine print that is often necessary in complex software designs. The authors' pragmatic approach and illustrative use of examples will help bring application developers quickly up to speed.

0-201-37940-6 • Paperback • 144 pages • ©1999

Smell	Common Refactorings
Alternative Classes with Different Interfaces, p. 85	*Rename Method (273), Move Method (142)*
Comments, p. 87	*Extract Method (110), Introduce Assertion (267)*
Data Class, p. 86	*Move Method (142), Encapsulate Field (206), Encapsulate Collection (208)*
Data Clumps, p. 81	*Extract Class (149), Introduce Parameter Object (295), Preserve Whole Object (288)*
Divergent Change, p. 79	*Extract Class (149)*
Duplicated Code, p. 76	*Extract Method (110), Extract Class (149), Pull Up Method (322), Form Template Method (345)*
Feature Envy, p. 80	*Move Method (142), Move Field (146), Extract Method (110)*
Inappropriate Intimacy, p. 85	*Move Method (142), Move Field (146), Change Bidirectional Association to Unidirectional (200), Replace Inheritance with Delegation (352), Hide Delegate (157)*
Incomplete Library Class, p. 86	*Introduce Foreign Method (162), Introduce Local Extension (164)*
Large Class, p. 78	*Extract Class (149), Extract Subclass (330), Extract Interface (341), Replace Data Value with Object (175)*
Lazy Class, p. 83	*Inline Class (154), Collapse Hierarchy (344)*
Long Method, p. 76	*Extract Method (110), Replace Temp with Query (120), Replace Method with Method Object (135), Decompose Conditional (238)*